The Secret Life of Captain X:

My Life with a Psychopath Pilot

by

MrsXNomore

TELEMACHUS PRESS

Cover designed by MrsXNomore and Telemachus Press, LLC

Cover art by MrsXNomore

Published by Telemachus Press, LLC
http://www.telemachuspress.com

ISBN: 978-1-940745-70-1 (eBook)
ISBN: 978-1-940745-71-8 (Paperback)

Version 2014.12.12

Printed in the United States of America

10 9 8 7 6 5 4 3 2 1

What the experts are saying about
The Secret Life of Captain X:
My Life with a Psychopath Pilot

"A profound memoir by a former pilot's wife telling of her marriage to a man who took her on a first class, one-way ticket to Hell, and from which she had to make her own journey back to the person she once was. What she discovered along the way was to change her forever. This is a must-read for all who live their lives walking on eggshells, trapped inside what might be, a not so grand illusion. An illusion created by a psychopath."

Thomas Sheridan, *Puzzling People: The Labyrinth of the Psychopath*

"For anyone who has had the misfortune of being in 'relationship' with a psychopath, MrsXNomore narrates eloquently and emotionally her journey, including the classic red flags she did not notice until she had been well and truly shafted both emotionally and financially: namely, the lack of empathy, parental alienation, and most importantly projecting their insanity onto their victims.

"Highly recommended for anyone who wants to understand what the hell went on in their relationship with a self-obsessed personality-disordered sex addict."

Sarah Strudwick, *Darks Souls: Healing and Recovering From Toxic Relationships*

"A courageous story of deception and survival shared to help others understand and overcome a traumatic encounter with a psychopath."

Barbara Bentley, *A Dance with the Devil: A True Story of Marriage to a Psychopath*

Table of Contents

The Secret Life of Captain X:

My Life with a Psychopath Pilot

DEDICATION

To all victims of psychopaths,
you are not alone.

INTRODUCTION

IF YOU WALKED past him at the airport dressed in his dashing, dark, militaristic pilot's uniform, both jacket sleeves adorned with four stripes indicating his rank, you would never suspect that Captain X was a socialized psychopath, a predator, a man without a conscience.

I was on cloud nine (really!) with my heart soaring from the minute I met and fell in love with Captain X. I just couldn't believe how happy and in love I was! At the age of 39, I had finally found a loving man to share my life with. Everything seemed just perfect.

Never in my life would I have thought that 22 years later my marriage would crash and burn, like a deadly aviation disaster, into a heap of massive deception. Captain X was left unscathed and at the controls of another woman's life to repeat his pattern of psychopathic destruction, all while he alienated me from family, friends and, most painfully, our daughter.

When we first met, I knew absolutely nothing about psychopaths. Captain X was incredibly skilled at masking his disorder, and I was swiftly and easily taken in by his charming personality. He appeared to have all the characteristics I was looking for in a mate: he was funny, intelligent, committed, family-oriented, successful, caring and loving. Psychopath predators skillfully present a perfect persona. When problems arose in our marriage Captain X expertly lied, deceived, and manipulated me, deflecting problems away from himself and pointing the finger at others, most often at me. Because of my ignorance of his disorder—his psychopathy with its defining characteristics—I was totally oblivious to this, and to his secret life. As a result, I lived for decades in a marriage filled with incredible confusion and abuse, eventually becoming a victim of parental alienation.

What happened to me could happen to anyone who is not aware that there are socialized psychopaths among us.

It took me three years to fully understand my life with Captain X. This understanding drove me to share my story and raise awareness of the evil psychopaths present in today's society.

When Captain X had his attorney craft a clause in our final decree of divorce preventing me from discussing the facts of our divorce, he continued to control me. I couldn't let this happen. I could not be silenced. I am no longer Mrs. X, wife of Captain X, but rather MrsXNomore and this is my story. The events in this book are all true. The names, locations, dates, and some identifying factors have been changed to safeguard myself as well as the privacy of certain individuals.

PART I

Chapter 1: Tango Therapy

AT 62 I'M still considered an attractive, vibrant woman, but to look at me you'd never know the arthritis in my right hip is cutting into me like a cleaver wedged into my coxal joint, while my left hip, with its three-year-old bionic replacement, is acting up with sympathy pains for its counterpart, scaring the shit out of me. In other words, from the outside I look great. My insides are questionable.

What in the hell am I thinking? I asked myself after signing up for a private tango lesson with suave Señor Miguel at a Centro Cultural in Costa Rica, where I now call home. Add recurring lower back pain due to scarred tissue from a spinal surgery to my mounting list of maladies, and I don't think I'll be quite ready to audition for a reality dance show anytime soon.

My immediate thought was that just maybe I could float away from the horrific memories of my 22-year deceptive marriage to Captain X while dancing on the planked wood floor to the tune of "Por Una Cabeza," the music Al Pacino danced to in the film *Scent of a Woman.*

I needed to dance, to tango. I needed to fulfill that promise my ex-husband made more than three years earlier in order to start the recovery process after all the years of hell and confusion I suffered while I was married to him.

"I promise you, just as soon as we get home the first thing I'm going to do is sign us up for tango lessons," Captain X said in a hollow voice, looking deep into me with his piercing green eyes while the overhead monitors in the Boeing 757 cabin rolled the movie credits of *Shall We Dance.*

It was March of 2008. We were returning from a week-long vacation at Captain X's and our 16-year-old daughter Gina's favorite all-inclusive resort in the Dominican Republic. I liked the resort well enough but we vacationed there far too often. I wanted to try someplace new but I was outvoted, so we returned, this time for Gina's school spring break. It was a typical family vacation using our Major Airways flight privileges. I could hear the other passengers' happy voices, filled with laughter, as they recalled their experiences in the Dominican Republic. I felt empty. The week left me with no loving memories, nothing to laugh about. All I had gained from the trip was a good tan, and I had read five books to try to let my mind relax. Gina seemed to have had a great time and that was all that mattered, I told myself. I had no way of knowing it, but this would be our very last family vacation together.

The film *Shall We Dance* was an entertaining romantic comedy. The plot involved a bored estate lawyer secretly taking ballroom dancing lessons; it concluded with the lawyer's wife relieved to learn he was just taking dancing lessons and hadn't been cheating on her, as she had suspected. The movie helped fill the boring hours in the cramped airplane cabin while we soared through the sky along with over 200 weary Major Airline passengers.

We had been lucky to get the last three seats available to Major Airways employees flying standby on the returning flight to Phoenix. "Here's your boarding pass," Captain X said, handing me one of the three he held in his hand. We were assigned two seats in a row together, with the other seat a row behind and across the aisle. Captain X sat next to Gina in the aisle seat. He always sat next to her on family vacations since I was often Gina's seatmate when we flew together to meet her father on holidays.

Stretching his arm back across the aisle, my husband firmly grabbed my hand, clutching it tightly for what seemed like a full minute, as if to add special emphasis, and made his public proclamation of yet another empty promise—this time for tango lessons. He continually tried to draw me in with his promises, but by that point I had no reason to believe him. He'd made too many promises he never kept. When he let go of my hand, I quickly turned my head away from him, eager to let my thoughts go elsewhere. I pulled out the *SkyMall* catalogue from the pocket of the seat in front of me and thumbed through the pages filled with innovative and unique products to enhance people's lives. I wished life was that easy.

As always, after returning from a trip, we ran through US Customs, exited the airport and walked to our car to drive back home, picking up fast food on the way for dinner. We were tired from the long travel day, eating silently while we caught up on the national news on TV. Gina gobbled down her food and bolted off to her bedroom to phone her high school friends, filling them in on highlights of her school break vacation and listening to how they spent theirs. Later I sorted through the family's vacation clothes for the next day's laundry.

The next morning Captain X picked up our mail that was being held at the post office and returned home to work in his office. I tended to the household chores, checked my email for my antiques business, and got Gina's clothes ready for school. After Captain X finished poring over his email and paying bills, he went on the Internet to locate local ballroom dance studios. Soon he was talking to them, showing an effort to keep his promise. After ten minutes he came to my office.

"It's just not going to work with my schedule. I just don't see how we can do it," he said flatly. I knew in my heart what he said wasn't true. He never kept any of his promises. He always used his schedule for an excuse. If he really wanted to take tango lessons with me, I knew he could find a way to arrange his schedule. I said nothing. I was too worn out from his constant excuses.

For some reason, the promise about taking tango lessons stayed with me for a long time. Was it because we never danced? I could count on my fingers the times we danced together. I always urged him to join some group or take up an activity with me, like dancing, something that would enhance our marriage and allow us meet new people. Maybe I just needed to dance, which always made me happy. We never did tango. The dance is just too intimate, and the music is too emotional. Captain X lacked the necessary intimacy and emotional capabilities.

Three years later so much has happened to me. I live alone in Costa Rica. My life is no longer dictated by someone else's schedule. For some reason, one day I decided to schedule a tango lesson on my own. I had no idea what to expect.

A week later I took a bus to the Centro Cultural building for my private lesson, feeling a bit apprehensive. I walked through a small hall to the studio where the lesson was being held. The entire back wall of the room was covered in mirrors and the room had a perfect sprung hardwood floor. It was a beautiful dance studio. This is the room where I would learn the basics of the popular Latin dance I had always dreamed of mastering.

"Hola! So you're here to learn the tango? Have you ever danced the tango before?" Señor Miguel asked, smiling through his sparkling white teeth. Señor Miguel was about five feet tall, four inches shorter than me, but in his tight black pants and matching open-necked long sleeve shirt I could see he definitely had a dancer's body.

My mind started to wander. I wasn't going to tell him that decades ago I danced professionally in New York. It was pointless. Since then I'd endured way too many physical and emotional roadblocks. I had most likely lost all my dancing ability. It would be a moot point revealing this. My mind continued to wander. It's hard to believe I'd traveled to Buenos Aires, Argentina with Captain X several times, yet we never attended a tango show, let alone taken one of the many inexpensive introductory lessons offered to tourists. He always had an excuse.

"Señora? Señora," Señor Miguel repeated, trying to get my attention. "I asked you, have you ever danced the tango before?"

"No, this is my first time, I just wanted to give it a try," I said softly to the teacher, desperately trying to hide my emotions.

I wanted to scream out the truth: I'm learning the tango in place of talk therapy. I had my fill of psychologists before and after my arrival in San Juan. They listened attentively while I poured out my heart-wrenching story, their facial expressions indicating that they were baffled about how to help me heal, how to help me sort out my feelings. I was positive they'd never met anyone as terribly deceived and victimized in a marriage.

My hope was that the dance lesson would give me some reprieve and I would feel alive again. By dancing the tango, I'd be fixing one the many broken promises Captain X had made to me. By dancing the tango, I would be taking care of myself, following just one of my many dreams that were lost in my confusing marriage.

I looked at my reflection in the mirror. My red hair was fastened back with plastic clips so it wouldn't flail across my face during the sharp dance moves. I was wearing a fitted, black, cotton knit, sleeveless shirt over white, stretch, pedal pusher slacks. I removed the bulky walking shoes I wore to navigate my way on the streets and replaced them with black high heel pumps appropriate for the dance. My skin retained the soft, flattering tan I acquired from my everyday life in the San Jose sunshine. Other than being 10 pounds over my ideal weight, my figure was proportionate, so my reflection in the mirror still looked good to me.

After 15 minutes of footwork instruction, Señor Miguel placed a CD in the portable player. The melodic intro echoed through the large cavernous room we had entirely to ourselves. He placed his hand on my back and his other hand found its place in mine. For the first time in decades I was dancing with a man. For one full hour I lost my thoughts to the tango, a dance where the man gently supports and protects the woman and lets her shine. As Señor Miguel guided me across the floor to the sounds of the beautiful Argentine music, I completely forgot the decades of pain and abuse I had endured.

Too soon, the lesson was over. I was glowing, elated that despite all the years that had passed, and my physical ailments, I still could dance. "You did *very* well, Señora!" Señor Miguel said with a smile, as he picked up a small towel to mop his perspiring brow. *Yes, I did do well during this first lesson,* I thought. With the help of tango therapy I finally got some gentle support and protection and was allowed to shine, feelings I sorely missed. After changing back into my bulky street shoes, I paid Señor Miguel his fee of 6000 Costa Rican colons, shook his hand, and promised I'd be back for lessons in the following weeks.

As I caught my bus back home, I realized I *was* shining. I felt alive for the first time in years. For one full hour I had lost my thoughts to the tango. It felt good. It felt really, really good.

Chapter 2: The Perfect Victim

"DADDY, SLOW DOWN!" we screamed as our dad, in a drunken state, pushed his foot down on the gas of our 1955 Chevy Bel Air station wagon as he usually did after visiting Grandma. "John, please slow down! You're scaring the kids!" Mom countered loudly. As if possessed, he clutched the steering wheel hard, speeding through traffic, the effects of the too many shots and beers he had just consumed.

I knew she couldn't make out the speedometer as it reached the 80 mph mark. Mom was legally blind. She could only feel the fear in our voices from the backseat as we kids rolled side to side, while dad swerved around autos in his way. These childhood road trips scared the crap out of us. As Mary Karr said in *The Liars' Club*, "A dysfunctional family is any family with more than one person in it." Many of us have been there; I know I'm not the only member.

I was born in 1948 to an uneducated, first generation Hungarian/Norwegian working class couple who made their home on Chicago's far south side. Our house was heated by a coal furnace; hot air seeped unevenly through the vents during Chicago's blustery winters. It was so cold I amused myself by sketching designs with my fingernail in the frost that coated the inside of the glass windowpane in my upstairs bedroom. I vowed to live in a warm climate someday.

Chicago's ungodly hot summers weren't much better; circulating GE table fans and open windows were our only methods to cool the sweltering house. Childhood summers were spent in a three-ringed blowup plastic swimming pool. Later we bicycled to the Park District's free swimming pools.

Family vacations consisted of driving trips to a rustic Wisconsin cabin that belonged to one of Mom's friends. There we would swim or fish with Dad in the picturesque lake setting. These infrequent vacations provided a few pleasant childhood memories—that is, if we blocked out our dad's drinking binges.

On occasion Dad could be a good man; he wasn't *always* a mean and abusive drunk, though this didn't happen often. Once Mom was in the hospital once for eye surgery and he made us kids pick violets from her garden to cheer her during her hospital stay. He also took us to the museum every Thanksgiving while Mom cooked dinner. He was a nasty drunk, but when he was sober he had some nice qualities. It was confusing.

Mom was totally dependent on my dad or neighbors for errands beyond a walking distance. My earliest memories of her are of her pulling us in a wooden wagon to go shopping half a mile away. How she managed to raise four children with her lack of sight, little income, and with little help from my dad, is beyond me.

Dad was a blue collar worker, a plumber employed by a small local company. When he was on one of his binges, usually on weekends, he filled our house with terror. He wasn't a constant drunk but when weekends came, we cowered.

I don't recall my parents ever being affectionate towards each other. They tolerated each other. Weekdays when Dad came home from work, his hot meal had to be on the table. Mom, the dutiful wife, gladly met his needs.

One day when Dad was in one of his drinking rages, his temper slowly escalated. We all knew he soon would begin to use his favorite phrases, "goddammit" and "son of a bitch," loudly—angry words we only heard during his rages. This time we were in the small kitchen and he grabbed the closest thing, a small, hot, half-filled coffee pot on the stove, and threw it at my mom. Luckily she put her arms up in time to protect her face, resulting in first degree burns on her forearms.

"Dad, stop it!" we kids screamed. "You hurt Mom!"

"I'm OK kids," she said, trying her best to soften the horrible situation through her tears. Dad disappeared into another room. My brother called the police, and soon two policemen were standing in our kitchen talking to our parents. The police instructed us to go to our rooms as they tried to get to the bottom of the situation. Mom didn't press charges. The next morning the incident, one of the worst, was forgotten. I was too young to understand what was going on, but I do remember being terrified. The term 'domestic violence' wasn't even known then. Mom used to say she kept the family together for the kids' sake. She was helpless to leave him; she couldn't get a job and was stuck in a bad marriage, totally dependent on my dad.

I loved my mom. On a good day when Dad was away at work, she'd dance around the house to Strauss waltzes playing from the Motorola radio on the telephone stand. Sometimes the emotion of the music brought her to tears. She was an extremely empathetic human being, a good soul. If empathy is inherited, I got mine from her. I always thought this was a positive trait. Years later I'd find my high levels of empathy made me a walking target. Maybe Mom was a target, too.

I have three siblings: a sister Margo, one year older, and two brothers, Charles four years older and Kevin, 13 years older. Margo was my constant childhood playmate. We had fun despite occasional family upheaval. Margo and I shared most of our friends. Susan was my favorite. Her family didn't seem to fit in our neighborhood. Her father was an airline pilot and I badgered her endlessly with questions about flying. "What's it like being in the clouds? What do houses look like from up there? How does it feel to land?" I often stared at the sky as a tiny plane flew through billowy clouds above, trying to imagine the flying experience. I was filled with envy. Our family never flew on an airplane; flying was for rich people.

There was no money for college, nor any guidance towards a continuing education. My high school guidance counselor was a disgrace to her job. As a result I floundered, just getting by in a Chicago public high school that took me two city buses to attend.

Success, in my loving mom's world, equated to a good marriage. Being married was instilled in me, despite the fact that my parents were far from good marital role models. One thing I was positive of: I wouldn't marry unless I found the perfect husband, someone loving and caring. I wouldn't settle for less.

Immediately after graduating from high school, despite our differences Margo and I moved into a cheap basement apartment in Chicago's north side. Our family home was too far from any city jobs we might find. We had to rely on public transportation since we had no car. At 18 and 19 we were off on our own.

We worked at a variety of clerical jobs while planning our separate futures. For our first real jobs, Margo worked as a bank teller and I worked for an insurance company, filing death benefits. I hated it. We were both young, pretty, and desperately trying to be sophisticated, all while we tried to find some career path or simple job that would lead to a decent future.

Eventually I steadily dated Mark, a young corporate lawyer. Mark had a deposition requiring him to fly to Milwaukee and he invited me to join him on the short flight. I was finally going to be an airline passenger! I loved breathing in the smell of jet fuel, which I equated to airline travel, when we boarded the shiny commuter plane at Midway Airport. Of course I insisted on the window seat. At the age of 19, my goal of flying on an airplane was almost as exciting as losing my virginity a few years earlier.

The flight attendant handed me a drink and peanuts soon after takeoff, but before I finished the flight was over. Mark teased me as I savored my first flying experience. Flying was becoming commonplace in the 1960s, but it was all so new to me. Months later Mark switched law firms and found a new girlfriend. He was nice enough, but not "the one" so I took the news in stride. I kept trying my best to make plans for some kind of future.

I had always wanted to be an artist or an actress. I had artistic talent, but lacked direction. Show business, or as I called it, the performing arts, won over as my main goal. People say that actors are looking for love, and maybe I was. I had been involved in community theater during high school and was good at it. I continued to sing and dance in theater in Chicago well after high school. I had never watched a musical comedy or play until *after* I had actually performed in one. Families like mine never attended live theater.

I worked a variety of odd jobs to pay for dance and singing lessons, honing my craft. I landed a low-paying job doing voice work for a small radio station, and followed that with a job as a singing/dancing waitress for a nightclub similar to the Playboy Club, a life of fishnet tights and big tips.

In my mid-twenties I answered a newspaper ad seeking a female singer/dancer for a Roaring 20s review. I aced the audition with my high kick Charleston and belting alto voice singing "Won't You Come Home Bill Bailey." Two days later they offered me a job with a show band in New York City. They were going to pay my way to the Big Apple. I was thrilled!

Greenwich Village became my home for the next 13 years. My tiny third-floor walk-up apartment made me happy every day while I auditioned for theatrical shows, sometimes getting the job. Soon I became a member of the theatrical unions, filling my resume with movie and commercial extras, voice-over work, dinner theaters, and two ill-fated Broadway shows. I was talented, but not star material. I didn't care. I was happy to be working in the theatrical world. I felt successful. I was being paid in a profession that I loved.

Like all actresses in New York City, I dated frequently. A social life and dinner were my goals. I dated all kinds of men: a news anchorman, a surgeon, an artist, an investment banker, an architect, a jazz musician and a long string of writers. These men loved to be in the company of a pretty actress while I, in turn, loved to meet successful, well-educated men. Dating took the place of a college humanities course. In reality I was always looking for true love, and eventually marriage. Even if these men were not marriage material, I certainly had fun with them.

I fell in love in New York. John Kelly was an investigative reporter working at a major tabloid newspaper. When news happened in the city he was there, with staff photographer in tow. The next day I would buy the paper, his byline on the first page, and read his story. John understood my theatrical life and I in turn understood his business. We dated steadily for two years; the problem was that John had no intention to get married, having already been through a bad marriage and divorce. I loved him and I knew he loved me. "Why can't we just live together?" he asked. The idea of marriage was just too ingrained in me, so I ended our relationship. I was brokenhearted. I was still young, I consoled myself. I continued dating, but never found Mr. Right, or Mr. Right never asked me.

As much as I loved New York, after 13 years it was time to leave. The theater world wasn't the place to meet Mr. Right. Most of the men in theater were gay. I had no problem with that but it put a dent in the list of eligible mates. As I got older most of the men who approached me were married, and I didn't date married men. I enjoyed my New York theatrical life but as you age in the theatrical world, there is no sound future unless you are extremely accomplished. I was good, but not *that* good. It was a fact I had to face. I dreaded becoming the proverbial "New York cat lady," an old single woman dying alone devoured by her cats.

"I'm leaving New York," I told my theater friends. They thought I was crazy. "Who leaves New York? Why?" they kept asking. I tried desperately to explain my list of reasons. By this time I was in my late thirties and acting parts for older women were increasingly difficult to come by. I was supplementing my income with an assortment of part-time jobs. I was tired of the cold winters. I needed a life change, a new adventure. I wanted to move south, to a warmer climate where a whole new world was waiting for me— or so I hoped.

I researched my relocation plan the best I could, before the Internet. For some reason Phoenix, Arizona sounded appealing. With my few belongings, $8,000 in savings, and two zero-balance credit cards, I headed to Phoenix to start my new life. I anticipated getting a sales position. *What actor can't sell?* I asked myself.

My ignorance of the magnitude of this major geographic move was astounding. Perhaps I was filled with optimism from the song "New York, New York:" "If you can make it there, you can make it anywhere." Not true. I had a terrible time making it in Phoenix. I was lonely and miserable.

I settled into a studio apartment located close to the airport, decorating it with my sparse furnishings. I was on a tight budget. Electric costs were high in the sweltering summers. I turned my air conditioning off to save money, cooling myself at the apartment complex pool when not looking for a job. Having access to a swimming pool was one of the few creature comforts I thoroughly enjoyed.

Although I knew how to drive, I had never owned a car. Like most New Yorkers, I relied on public transportation. That was impossible in Phoenix, so I purchased my first car, a Ford Escort which I named "Ellie

Escort" after Miss Ellie, a character in the then-popular TV show *Dallas*. Right after I purchased Ellie, I had my first major auto accident. Alone, frightened, bruised and without a job, I kept repeating my mantras: "I can do this." "I'll be OK." Ellie was a total loss. I replaced her with a used Subaru I no longer cared to name.

I finally landed a job in radio advertising sales for a station with a soul music format, as their token redhead employee. I loved the people but hated the long distance driving required to make sales calls. My nerves were frazzled, maneuvering the endless freeways. I quit the job in hopes I could find something better with less driving.

Weeks turned to months. The only job I could find was commission cosmetics sales at an upscale shopping mall. I was one of those annoying fragrance-spraying women in the cosmetics department. My job required me to beckon women over for a free makeover; I received a substantial commission on their purchases. My New York experience made it easy for me to spot and do makeovers on cross-dressers, many of whom spent plenty of money purchasing cosmetics from my specialty line.

I was mortified to be selling cosmetics, and cried myself to sleep most nights. On the surface I appeared to be a strong, confident person but I was slowly breaking down, realizing how difficult it was to make a new life and start a new career, lacking a college education. My self-esteem was at an all-time low.

I had few friends in Phoenix. Many did not appreciate New Yorkers. I was lonely, sad and miserable. *What the hell was I thinking, moving here?*

I soon made friends with a few flight attendants living in my complex. One day, while sunning myself at the apartment's pool, I found myself chatting with them as they relaxed on their day off. The conversation quickly turned to men. "I'd love to meet a nice guy," I added. Like magic, one gal went into her purse and pulled out a piece of paper with a name and phone number. She said, "Honey, give him a call. He's nice, a pilot, and good-looking, too! He's not my type, and besides, I'm dating someone." I figured I had nothing to lose.

Once I got back to my apartment I took out the piece of paper, held my breath in anticipation, and dialed the neatly written number. After a few rings, he answered.

"Hello, is this Captain X?" I inquired.

"Yes, who's this?" he asked.

"I know this sounds a bit crazy, but I live in the same apartment complex as a flight attendant you just flew with, Sue. She gave me your name and number and said I should call you. Maybe we could get together," I said somewhat apprehensively.

"Oh, yeah, Sue, I just flew a trip with her, nice girl," he said in a pleasant tone. His voice sounded young, almost boyish.

"Well, she said to give you a call," I repeated, feeling awkward. "I've just moved here from New York and I don't know many people."

"Yeah, I know the feeling. I just moved here too. Being a pilot it's difficult to meet people when you travel, and change bases," he said. His youthful but commanding voice began to put me at ease. He told me he had just returned home from a three-day domestic trip with Major Airways.

I had never dated a pilot and knew nothing about the profession. He explained the basics of the airline industry, telling me that everything works on a seniority system, a number tied to the date you were hired. He was a flight engineer, the third pilot of a three-man crew flying domestic routes on a Boeing 727 airplane. He explained that as his seniority rose he would become a first officer and eventually a captain. With each new rank advancement and larger airplane he was assigned, his income would increase.

"Someday I'll be the one in charge of my own airplane. I just wish that time would hurry up! I'm tired of sitting next to a captain who makes the big bucks, watching my every move," he added. His monthly trips were assigned by a bidding system, with a monthly bid sheet. The results depended on his seniority.

During our first two-hour conversation I was immediately enthralled by his intelligence and charm. He told me he grew up in the San Francisco Bay area where his financially comfortable family had a successful restaurant business. They still lived in the house he grew up in. I countered with a very brief description of my family life, mentioning I wished we were closer, glossing over the dysfunction. He immediately responded, proclaiming strongly, "I'm Greek. *I have the best family in the world.* We're really close," he boasted. I listened intently with admiration and envy. As the conversation progressed we discovered the uncanny coincidence of my having the same birthday as his mother. "Wow, that's incredible. Wait till I tell my mom!" *He hadn't even met me and he was going to tell his mom?* I wondered. He instantly showed lots of interest in me. "Hey, let's get together now," he said. "No, let's talk more before we meet," I said cautiously. I was in no hurry to meet. Still, my curiosity was getting the best of me. I wondered what he looked like, but there would be time for that.

The phone calls flew back and forth constantly over the next few days as he bent my ear with stories demonstrating his wit, intelligence and charm. It had been a long time since anyone had paid that much attention to me. I was more than flattered. I gathered that he assumed I was attractive since I had worked in the theater. When I asked him what he looked like, he teasingly answered, "Now you'll just have to wait and see, won't you?"

He loved music and concerts. He loved to cook and dine out. He repeatedly mentioned the closeness of his family. I kept saying to myself, *is this guy for real?* He made me so at ease I couldn't believe it.

We exhausted ourselves learning about each other over the phone, but I was still apprehensive about meeting him because he sounded too good to be true. In the back of my mind I kept thinking *something has to be wrong with him.* It seemed odd that he gave his phone number to a flight attendant and asked her to pass it on. When I questioned him about that, he said, "Well, I really don't know Sue. We just met this trip and I gave her my number. When I found out she was dating someone, I told her she could fix me up sometime. It couldn't hurt. When it gets down to it, it's difficult to meet people in my job. I had nothing to lose by giving her my name and number." That made sense to me. Besides, *I* was the one who phoned him.

The endless telephone conversations filled with flattery and interest were exhilarating. I finally gave in to meeting him in person. The evening we were to meet at my place I agonized over what to wear. Nervously I rechecked my hair and makeup, wondering what he looked like. When the doorbell rang in December of 1987, he covered the peephole of my door with his finger. "That's not fair!" I said, laughing as I opened the door. I took this as a joke and never realized it was a controlling behavior.

I was pleasantly surprised by his appearance. He was tall, over six feet, with a crop of thick fading black hair, the temples showing signs of gray. He looked nothing like I'd imagined when we talked on the phone.

"Well hello! We finally meet," he said, smiling. He was wearing a Members Only jacket over a royal blue dress shirt and professionally pressed jeans. Although he was five years younger than me, he appeared my age or slightly older. My first impression was that he looked like a soap opera actor, straight from central casting. His sparkling green eyes were stunning. Along with his roguish grin, he instantly won my trust.

"God, you're beautiful!" he said as he made his way to my futon couch, his eyes following my every move. When they weren't sparkling, his eyes had an intense gaze as he looked into mine as we continued to learn everything about each other, this time in person.

He excelled in conversation. He had a non-stop sense of humor, a great command of words, and even a flare for impressions and foreign dialects, all with the expertise of a Broadway actor. I joked he must be an actor. "No, this is not so, I am an airline pilot," he replied in a perfect Indian accent, causing me fits of laughter. As an actress I always had difficulty with accents. He was a natural! I was enamored. I laughed constantly at his endless stories while a warm and fuzzy feeling engulfed my entire being. I just couldn't wait to spend more time with him. I could tell he really liked me from the way he looked at me, like I was a prize he desired. From that day on he never left my side unless he had to fly one of his scheduled flights.

Everything happened so fast. We dined at Phoenix's best restaurants, him ordering for me, all while flattering me with attention. He was a perfect gentleman, always opening the car door for me. When we were not dining out, we spent hours at my apartment talking endlessly, drinking his brand name scotch and the expensive bottles of wine he brought along. My meager income had afforded me an occasional box of wine.

We shared more and more of our histories. I soon recognized that although we came from completely different worlds, we shared the same values. He told me how hard he worked to be hired by Major Airways, how much he loved his family and friends, quickly skimming over their names. His parents, Allegra and George, were nearing their 40th wedding anniversary, and he emphasized how close their marriage was. Like me, he believed "marriage is forever." He just hadn't found the right person. *That's exactly how I feel,* I thought! He was my mirror image when it came to ideals. I told him so. Everything he said made sense to me. I thought marriage should be forever.

Each day blurred happily into the next with his constant attention, making me feel like the most important person in the world. I was living in some romantic fairytale—or was I spellbound? He was insightful, delightful, enthusiastic, and fun to be with. He had a secure job in a wonderful profession.

I was 39 and had dated a lot of men in my time. I had acquired street smarts from my days dating in New York. I trusted myself in my relationship choices. I was positive I could identify a good man when I met one. I was smitten. He swept me off my feet from the day I met him. I used to say it was love at first sight, with his twinkling green eyes peering deeply into mine. I had never been so happy in my life.

He phoned me from his layover hotel. "Hey beautiful, whatcha up to?" he asked sweetly. "Oh, just doing laundry and chores," I answered, smiling at being addressed as beautiful. During one conversation I told him I was having problems with my boss at the cosmetic counter. "Don't worry about it. It's nothing," he said in a comforting tone. "You know no one understands you like I do," he continued, inching his importance into my life. I believed him. We shared so much in our conversations that I truly believed he understood me.

We became inseparable. Adrenaline, dopamine and serotonin were on overdrive in my brain. Soon I was addicted to him, but I didn't realize it.

I really don't remember the exact number of days we had known each other, but in a very short period he looked at me with his engaging green eyes and the word "love" came out of both our mouths. I was in love. I was positive I'd found the perfect man, my soul mate, my Mr. Right. I had no idea I had just been love bombed by Mr. Wrong.

Chapter 3: Marry Me and Fly Free

MY NEW LIFE with Captain X was incredibly exciting. I was propelled from being extremely lonely, floundering professionally, and nearly broke to soaring in love with a charming, prestigious airline pilot with strong family values and a loving family.

I now had an attentive partner who showered me with compliments, listened to my concerns and tended to my every need. "Don't you worry, I'll take care of your car for you," he assured me, and he did, changing the oil, checking the tires, tasks totally foreign to me. He also showed a constant interest in me. One day I pulled out a box containing my collection of small antiques I'd picked up for a few dollars at New York flea markets. As I showed him the collection he looked at each piece with intense interest. "Wow, I've never seen anything like that," he commented. Soon he was taking me to every flea market in the area, sharing my passion, scouting the aisles for items of interest to me. Then we would go to lunch celebrating my $10 purchase I was positive could be valued between $75 and $100. We laughed, rehashing how I bargained with dealers. It was fun sharing my passion with him.

Almost immediately after we met we became intimate. "God, you're beautiful and sexy!" he said. I fell into a sexual seduction with someone who told me what I had longed to hear. It had been a long time since I'd had sex. I wanted to be held, to be intimate with him. The first time we had sex he seemed nervous, almost boyish, fumbling like an inexperienced teenager. Then, all of a sudden he seemed to devour me. It was over before it began. *Never mind,* I told myself, *give it time. Practice makes perfect.*

In time, our sex life became somewhat fun and adventurous, despite the fact that he was preoccupied with the size of his manhood. At 39 I'd had my share of lovers. "It's not the size, it's how you use it," I told him gently, trying to put him at ease.

I enjoyed wearing the expensive sexy lingerie that he purchased for me, playfully parading around the bedroom as a prelude to sex. "I've never been with a woman who was as sexy as you," he said, just one of a non-stop barrage of compliments, continually feeding my ego.

One evening at my apartment I suggested we take a bubble bath together. Captain X never took baths, only showers. "Come on, you'll like it, I promise," I urged him. I lit candles and brought in our cocktails for the romantic bath. I turned off the overhead lights and the candles flickered while we sat in the bubbly, warm, relaxing water, sipping our cocktails. Captain X was at one end and I at the other, our toes teasing each other's bodies. He seemed to enjoy this new form of relaxation I'd just introduced him to.

Suddenly the conversation veered to children. "I've always wanted children," I confessed, "but at my age I'll be lucky if I have one."

"Well," he said, "we have to follow a family custom. If it's a boy it has to be named after my grandfather, Theo. If it's a girl, it would be nice if it was a Greek name too." Then and there we came up with the names Gina and Theo. We weren't even engaged and we were naming our children! *There's definitely a future here,* I told myself, feeling emotionally as comfortable as the warm bubbly bathwater we were lying in.

Wherever we went he constantly held my hand, making me feel warm, fuzzy and attached. He called me his special lady and that just reinforced how I felt. I was special to him. He made me feel *very* special.

For some reason I felt compelled to reveal my personal finances. Maybe it was because I wanted to prove myself, to show that despite my low-paying job I was a good, frugal person. Although I had no savings, I had no debt and excellent credit. Whenever I charged something on my credit cards, I paid it off immediately.

My small antiques collection started with a handful of items I traded up through a national collectors club I belonged to. Eventually the worth of these items added up to three or four thousand dollars. I felt compelled to show him I was clever and thrifty. It may have been a small nest egg, but at least I had one. My life in New York had taught me to be extremely frugal. I told him that I often shopped in thrift shops and even sewed many of my own clothes. "That's great. You certainly know how to handle money, don't you?" he said in admiration.

I told him about all my friends in the antique world, some of whom I'd known for years. All lived in other cities but nonetheless were special to me. I would see them annually at antique conferences, keeping in touch by letters. I also shared stories about my remaining friends in New York. Having good friends meant a lot to me. He mentioned a few childhood friends and some from his early flying days, but he quickly changed the topic.

He had excellent taste in everything. *Of course he did*, I told myself, assuming everyone who grew up in northern California had good taste. I considered myself a New Yorker with street smarts. I knew little about California, so I listened to every word he said. I loved hearing about how his family started with one small restaurant and now owns restaurant chains, buying and selling them, leading to their financial success.

I had butterflies in my stomach the day he surprised me by meeting me for lunch at the mall where I worked. I had just expertly completed a cosmetic makeover on one of the many moneyed Arizona women who purchased hundreds of dollars of cosmetics to feed their retail habits. As soon as our eyes met, I tore off my smock and he whisked me off to lunch at the best restaurant in the upscale mall. Before returning for my afternoon shift he insisted on stopping at a high-end jewelry store.

Holding my hand tightly, his free hand pointed at the glittering window display. "Those would look just great on you," he said, indicating a pair of large 14K gold hammered loop earrings dangling on a grey velvet stand. I was 39 and had never purchased jewelry from a high-end jewelry store. Before I knew it, I was trying on the earrings. Admiring my reflection in the mirror, my beaming face framed by the large gold loops, he handed his credit card over to the sales associate. "You just have to have these," he said. He had just purchased $700 earrings for me a month after we met! To me, his wish for me to have the earrings was just another indication that we definitely had a future together.

We continued to dine at the best restaurants, places I had only read about in magazines. Captain X ordered confidently, selecting the best of everything. I was a bit out of practice in fine dining, so after he asked me what I wanted from the menu, he took the lead, telling the waiter what I wanted. "She'll start with the mixed green salad and house dressing and the rib eye, medium rare, and I'll have the same, only make mine with Ranch dressing." He ordered for me like it was the most natural thing in the world. I took his ordering for me as being protective and knowledgeable, enhancing our dining experience. He was a take-charge kind of guy, a man who could take care of me.

Everything was happening so fast. I remember clearly the night we finally stayed at his nondescript pilot's crash pad, a one bedroom apartment about 10 miles from mine. It was not what I had expected: it was dark and filled with unpacked boxes from his move. There was a huge, ugly, wide projection TV that took most of the living room, along with a nondescript leather couch and chair. Nothing was decorative or homey. There were no photos of his family. He lived like a bachelor who had yet to unpack. *He's busy flying*, I told myself.

That night, right after we had sex, his conversation instantly took off in another direction, focusing on the future. We had been together less than two months when he pulled out a huge binder from his closet, his Major Airways benefits book. "I want to show you something important," he said as he opened the binder. He went on to explain his airline retirement plan, and the pilots' pay scales, indicating his pay would just about double as his career proceeded. Then he added, "And you get to fly free!" My life was soaring. He was actually *talking about getting married* when he mentioned the travel benefits associated with being married to an airline employee.

At the time, flying as a spouse on Major Airways was not really free; the airline deducted a small service charge from the employee's paycheck. He did, however, buy me a T-shirt from the company store emblazoned with "Marry Me and Fly Free," an industry joke. The marriage part, however, was not a joke. I was positive he was going to propose.

A few weeks later, Captain X invited me to fly with him to Colorado, paying for my airline ticket with his industry discount. It was February 1988, Martin Luther King Day, a national holiday. Martin Luther King had a dream, and so did I.

Captain X was due for his FAA physical. He hadn't had time to find an FAA physician in Phoenix he felt comfortable with, and preferred to fly to his former FAA physician for the exam. I thought it odd to fly to get a physical, but I soon I learned he was not alone. Many pilots do. They're nervous changing FAA physicians. If a physician finds any medical problems and the pilot "busts his physical," he can lose his flying license. Pilots tend to trust physicians they know well for these mandatory physicals.

"I'm booking us a room at the Doubletree. They're famous for putting great chocolate chip cookies on your pillow," he said, grinning. It was our first trip together. I was so in love I couldn't see or think straight. I remember sitting in the waiting room as he went through the check-up and then going off to an upscale restaurant near the hotel. He ordered a bottle of champagne, something he did often when we dined. We toasted the passing of his physical, although he had no medical concerns.

I wondered if he was going to propose. *No, it's not going to happen here*, I told myself as I sat on the edge of my seat across from him in the restaurant, hanging on to his every word, glancing occasionally at the patrons around us in the restaurant. As soon as we returned to our standard hotel room and he closed the door, he got down on one knee in a mechanical way, looked into my eyes with his deep penetrating eyes and said, "Will you marry me?"

"You're kidding," I said, shocked, laughing in happiness. "I mean YES!" I said resolutely. I was over the moon. I wondered why he proposed there, in a private hotel room, and why there was absolutely nothing romantic about the proposal. There was no ring. I don't even remember him saying, "I love you," or "I want to spend the rest of my life with you." This quick proposal was just one of the many relationship red flags I missed. I was too naive and too much in love.

I wasn't the least concerned about marrying a pilot, having him away about 15 days each month. I had traveled on the road in theatrical productions. I certainly understood a lifestyle of work-related travel. I was positive that the time he would be flying away from me would give us both a degree of independence that could actually enhance our relationship, making our time together more valuable and exciting. After all, cheating isn't linked to any particular profession but is rather a matter of a person's moral character. If there is trust in a relationship, there shouldn't be a problem.

In our whirlwind romance I had somehow acquired blind trust, partly because he presented exactly what I was looking for in a mate. He had none of the qualities of my father. He said he believed marriage was forever. He said he had a close and loving family. During our time together we had learned everything (or so I thought) about each other's lives. I was so incredibly happy. I completely trusted him. I didn't realize that trust is gained by a series of completed promises in time. Our relationship was going so fast that I had no time to think.

Early on he told me that his parents hoped he would marry a Greek, but he had convinced them that I was the one for him. He immediately called them to tell them of our engagement. After he shared the news, he said, "Mom, you're going to *love* her, she's really great," all the while his twinkling green eyes never left my gaze. "Here, talk to her," he commanded as he handed me the handset. His parents sounded warm, loving and genuinely happy for us, just as he had said. I was giddy and nervous. "I can't wait to meet you!" I gushed excitedly into the phone. For a girl from a somewhat poor and misguided family, I was gaining a whole new loving family, and a storybook life. Totally unlike the large typical Greek wedding, we chose to make it a small affair, due to his work schedule. We picked a day in August, giving us six months to plan.

Allegra and George immediately booked a flight to Phoenix to meet me, their soon-to-be daughter-in-law. I knew I looked perfect, dressed in my fashionable red two-piece classic pantsuit Captain X had just purchased for me. Everything was going faster than the speed of sound.

My first impression of his parents was that they were just as he had said: wonderful. Captain X's mother, Allegra, was just like the character Marie Barone, played by Doris Roberts on the popular TV show *Everyone Loves Raymond*. Bouffant blonde, full-figured Allegra was talkative, just like me. Allegra and I shared bubbly conversations getting to know each other. She was exactly 21 years to the day older than me and nothing like my own mother. Despite her full figure, she was fashionable and youthful. I imme-diately liked her.

Sometime during his parents' short visit Allegra took me aside and confided, "He'll make a wonderful husband. We were kind of worried about him when he was dating that other woman, the one 14 years older, so your little age difference is nothing." Captain X had briefly confided in me about a relationship with an older woman. He said they broke up because she was an alcoholic. That was history, but I didn't realize that his parents *had actually met her*. I was confused about why he hadn't he told me this.

"We didn't understand that relationship, but you're just perfect for him. We're so happy for you both. You know, he'll make a great husband, just like his father. He'll never cheat on you," Allegra proclaimed. I found her statement odd, although Captain X had once confided the family secret that Allegra's father, Captain X's maternal grandfather, cheated on his wife. *Perhaps that's what Allegra is referring to*, I told myself.

Allegra dominated every conversation, filling me in on the family all the while doting on her son. George, on the other hand, had few words to say, spending his time taking care of Allegra's every need. I got the feeling they were sincerely happy for us, happy to have their son married. I also believed they liked me and welcomed me into the family—the family of my dreams. To my surprise, before they left, Allegra pulled out her purse and wrote a sizeable check made out to Captain X, one of many she would hand him throughout the years. "Here, this is to help you start your life to-gether." *How unbelievably lucky I am*, I thought. *I have a whole new life with a lov-ing and generous new family!*

I soon quit my job at the mall selling cosmetics. Captain X wanted me to take on a new job as a homemaker. I was only too happy to do so, after endless floundering to get a decent job or start a new career at the age of 39. I was ready, willing, able and ecstatic to become a wife, and to start this new exciting chapter in my life.

Captain X found us a small but new $100,000 starter house in the sub-urbs. Actually *he* picked out three houses without me and then told me I had my choice of the three. I kept saying to myself, *I'm not yet married. He's paying for this. I'm lucky to have him.* When I look back, what choice did I really have? I knew nothing about buying houses. Everything was going so very fast.

Soon after we moved into our starter house, Allegra and George flew in to visit and took us furniture shopping at a suburban strip mall. There, along with Captain X, *they* picked out our living room furniture. "That will look just great, and it's so durable and the pattern won't show dirt," Allegra said. *What could she possibly know about that*, I thought. She had an interior decorator design her home and a weekly housekeeper. I couldn't get a word in. I was speechless as Allegra handed over her credit card to purchase the furniture. I just couldn't believe their choices! The upholstered couch and matching arm chairs were covered in a modern print with ugly splatters of bright colors on a dark background. I despised it, but it was three against one—I was outnumbered. I didn't want to be considered unappreciative, so I nodded my head in agreement to the gaudy purchase. I silently consoled myself with the fact that I'm extremely creative. I could make the awful pattern work by accessorizing with large solid colored pillows. Just as my mother used to say, I remember saying to myself, *we make do the best we can with what we have.* Although I loved my mother, later I wished I hadn't taken all she had said to heart.

I still had no engagement ring. Being economical I suggested that since Captain X had New York layovers that month, he should go to the diamond district where he could definitely get a good price on an engagement ring. I always thought I would be pleased with any ring I received from the man I loved, but I was disappointed when he returned with a very simple diamond solitaire ring, less than three-quarters of a carat on a white gold band. I was confused. He had a good income and came from a wealthy family. He had lavished me with expensive gold earrings, and now he handed me a simple stock engagement ring with a diamond that was considerably small. I admonished myself, thinking how terribly ungrateful I was. I vowed I would never take it off until it was reset in pretty setting, as he promised.

Captain X told me he didn't want a wedding ring, saying lots of men don't wear wedding rings. My mind was in such a wedding preparation whirlwind I didn't take this personally. He loved me. If wearing a wedding band was not important to him, I certainly didn't want to make a big deal about it, so I put it out of my head.

I had few people in my life in Phoenix to help me get ready for my wedding day. My sister Margo had become increasingly distant and jealous of my impending marriage to a pilot so I had no sisterly wedding planning help from her. All my friends lived out of town, so my bridal experience was spent very much alone. It didn't matter because soon I would be Mrs. X and soon, I told myself, everything would be perfect.

My white Douppioni silk cocktail-length wedding dress cost less than $200 to have made. I had planned on sewing it myself, but I worried I might prick my finger and bleed on this dress that signified my new life so I left the sewing to a local dressmaker. Captain X wore an $800 Ralph Lauren suit, the cost he justified since he never got to wear suits, just a uniform. *He sure does like expensive things*, I told myself. Again I admonished myself; he was the breadwinner and it was his special day, too.

Our immediate families flew in for the festivities which were held in an upscale hotel near the airport. The sound of rain pelting the hotel windows didn't dampen my excitement. Rain on your wedding day was supposed to be lucky. A harpist played "Pachelbel's Canon in D" as I walked next to my brother Kevin, happily approaching my groom. A local judge conducted our ceremony, and read our original vows where we publicly promised to "love, comfort, and keep in sickness and in health, forsaking all others for as long as we live." The harpist continued to play softly in the background while our 28 wedding guests dined on grilled chicken over a bed of seasoned angel hair pasta, while champagne was poured.

After the luncheon and goodbyes, we drove off to another hotel in my simple car with the radio blaring "Don't Worry, Be Happy," the popular hit tune of the day. We spent our wedding night in the top hotel in Phoenix, compliments of Allegra and George, of course. There we consummated our marriage.

I remember an odd, empty feeling afterwards. I was sexually satisfied, but something was missing. *So this is what it is like to be married*, I said to myself. It felt like we were having sex, not making love. I still can't remember if Captain X even said "I love you" when we consummated the marriage or while we sipped champagne afterwards from the complimentary bottle in our honeymoon suite. *Something is missing*, I told myself. *No, I'm just a nervous bride. Of course he loves me*, I reassured myself.

The very next day, Allegra and George met us at the Major Airways VIP lounge where we were their guests. I'd never been in a private airline lounge. I was giddy over sharing mimosas with my new in-laws, my new family, as we said our goodbyes. They were off to San Francisco and we were off to enjoy our five-day Acapulco honeymoon.

I remember my modest trousseau consisted of inexpensive sportswear, many outfits well over two years old, while Captain X packed smart designer resort wear. I didn't care. I was a happy, newly married woman. By the time our plane touched down in Acapulco, I was lightheaded from the complimentary champagne the first class purser kept pouring. My honeymoon flight was the first time I had flown in a first class cabin. I loved it. George and Allegra had paid for first class tickets so we wouldn't have to wait flying standby.

After exiting customs and a short taxi ride, we arrived at our honeymoon hotel, which was decorated in a pink motif. The beautiful white stucco casita had a stunning view of the property, with lush cliffs of cascading bougainvillea. The soft modern Mexican white stucco and bright pink décor continued into the honeymoon suite where the large, inviting bed was waiting for us. It was decorated with freshly cut fuchsia bougainvillea blossoms forming a large heart on the pink bedspread. The resort was constructed so most rooms had a private outdoor living space, each with its own private swimming pool.

As Captain X disappeared into the bathroom, I immediately stripped off my clothing and jumped naked into the pool, its water warmed by the afternoon Acapulco sun. I remember his reaction well. He was shocked that I had jumped in naked. "What are you doing?" he asked. "I'm starting our honeymoon with a splash!" I said, laughing. He looked confused and I had absolutely no idea why. We were married, for God's sake! No one could see us. I was starting to notice that my new husband was surprised by what could be considered a perfectly normal situation. He mentioned this, my skinny dipping in our private pool during our honeymoon, in social conversations for many years to come. *What's the big deal?* I asked myself. I came to realize that he often repeated the same stories over and over in conversations, this one being one of his favorites. *It's just an odd quirk*, I said to myself.

The mountaintop resort was filled with newlyweds and for some reason, instead of being alone we all celebrated our evenings together. I was missing a romantic honeymoon with long, intimate lovemaking sessions, but I assured myself the romance would soon follow. After many dinners and many drinks Captain X captivated the other honeymoon couples with his compelling airline stories, becoming the life of the party while I sat attentively by his side happily listening, basking in my new title of Mrs. X, enjoying the balmy tropical breeze.

Five days later, after settling back into our little suburban Phoenix house as Mr. and Mrs., Captain X flew off on his first trip as a married pilot while I busied myself as a homemaker, economically decorating our new little home.

"I changed my mind. I want a wedding band," Captain X proclaimed after a month of marriage. "Why did you change your mind?" I asked, dumbfounded. "I just did, that's all. Don't you want me to wear a wedding band?" he asked indignantly. "Of course I do." I was perplexed. So off we went to a high-end jeweler for him to buy his gold wedding band. The purchase felt strange. It was as if we were going to get a house key made, not purchase a wedding band, the symbol of eternal love. *I am married*, I thought. *Don't make a big deal about it. Be happy he wants to wear it.* His complete turnabout on wearing a wedding ring was the beginning of the mixed messages that would dominate our marriage.

In 1986, *Newsweek* magazine published a story stating, "A woman over age 40 has a better chance of being killed by a terrorist than of getting married." I thought I had just barely beaten those odds by getting married for the first time at 39. At the time I didn't know I hadn't actually beaten those odds. The terror was just beginning, but I would be oblivious to it for a long time to come.

Chapter 4: Infertility, Adoption and Baby Gina

CAPTAIN X ALWAYS left a computer printout with his assigned flight sequence and the phone number of his layover hotel, in case I needed to reach him, but I seldom used it. He always stayed in touch, phoning me from his layover hotel. I know my face glowed as I ran to pick up the phone to hear my new husband's voice.

When he returned home, I proudly showed him how I had spent my time decorating our starter home. He would nod appreciatively, saying, "Looks great." Then he'd change out of his uniform, shower, and slip into sportswear. We'd drive to a nearby restaurant where he would unwind from his trip. There he would fill me in about his crew, hotel, and any flight disruptions. He mostly focused on the captain he had flown with. "He was such an asshole. He was on my back the entire trip." Captain X was not yet in charge of the aircraft. I could see he didn't like taking orders. He wanted to be in charge.

Afterwards we would go home to bed and make love. I longed for him to hold me afterward. I'm one of those people who loved to spoon, to cuddle after sex. "Honey, just hold me a little," I would say. Looking intently at me he'd say, "Look, I've had a very long day. I've been up since four this morning. I'm really tired. I have to get some sleep." *He did have a very long day and of course, he was tired*, I told myself. I had to get used to being married to a pilot, to him coming home dead tired.

Captain X could fall asleep immediately. He'd say, "Goodnight, I love you," give me a quick peck on the lips, then turn his body opposite mine and fall fast asleep in less than a minute. I was amazed! I thought this must be some pilot trick, something he'd conditioned himself to do because of his erratic schedule. In the beginning he would cuddle for a minute or two, but soon he'd say, "You're just too warm to cuddle," or "I'm dead tired," turning away. As a result, there was none of the post-coital lovely-dovey snuggling I longed for. I kept the bedroom television low while he slept, distracting me until I could sleep.

I tried to initiate morning sex. We developed a morning custom of bringing a carafe of hot coffee and two cups into the bedroom. This new marital pleasantry led to morning sex. But right after our morning orgasms he would pop out of bed. "I've got to get started on mowing the lawn," or "I have to go over the bills," he would say. There was always something to attend to. Maybe he was just one of those people who felt so fulfilled by the sex experience that he was just done. *He doesn't need more*, I thought. I stopped focusing on this because I had something more important on my mind. I wanted a baby.

Immediately after our wedding we tried to conceive a baby. Being 40 meant my fertility days were speeding off at a velocity of their own. After decades of avoiding pregnancy, I now longed for it with a passion. I couldn't wait to place a "Baby on Board" sign in my car window and to have a Little Tikes Cozy Coupe in the yard. "Honey, this is just not work-ing. I need expert advice on getting pregnant," I told him after my fifth pe-riod after we married had arrived. "Yeah, I guess you'd better do that," he said, his voice lacking enthusiasm. I immediately sought gynecological help.

I'd suffered from painful menstrual cramps so my physician suggested I undergo a laparoscopy, a day surgery to diagnose any problem that might cause infertility. My gynecologist said if my problem was endometriosis, I'd have a good chance of conceiving after a procedure. I wasn't at all fright-ened by the surgery. Captain X said little, just keeping on top of the medical expenses and insurance.

He was right. I had endometriosis, a disorder where cells from the lining of the uterus attach to other areas of the body. My physician pre-scribed Lupron, an injectable drug to put me in a chemical menopause for three months to keeping the endometriosis at bay. After that I'd have a better chance to conceive. The doctor neglected to tell me Lupron's side effects: hot flashes, mood swings and a low sex drive often associated with a normal menopause.

My three months on Lupron was my first medical problem that clearly affected our marriage. Captain X now seemed to want sex more often but I had little feeling for it. I felt like a non-sexual "it" instead of the woman I used to be. I tried my best to please Captain X, but it was difficult. "I hope you're not going to be like this for long," he said, referring to my diminished sex drive. Couldn't he understand that this was part of the path we had to take to make *our* baby?

I filled the three Lupron months decorating the house and joining Captain X on a few of his layovers. These trips were difficult. I'd meet married flight attendants who had kids *and* a fun job with friends and a social life. I felt I didn't fit in, so I stopped joining Captain X on layovers while my body was in the chemically induced menopause.

Soon I was off Lupron and back to my normal self. I was prescribed Clomid, an oral pill, to help me ovulate. Captain X had to be checked by a urologist, and he did so grudgingly. I gave little thought to his fertility work-up. "The urologist says I have a low sperm volume," he said in a flat tone. "It seems I have enough little guys floating in my stuff, I just don't shoot enough stuff to get them to the right place," he said. This biological information about my husband would come back to haunt me.

When the topic of our infertility came up in conversation, Captain X immediately mentioned my endometriosis, but never mentioned his problem. *Just male ego*, I thought. I certainly wasn't going to hurt him by mentioning his low sperm volume. Something so personal could only be shared with my infertility support group, who provided me with a social life. Since we never mentioned his problem I eventually came to believe it was entirely my fault that we couldn't conceive a baby.

There had not been a baby born into Captain X's family since he was born, something I considered extremely odd. His older brother Nicholas and his two female cousins were childless. His Uncle Kostas had been married four times, yet never fathered children. My siblings all had children, as did my cousins. *This is strange*, I thought. Before we married, Captain X wanted a baby but said "adoption was not an option." I halfheartedly agreed, never imagining I would have such a problem conceiving.

My mother's health was slowly failing. She lacked knowledge of infertility. She was, however, compassionate in her own way. "Don't worry honey, it will happen," she said over my tears on the phone. She was a grandmother of four. Her love of children was undeniable.

Nothing could prepare me for what my new mother-in-law said during one of our phone conversations. "Are you sure you want a baby? Children can be a lot of work." I was shocked! *What kind of woman doesn't want to be a grandmother*, I asked myself. I just couldn't understand Allegra's lack of interest in becoming a grandmother. It was completely foreign to me. *Perhaps this is her way of telling me she loves me, her new daughter-in-law, not wanting me to endure the arduous infertility treatments*, I comforted myself.

Trying to get pregnant while being married to a pilot often away from home was stressful. When Captain X was home, I wanted to be held and reassured that I was loved. Our lovemaking was becoming mechanical. I was growing increasingly uneasy with Captain X's detachment from me afterward. I now attributed this disconnect to my infertility.

I knew Captain X loved me and I loved him. He showed this anytime we were with people. He was always close by my side, his arm around me, charming everyone with colorful stories. He entertained everyone at infertility group socials, and the doctors we came in contact with, and even me.

Now that I was on Clomid, I began to join Captain X on an occasional layover. I appreciated the fact that he wanted me to be with him, to learn firsthand about his profession. I walked proudly beside him in the airport when he was dressed in his dashing uniform. I remember joining him in Guadalajara where I enjoyed his layover at a resort with a swim-up bar. While Captain X napped in the hotel room, I joined a group of Americans for a city tour. When I struck up a conversation with my seatmate, I discovered she was a retired ex-pat living in Mexico. I had no idea Americans could easily live in a foreign country, and I filed the information in the back of my mind.

I just couldn't get pregnant. My gynecologist suggested we come into her office and learn how to do intracervical inseminations, a procedure where Captain X could do the insemination process by himself with his own sperm on the days I was fertile. I was surprised by how well he took on this job of mechanical baby-making.

After the procedure, instead of holding or stroking me, or verbally encouraging me during the 10-minute wait on the bathroom carpet with my buttocks propped high on a pile of pillows, he immediately left the room. He'd say, "I've got bills to pay. My desk is piled with papers since my last trip." He did his part and left. No "I *know* this is our lucky day." No kiss or caress. "Stay with me," I pleaded. "I've got stuff to do," he said firmly. I tried my best to relax, envisioning his sperm working its way into my cervix. We tried this unromantic clinical procedure for three months. It never worked.

Soon we made an appointment to an infertility specialist. The physician had a new plan: Captain X would give his sperm sample at their reproductive center where it would be washed to prepare it for the insemination, which now would be done by the physician.

We did this for three cycles, and the third I remember well. It was St. Patrick's Day, so I focused on the luck of the Irish. People in the throes of infertility often become superstitious; many members of our infertility group resorted to psychics, fortune tellers and lucky charms. Soon I was late for my period, and this being in the early days of reproductive science, I had to go to the doctor's office to get a qualified laboratory pregnancy test. We anxiously waited for their call with the test results. Captain X and I were in bed when we got the news. I was elated. My dream came true: I was pregnant!

As soon as we hung up the phone with the results, we excitedly phoned Allegra and George, then my mother, and then friends and family on our list, sharing our exciting news. I remember calling my sister-in-law, Sally, who sounded oddly apprehensive about our news. I had forgotten she'd suffered a miscarriage early in her marriage.

I never gave a thought to the possibility of having a miscarriage. I remember the day it happened, not only because of the tragic end of a pregnancy, but as yet another clue to how confusing life was becoming with Captain X. At first I felt minor pain, then major cramping and heavy spotting. Captain X called the doctor, receiving instructions to monitor me. Soon I was on the toilet experiencing heavy bleeding and severe pain. I was holding my stomach to ease the pain when a large clot of tissue fell out of me.

I fell to the floor and went into shock, screaming and crying at the same time. "Noooooooo, nooooooooo," I wailed. I knew instantly my dream was over. I sobbed as I asked him, "Should we save it? Bury it?" I really didn't know what to do. I was flooded with extreme sadness and I looked to him for comfort and understanding. In a hollow, emotionless voice he said, "Are you crazy? Flush the damn toilet." He didn't even hold me, comfort me. Then, in an instant, his demeanor changed. His eyes welled and he started to cry in a strange fake sounding way. I had never seen or heard my husband cry before.

Somehow I found my way to bed, sobbing, with a towel between my legs and a heating pad over my abdomen, clutching a box of tissues. I was shocked by this unexpected loss. I have no recollection of him comforting me on this day, a day we should have been comforting each other.

Major Airways' insurance did not cover expensive infertility procedures such as IVF, in vitro fertilization, at the time a new and often successful procedure. Because of its high cost, Captain X said that IVF was definitely out of the question.

I willingly allowed Captain X to handle the family money because I trusted him as the family breadwinner. He appeared to be financially savvy, and always talked about future pay increases. I had enough on my plate with infertility stress. I believed ours was a solid marriage founded on mutual love. I believed "what's yours is mine and what's mine is yours" when you are in a marriage.

Soon after my miscarriage I was prescribed Pergonal, a strong and expensive infertility drug. I was instructed to inject the drug subcutaneously into my thigh five times a week each month, and have my hormone levels checked at the fertility clinic. I had never given myself an injection. I soon became a pro.

Since Pergonal was expensive, I opted to fly Major Airways to the Mexican border where I purchased Pergonal at a local farmacia for nearly half the U.S. cost. I did this twice, carrying cash for the Pergonal purchase. Although I was doing nothing illegal, I felt uncomfortable with these borderland drug purchases, despite carrying a legitimate drug prescription. I purchased two cheap two margarita glasses, somehow thinking this might help me not stand out as a drug dealer while returning through customs. I hoped someday we would use those margarita glasses for a toast when we achieved our goal of parenthood. Captain X hated those margarita glasses, saying "They don't hold enough!"

When Captain X was flying a trip, I was so lonely in the house with my mind wandering while waiting for the baby. I often felt compelled to get out, driving to a secluded area, to cry in frustration and confusion. Weekly phone calls to Allegra didn't help; she constantly talked about herself, avoiding any conversation about my baby quest. On the other hand, my mother, despite her age, listened compassionately.

I tried to reach out to my sister Margo, but sibling rivalry got in the way. By that time she was divorced with a teenage daughter. Her envy of my marriage to an airline pilot was obvious. I received no comfort from her. Other than my infertility support group friends, I had few people to talk to. Why was I feeling so lonely and unloved? I blamed my feelings on the infertility drugs. Too many drugs, too many procedures, too many Pergonal injections, too many doctor visits, too much to live through alone. *This too shall pass*, I told myself.

To get a social life and to keep my mind off of baby-making, I joined a Major Airways Pilots' Wives group. The Pilots' Wives was modeled after military wives clubs. Everyone in our local chapter was aware of my infertility problem, and sympathetic. We attended one of their evening functions held for couples only at a local restaurant banquet room. Captain X and I both looked forward to it. *Good, no babies, just grownups*, I thought. Most women going through infertility do not want to be surrounded by babies, a reminder of a goal they're struggling to achieve.

That evening one of the pilot's wives showed up without her spouse, who was out flying. She couldn't find a babysitter, and despite the fact that the function was adults only, she brought along her newborn. Immediately she approached me saying, "Here, do you want to hold her?" She shoved her baby against my chest, never allowing me to get a word in to decline. I carefully handed her baby back, breaking into sobs as I darted into the nearest ladies room. Having a newborn shoved into my arms so soon after my miscarriage was more than I could handle in my fragile emotional state.

I pulled myself together, splashed cold water on my face and fixed my makeup. I returned to the function as if nothing happened and downed a stiff scotch, the same drink Captain X was drinking while he chatted away, oblivious to my pain.

Sonograms were required during the Pergonal cycle to monitor follicle growth. Due to my age, many of my eggs were not viable. Still, there were promising days. One day, early in my Pergonal cycle, I went alone for my sonogram. Looking at the video monitor, the specialist said, "Everything looks perfect! You have five viable follicles ready to be released."

"Are you sure?!" I said. "Isn't this early?" He answered by pointing to the images on the monitor. Captain X had just left for the airport on his scheduled trip. We needed his sperm immediately! I phoned him, hoping his flight had not yet left.

"Honey, I'm really sorry to bother you but I need you now. The doctor said everything looks perfect today. I know it's sooner than we anticipated, but we really need your sperm sample. Can you call in for a family emergency and get here?"

"You're kidding aren't you? We're just about to close the cockpit door! Are they sure?" he asked in an angry tone.

"That's what they said," I answered.

"You know I'll get a mis-trip for this and we're going to lose a lot of money," he said indignantly. "OK, I'll be there as soon as I can," he said flatly.

Captain X drove directly from the airport to the reproductive center, gave a sperm sample, then drove back home. Soon I was inseminated with it by the best reproductive team in Phoenix. With five viable follicles I had every reason to be optimistic. My mind wandered off to the possibility of having twins. But it didn't work. My period came and I was heartbroken. Captain X was visibly angry that he had lost his trip, and I was sad because this cycle seemed so promising. I didn't know how much longer I could endure this. I also didn't know how much more Captain X would participate. He seemed to have lost sight of our goal of having a family. I was living month to month trying to have a baby.

Our marriage was stressed. I comforted myself knowing that every infertile couple goes through the same thing. Again Allegra and George came to the rescue, inviting us to join them on a fall trip to the wine country to "see the fall leaves." This was foreign to me, that people actually spent money to view fall foliage. If my mother had been more alert I would have shared this with her. I'm sure she would have said, "Don't they have better things to do with their time?" and we would have laughed. Captain X and I were from two different worlds.

It was there, during this gifted Napa Valley holiday, I once again got my unwanted period. I sobbed, sitting down on the hotel's cold marble bathroom floor in tears.

"What's wrong? Why are you crying?" he asked, quizzically. Captain X was oblivious to my monthly fear.

"I got my period again," I cried.

He looked down at me, not even touching me, and said in a matter-of-fact tone, "You have a choice, one IVF cycle or adoption."

I didn't hesitate. "Adoption, *YES adoption!*" I answered, thrilled as if I had won the lottery. IVF was a gamble, but adoption was a sure thing. I hadn't told him but I had already looked into adoption in hopes he'd change his mind. I was so happy at the prospect of becoming a mother I never realized he hadn't comforted me about not being pregnant, that he wasn't talking about adoption in a loving manner. It was a blank statement, his voice void of any emotion.

We shared our adoption news with Allegra and George. George broke into a huge smile at the prospect of becoming a grandfather while Allegra reached into her purse and pulled out her checkbook. My husband put on a new face. Beaming, he pocketed the check. "Thanks folks, you're great. This will really help with the adoption expenses," he said. Again his family came to the rescue with a sizeable check. It seemed Allegra always expressed her affection with money.

Like infertility, the adoption process was stressful, but in an entirely different way. We decided on a closed adoption, having no contact with the baby's birth mother. Adoption requires a lot of paperwork, interviews with lawyers and a home study with a state social worker. We were also required to undergo psychological testing.

Our adoption agency required us to visit a psychologist. After a brief interview we had to take a test, the MMPI, Minnesota Multiphasic

Personality Inventory. The MMPI was commonly used to assess psychological stability in workers in high-risk professions, including police and pilots, to reveal any emotional deficit or psychopathic tendencies.

I couldn't recall ever having taken a psychological test. Captain X assured me, "It's nothing. I've taken these to get with the airlines." Sitting in the waiting room he turned toward me and confided, "There's nothing to be concerned about. I actually know how to beat it." What an odd thing to say to me as we went in to be tested!

"Everything will be OK. We'll be matched with a baby in no time," he said afterwards, patting my thigh as he started the car to go home.

"How do you know?" I asked, emotionally drained.

"Because they like me," he answered matter-of-factly.

Five months later our adoption agency matched us with a birth mother due to give birth in March. Our baby was on its way! Captain X wanted to forget infertility, and I readily agreed. Since I still lacked family support other than my mother, I needed someone to talk to while waiting for the baby to be born.

I join an adoption support group. Instead of hearing about IVF procedures, eggs and inseminations, I'd moved to a group that talked about bonding, closed versus open adoptions, and Moses baskets, something I never heard of, which turned out to be a straw basket to carry a newborn. I didn't want a Moses basket. I wanted a baby.

I tried to feel positive, and Captain X, his family, and everyone I came into contact with—with the exception of my support group—thought adoption was a sure thing. But it's not. A birth mother can change her mind. Adoption is only a sure thing when the adoption is finalized in court.

Captain X wanted his "sexy wife" back, but I needed love and we did not make love. Soon I became a sex partner out of what I saw as my marital duty. I blamed the lack of lovemaking and intimacy in our sex life on the stress we had been through. I worked hard to please him. I kept telling myself, *After all, he did change his mind about adoption for me.* Never once did I notice that my trying to have a baby was something I seemed to be doing all alone.

Home alone waiting for a baby was tough. I had trouble passing the empty nursery, fearing something would go wrong with the adoption. I cleverly decorated it; Martha Stewart would have been impressed.

I eased the wait with endless phone calls to fellow support group members. Meanwhile, Captain X kept in touch with quick phone calls from his layover hotel before "going out for a quick bite to eat," or to "dinner with the crew."

The week our baby was due I called him out of frustration, begging for emotional support. "Why can't you just let go of the baby stuff for now?" he lashed out at me. "I'm all alone. You have people in your life with your job. They're your distraction." I replied.

I really needed to be with him. The baby was due any day and I was going crazy in anticipation, alone in the house. He was headed to a Detroit layover. I pleaded with him, "*Please* let me be with you! I need to be with you!"

"All right, get on a flight and come here," he replied, "but I don't want to talk about the baby." Oblivious to this odd invite, I quickly packed an overnight bag and caught the first flight to meet him. Once there, I proceeded to get mildly drunk with Captain X and crew, with his arm around me, all the time assuring myself how much he loved me and how this baby would soon change our lives.

The next morning I flew back home while he went finished the final leg of the trip. I felt better for getting out of the house. No sooner had I walked in when the phone rang. It was the adoption agency. "You have a beautiful baby girl! She was born yesterday and you can come tomorrow to get her." After scribbling down the specifics, I hung up the phone and let the news sink in. Gina had just been born. I walked into the nursery with tears rolling down my face. "You're going to love this room, Gina," I said out loud.

I called Captain X's crew schedulers and told them we had a family emergency, to have him call me as soon as possible. I couldn't wait to share the news.

When he arrived home we went out to dinner to celebrate, knowing the next morning we would be parents. I didn't sleep a wink that night knowing that Gina, my baby daughter, would soon be in my arms.

Chapter 5: The Standby Family

"WOULD YOU LIKE to hold your daughter?" the neonatal nurse asked. It was love at first sight when Gina was placed my arms in the hospital chapel. The nurses dressed her in a white Baby Dior onesie we brought for her to come home in. *Nothing but the best for this kid*, I thought. I was bursting with happiness with the perfect little family I'd always dreamed of.

From the second Gina joined our family, Captain X found a new purpose in life. It was amazing to see how he quickly he became a doting father. He was in Gina's room every morning he was home, the first person she saw when she woke up. I didn't mind one bit that he took fatherhood with such enthusiasm. In fact, I welcomed it. He was bored with his job and life in general. Gina became his newfound focus.

Gina was the perfect baby, never developing colic or feeding difficulties. We willingly jumped to attend to her needs. "I'll get her," he commanded me. Early on I loved this, my husband being such a doting father, but it came to feel like I was competing with him. When I look back, he *was* doing that, competing with me over parenting.

As we settled into our little family routine, we only did things as a family if I instigated them. Captain X never planned ahead, had no long-term goals, and lived very much in the present. I always had to come up with plans for holidays, birthdays, vacations and family outings.

A pilot's profession is regulated by the FAA (Federal Aviation Administration). Captain X was limited to flying 100 hours a month, flying up to 8 hours a day. He usually had 15 days off a month dispersed between trips. He left home and returned at all hours of the day. His work schedule changed each month. His profession dictated our lives, or so I felt. Everything depended on his bid sheet, the next month's schedule of flying.

Each month Captain X received an electronic bid sheet showing all the flight sequences (trips) available for the following month. He put his selection of trips for the following month in when the bidding closed, about five days later. The results came back about a week later. Open time, or picking up trips (if his bid result came up short on flying time and he needed more hours) came later in the month.

Every month's bid sheet was different. New routes or equipment (types of airplanes) may have been added or changed. Pilots may be on vacation, off for training, retired or they may even have died, leaving open sought-after trips. "Hey, guess what," my husband would say, "Captain Ray Smith just died! Great guy, Ray, good guy to fly with." The mourning period was less than a minute. "My seniority just moved up a number!" Captain X would announce happily, in what I took as black humor.

"The bids are out," he announced like clockwork every month. He would spend hours arranging his preferences. He usually selected trips with important days off, like Gina's birthday, and high time trips (which paid more) with the best layover location, all in the hopes that someone with greater seniority didn't pick up the trips he bid for.

"I got my fourth choice," he would announce, or whichever choice he was awarded. This meant nothing to me; I was only interested in the results. I would mark my calendar accordingly. Captain X was also able to trip trade part of his next month's sequence with other pilots. He trip traded often, telling me he did it to make more money.

Now that there were three of us, I needed to get involved with the family finances. "Honey, can we go over the finances?" I would ask. "Now's not the time," he'd answer. "I'm just too tired from flying. Besides, I've got a lot of stuff to do around the house. Anyway you know that it's all here," he'd say, pointing to his file cabinets and computer. "We'll go over it. I give you my word." Then he'd skillfully change the subject. Captain X always had a plausible excuse for not wanting me to get involved in family finances.

He did, however, share complicated information about his union contract negotiations, information he knew was confusing to me. "Why don't you become active in your union?" I asked when he complained about his union. He had no hobbies other than Gina and cooking. It seemed a good idea. "Yeah, I should do that," he answered, but he never did.

Gina's first airplane ride flying standby was when she was four weeks old. I thought it would be special for Gina to take her first flight with her daddy as the captain. He mentioned he was short on flight time. "I can pick up a short Phoenix-Tucson turn tomorrow."

"Honey, can you check and see if there are any open seats on it? If so, could we join you?" I asked. Seats were available, and soon Gina and I were bound for Tucson with her father at the controls of the airplane. When we landed, Captain X held baby Gina in the cockpit while I snapped photos.

From the beginning I'd thought I would be smothered in Greek culture, but Allegra and George didn't do that. I was even more surprised they didn't celebrate traditional holidays. Perhaps it's because they'd spent so many long days and years in the restaurant business and they never developed the habit. They seldom visited us, despite my constant invitations, and only invited us to visit them a few times a year. They definitely were not hands-on grandparents, but rather the gifting kind. *I have no right to complain*, I consoled myself, since they were so generous with checks, which they handed directly to Captain X. Still, I thought it was off-the-wall strange how his family never cared to be with us. My dad had passed and my mom was fading in a nursing home. Allegra and George were Gina's only active grandparents. *So much for warm and fuzzy family holidays with family*, I told myself. When we first met, Captain X said his family was "really close." I thought close families spent holidays together.

One of the few Christmases that Allegra and George did visit us was when Gina was four years old. Gina never left her grandparents' side from the second they arrived and unpacked in the seldom-used guest bedroom. Allegra handed Gina her presents immediately, rather than waiting for Christmas morning. "Honey, I wish your parents would have waited until Christmas morning to give Gina her presents."

"Let them do what they want," he said. His family just didn't seem to get opening presents on Christmas Day.

"Why don't you two go out to a movie together? We'll stay with Gina," Allegra said. That sounded good to me so Captain X and I got into his car and drove to a movie theater in a mall. As we were driving I politely asked my husband, "Honey, why don't your parents get the idea of Christmas Day surprises?" He instantly became enraged. "Why can't you just leave it alone? Bitch, bitch, bitch, that's all you do!" he yelled at me, as he pulled the car into an open space in front of a bookstore filled with last minute shoppers.

Tears flowed down my face and my head filled with confusion. I wasn't confrontational. I'd just asked a question. Now my husband was yelling at me on Christmas Eve! When he parked he commanded, "Stop your bitching *NOW!*" I quickly walked ahead of him towards a store, with tears streaming down my face. Suddenly he grabbed my arm and jerked it hard. "Just shut up!" he yelled. He didn't let go, still pulling me toward him. "You're hurting me!" I yelled through my tears. Soon a shopper appeared. "Lady, do you want me to call the police?" he asked. "No, no, I'm OK," I said softly, not wanting to bring attention to what I took to be an unusual marital spat. But I wasn't OK. It was Christmas Eve and I was in tears. His piercing eyes glared at me with a predatory stare.

Then Captain X instantly turned off his rage and acted as if nothing had happened, saying nothing. My emotions were all over the place as he purchased the movie tickets. We had 15 minutes to kill until the movie started so we walked silently around the shops. I stared at the Christmas windows, half trying to look through them, and half trying to look at my reflection in the glass in an attempt to hypnotize myself into forgetting the incident, trying to find excuses for his behavior. *He's stressed over his parents' visit*, I thought. *That has to be it. What else could it be?* I sat rigid in the seat next to Captain X staring at the movie screen, trying to focus on the film. I must have done a good job of hypnotizing myself over what had happened. I don't remember one bit of our conversation as we drove back to the house.

"Did you two have a good time?" Allegra asked. I filled her and George in on the movie plot. I have no idea how I did it. It was as if the whole incident had never happened.

I had done this before Gina joined us. Captain X was assigned to fly to Hawaii during Christmas. I was thrilled to get away from infertility and be in Hawaii. I remember going down the escalator of the layover hotel to the main lobby to meet the crew for dinner. I was wearing a sleeveless sundress. Pointing to a bruise on my forearm he asked, "Did I do that?" I had forgotten he had grabbed me the day before during an argument. "I guess so," I said meekly. I didn't know I had a bruise or I wouldn't have worn that dress. He said absolutely nothing. I buried the whole incident somewhere in my mind. I didn't realize it, but I was living in denial and confusion.

Since Captain X's family made no attempts to share any holiday time with us I encouraged him to bid to fly holiday trips. He could easily get his choice of destinations flying on Christmas or Thanksgiving, days most passengers had already arrived at their destinations. That way Gina and I could easily get space-available non-revenue seats. We three could be together and celebrate at a unique locale. This became our common practice most every holiday throughout our marriage.

Traveling standby on Major Airways meant getting to the airport two hours ahead of time for domestic flights and four hours ahead for international to be first in line on the standby list. We never checked luggage, always traveling with our rollaboard suitcases. Little Gina and I endured long airport waits with what we called "suitcase races," running from one airport shop to another so she would be tuckered out for the flight. Gina was responsible for her own rollaboard from the time she could handle it. I wonder if she knew I always let her win the races.

As a flying mother, I learned to keep my toddler active before boarding a flight so she would sleep on the airplane. I always said to her, "no dillydallying." The phrase set her off into a fit of giggles. Once aboard the aircraft, she would soon be asleep wearing a Major Airlines eye mask.

We spent one Thanksgiving in Reno at a layover hotel and casino, dining on casino buffet fare. Gina, the only two-year-old in sight, shoved mashed potatoes into her chubby little face from her red-striped umbrella stroller tray table. Captain X, his crew and I sat at a long dining table, eating and drinking while being serenaded by the cacophony of slot machines with their constant clink-clink-clink-ringgggg. To this day, every single time I think of Thanksgiving, I think of that trip and Gina with her mashed potatoes. Little Gina was fun to travel with. I was the happiest person in the world when I fastened the seat belts snugly around our waists and we were soon at 35,000 feet in the sky. Next to Gina I was never lonely. Travel helped me ignore the ongoing lack of intimacy in my marriage.

I'll never forget the time we went on a trip with Captain X to London. Gina was five at the time. Gina and I stayed on a few days, visiting my friends and enjoying the sights—her favorite, going into each red telephone booth. We rushed through London's Heathrow Airport to get on the standby list to return home. Gina wore her black travel dress, tights and patent leather Mary Janes, with a navy blue Chesterfield coat with a matching hat. She looked as cute as a button. We took a lengthy escalator up to get to the main floor of the busiest airport in the world. Approached the landing, a group of Arab sheiks dressed in white thawb robes came into view. "Look Mommy, angels!" My heart swelled with motherly love.

When Captain X flew internationally, he had flights to Frankfurt, Germany. When Gina was six and on a school break, we both flew on his flight. Traveling standby I always wore a stylish travel pantsuit accessorized with a silk scarf. After saying goodbye to Daddy, Gina and I made our way to the bustling Frankfurt underground train station to visit my friends a short train ride away. As we passed a Tie Rack shop, a chain store selling inexpensive ties and scarves, Gina bolted toward the shop's display of colorful scarves. "I want one Mommy, *puleeze, just like yours!*" She looked closely through the rack and said, "I like this one. It has doggies." After purchasing it, I tied the scarf around her neck. I would keep my eyes on her "doggy scarf" for years. It became one of my most prized mementos.

We found a competent neighbor willing to babysit Gina for extended periods of time, so Captain X and I decided to embark on a Hong Kong vacation that I planned on a budget. As usual, he was concerned about getting home even before we departed. "I sure hope that return flight stays open. I barely have enough time to get back for my next trip," he said. I could never understand this; he could get the jump seat (a cockpit seat used for crew members not working the flight) or if worst came to worst, buy a ticket at a discount on another airline. We always allowed adequate time to catch the next flight. His need to control was confusing, putting a damper on trips before we even took off. Most people in the airline industry feel "where there is a will there is a way" to get to get to their destination.

Together we flew to Japan, where we caught another carrier to Hong Kong. Seeing the highlights of the bustling Asian city we had a pleasant time, but little romance. Hong Kong was a shopping paradise. Not being a shopper, my only purchase was an Asian doll for Gina styled like the popular Cabbage Patch dolls. Rather than holding a birth certificate, the Asian doll came with a passport. When we arrived home early, I handed her "Hong Kong dolly," which she gleefully embraced.

Since Captain X still had remaining vacation days, we came up with an idea. "Hon," I said, "you still have days left. What if we took Gina to Puerto Vallarta as a family? Gina missed us and she'd love it." He agreed and so we repacked our rollaboard suitcases, this time filled with resort wear, and we flew to Mexico, booking an industry-discounted hotel. As we entered customs, five-year-old Gina presented both her and Hong Kong dolly's passports to the Mexican customs agent. The agent broke into a broad smile as he obligingly stamped both passports.

When Gina was six, we flew to Honolulu where Captain X's flight would arrive the following day, Thanksgiving. There wasn't a child in sight at the crew hotel. I tried my best to make our holiday special. Gina wanted to go to the beach, so off we went. Gina couldn't wait to meet her daddy as the crew bus pulled up to the layover hotel.

After having a good nap, the three of us went off to a typical tourist luau. The crew made excuses not to join us. I wondered why. I would have welcomed their adult company. Some crews socialized together, and other times they went their separate ways. It was just the three of us for the Thanksgiving luau where we watched a Hawaiian show. Gina and I made silly foul faces after tasting the purple Hawaiian poi.

In the early days of our flying, prior to 9/11, I used to pack a tiny artificial Christmas tree, miniature lights and ornaments to decorate the Christmas layover hotel room. I strongly encouraged Gina to ask Santa for small gifts like jewelry or gift cards so I could put tiny boxes under the tree, keeping my carry-on baggage light. "Isn't that a pretty necklace?" I would say. "Yeah, Mommy, pretty." If she asked for a large item like a bicycle, Santa Claus brought it early, the morning we left on our holiday flight.

Gina was six when we joined Captain X in London for Christmas, spending it at an airport hotel. At least we would be together. Gina and I passed the time making paper chains with red and green construction paper, using a glue stick and toy scissors (again, pre 9/11) to decorate the layover hotel room. Flight attendants decorated the back of the airplane with the chains.

That evening Captain X made a few phone calls, persuading a Major Airways official to pay for the crew's holiday dinner. I had hoped some crew members might have brought their families along (which sometimes happened on holidays), but Gina was the only child. Captain X had his arm around me and Gina next to him, captivating his crew audience. Despite his talent for conversation I noticed again the way he repeated the same stories over and over, and increasingly talked about his wealthy family. His bragging behavior was becoming embarrassing.

This crew soon became a bunch of party animals. It wasn't the family holiday I had envisioned. The only holiday spirit Captain X had was the scotch he drank. I never heard a "Merry Christmas," or "I love you for bringing Gina." After I tucked my daughter in the roll-out bed we'd ordered, I slipped into bed next to Captain X with mixed emotions. I wondered if it had been worth it joining him for Christmas. He was fast asleep, and I felt lonely in the hotel room that we three had squeezed into. I reminded myself that had we stayed home in Phoenix, I would have been lonely with no family around except Gina. Besides, Gina wanted to be with her daddy.

Once Captain X was assigned a month of Sao Paolo trips. The hotel gave him their best available room, a huge suite with an extra bedroom and amazingly, a sauna. "Wow, you just wouldn't believe the room I got!" he said excitedly when he returned from his first trip. Gina was seven and on a school break. She and I had developed a terrible bronchial ailment we just couldn't shake. I was exhausted and drained. Since the Phoenix weather was dreary and it was bright and sunny in Sao Paolo, I suggested that we join Captain X on his Sao Paolo trip. We were on a series of antibiotics, so we weren't contagious. "Can we go with you?" I asked. Captain X checked the computer and seats on his flight were available. "If you want to," he answered. We quickly packed our rollaboards and headed out to the airport with Captain X. Seated far back in the coach section, we slept most of the lengthy flight. When we woke, we ran through customs, boarded the crew van with Captain X, and soon were in Captain X's luxurious suite. Gina and I immediately disrobed. "Follow me," I said, leading her into the sauna to breathe in the wet steamy air. "Neat, Mom!" Gina said, never having been in a sauna. It was a long way to go to get healthy, but the weather and hotel's sauna and pool were therapeutic. Gina and I returned home revitalized.

One year we flew a few days earlier than Captain X's flight to Buenos Aires. As a typical teenager, Gina's main interest was shopping. For Christmas we gave her $100 to shop with. The next day, Gina and I hit Florida Street, a pedestrian shopping strip filled with shops, arcades, vendors, restaurants and street entertainment of tango dancers and living statues. It was a fabulous place for a teenager to spend her Christmas loot. At the time I was swallowing lots of ibuprofen; I was in constant pain due to my arthritic back and hip. "Mom, how do I look?" Gina said, smiling as she modeled a colorful skirt. "Beautiful, baby," I said, leaning against the wall in pain in the chairless boutique. She hit every shop in the area, with me following closely in tow. Gina grinned from ear to ear with her piles of purchases. We were lucky. The exchange rate made the dollar go far. Gina had a ball and she couldn't wait to show her dad her purchases. I was just thankful to be in a warm climate that holiday; arthritis and cold weather don't mix well.

One of the most difficult holiday trips I shared with Gina sticks out prominently in my mind. Gina was five and we were trying to meet Captain X in Miami, where he had a Christmas layover. Gina and I had a four-hour layover in New Orleans on Christmas Day in the nearly empty Armstrong International Airport. We were starving, after declining bad coach food. I anticipated finding a restaurant in New Orleans, never thinking everything would be closed on Christmas Day except a hot dog stand. We consumed day-old sodium-filled sausages on stale buns slathered in mustard for our Christmas lunch. We had spent nearly eight hours in airports just to keep our three-member family together for Christmas.

I approached two Major Airways pilots to ask them to check our standby status for our connecting flight. As a spouse I was not privy to this information. When they asked my husband's name, I got an odd look from one of them who said, "Oh, him," in a strongly dismissive tone. I was really perplexed by the pilot's response; I'd assumed Captain X had an exemplary image. Before I could get the pilot's name, he disappeared from sight. *You can't be liked by everyone*, I thought. Once we met Captain X at his Miami hotel, we dined on Chinese food from the only restaurant open late that Christmas night. Gina didn't care. She was with her daddy on Christmas.

When I was on any of Captain X's flights, he often introduced me to flight attendants he knew. "He talks about you and Gina all the time. What a wonderful husband you have," they would say. He had them charmed. Before his assigned nap break on long international flights, Captain X would come back to my seat and say, right in front of the flight attendant working my section, "How are they treating ya?" I always answered "Great!" since the flight attendant was in earshot. In truth it was a coin toss. His concern over how I was being treated seemed fake, like he was putting on a show, but he did it with such style that I took it for the real thing for quite a long time.

I often used my flight pass privileges to visit my European friends. I planned these trips around Gina's extended sleepovers or when I could get a good sitter. I kept expenses down, staying with my friends, visiting museums and flea markets. I loved small antiques and found my way around the flea markets, including London's Portobello Road, Paris's Puces de Clignancourt and the San Telmo Antique Market in Buenos Aires.

These trips gave me a great idea for start-up business. With my outgoing personality, love of travel, and expertise with antiques, I thought I would the perfect person to organize small guided tours to European antique markets. I proposed my idea to Captain X. "I've got a great idea. What do you think of me starting up an antique tour business taking small travel groups to European flea markets?" I said excitedly. I never anticipated his response. "Don't be silly. You can't do that. You wouldn't even know how to do that," he said with a smirk. I didn't know how to react to his sarcastic, cynical answer. He shut me down, making me feel as if I had no talent or intelligence.

Captain X sabotaged every idea I came up with to make a life independent from him. *Maybe he's right.* I stopped questioning him. My self-confidence and self-esteem were slowly being eroded. Soon the ideas were forgotten. I was slowly being conditioned by Captain X, though I didn't fully recognize it. In the back of my mind I was beginning to think that my perfect life was being controlled by Captain X, but at the same time *I did have a perfect life*, I assured myself.

What's my problem? I asked myself.

"Hey! Guess who just made captain? The bids came out, I found out I've just been awarded captain!" my husband yelled excitedly from his office. We had been anticipating this. His captain training would take place the following month. Captain X was manic when he was in training. There would be no chance for me to get involved with our family finances. He would be away for weeks, staying near the airport, and in no frame of mind to answer questions. Our family had reached another goal. Making captain meant more money. I celebrated with my husband that he finally reached his goal, all while keeping my nagging thoughts somewhere in my mind, on standby.

Chapter 6: The Captain's House

IN ORDER TO get the flight hours required to be hired by a legacy carrier—an established airline—George and Allegra had purchased a small airplane for Captain X, which they wrote off as a company expense. This was foreign to me: "I know! Let's buy the kid an airplane!" I later discovered they'd also bought him a college degree from a diploma mill to help him land his job. In reality he only attended one year of college. Captain X was employed by a smaller airline prior to joining Major Airways, and the family plane helped him accumulate flight time to become a commercial pilot. Captain X had told me he worked hard to get to where he was in his career, but as time went on and I received more bits of information, I wondered if he realized how lucky he was.

His income nearly doubled when he achieved the rank of captain. To celebrate his promotion, we agreed that he would buy a new luxury sports car, which we nicknamed the "datemobile." We could enjoy it together when we went out to dinner, like we were on a date. The car had deluxe leather seats in the front, but the back seats were cramped. Gina could just barely squeeze in the back during short trips so we used my car for family outings.

When he was not flying and Gina was with a babysitter, we occasionally had a nice dinner out at a restaurant that catered to adults. On the way home, with a few cocktails under his belt, he would retract the hard top and pop in a CD, blasting it loudly while maneuvering through traffic at speeds of up to 100 mph on the expressway. Somehow he was never stopped for speeding. I yelled, "Slow down, please!" He'd answer, "Come on now, I know what I'm doing." By this time I was so confused, I actually enjoyed the exhilarating feeling, sharing something with him—a better version of my father—despite the danger we might be in. Sometimes he developed road rage. When this happened, I begged him not to confront the person who had cut him off. This frightened me and when I told him so, he calmed down.

Soon we were looking for the "Captain's House," a bigger, better house than our starter home. Most airline captains buy larger homes after achieving their new financially rewarding rank. Like most families, we looked for a home located in an excellent school district. Captain X always made it very clear: "I don't want to live near other pilots" in what he called pilots' ghettos, subdivisions 20 minutes from the airport where pilots made their homes. These subdivisions were far from ghettos, since airline captains' salaries could reach as high $200,000. He added "They don't like non-military trained pilots. Most of them are assholes." Captain X was civilian trained. I thought this explanation was plausible.

After my husband's promotion to captain, I wasn't the least bit worried about money. My mind was busy with the new house. Again I resigned myself to letting him control our finances. He seemed competent, poring over his computer, always appearing to be looking at a spreadsheet like a trained accountant.

He repeatedly mentioned his financial inheritance. "My family is worth about four million. Someday half will be mine," he boasted. He still slipped bits of this into conversation when we were out with other couples, which I found embarrassing. *Then again, maybe this entitlement attitude is something all rich kids have,* I said to myself. I had no experience with moneyed families. Somehow I accepted what he said as a fact, rather than a clue to his arrogance and grandiose manner. My naiveté about our financial situation was just one of my many errors in judgment during the marriage.

I remember the day we went house hunting in a luxurious gated community called Elmdale, with houses starting at $650,000. As we slowly drove through the stately community, he stopped at an elaborate mansion still under construction. He commanded me to get out and follow him into the elaborate mega-house. "Do you like it?" he asked with a grin. "I bought it, it's ours!" My jaw dropped! "What, you're kidding? REALLY? REALLY? IT'S BEAUTIFUL! I can't believe it! Oh my God, this is WONDERFUL!" I answered in amazement. I was dumbstruck! My head was spinning as I tried to absorb this huge revelation. This surprise was shocking, but not at all inconceivable; after all, he came from a very wealthy family, and had bought our first home without my input. A full minute later he said with a slight sneer, in an even-toned voice, "I'm only kidding. Can't you take a joke?" My stomach dropped. His cruelty cut deep into my heart. "Don't EVER do that again," I said through tears. He laughed at me as if what had just happened was funny. We got back into our car. "Come on now, you know I was only joking!" he said smiling, patting my knee as he started up the ignition. As we drove off silently to look in other neighborhoods for a house, I was frozen by the shock of having been duped by him. Confused, I thought that he was probably right; I should laugh at the joke he'd just played on me. *What's wrong with me? Can't I take a joke?*

Eventually we built the Captain's House on one of the few remaining empty lots in an affluent subdivision called Foxhollow. We hired the same architect who designed another house we'd both liked, but with modifications that would work on the lot we had chosen. When he returned from each trip, Captain X was totally preoccupied, overseeing the process step by step. We made frequent trips to the property to check the progress. Gina was a toddler at the time, keeping me extremely busy. When Captain X wasn't flying we were picking out cabinets, drawer pulls, carpets, tile, countertops, lighting and plumbing fixtures, door knobs and the millions of other decisions that had to be made to ensure our home would be completed to our specifications. These were our family outings for much of the year, many with Gina in tow.

Some people love the process of building a house. I hated it. Captain X loved it. The house was way behind schedule. I longed for its completion after the difficult I years endured trying to have a baby. I wanted to live life, not spend time making a place to live it.

The home fit right in among the neighborhood's homes. At 4,000 square feet, the contemporary house looked beautiful on the tree-lined cul-de-sac. After we moved in, I spent months scheduling and waiting on workmen to make adjustments, to fix things that were improperly executed or working incorrectly. Gina was enrolled in a Mother's Day Out program which gave me some relief, but the whole house building process drained me. I had very little social life. It took close to a year before I could feel somewhat comfortable in the house. The sight of Gina happily riding her Little Tyke's Cozy Coupe in the house soothed me.

When the construction workers poured the concrete sidewalk in front of the house, we were there. I made a suggestion. "Honey, wouldn't it be nice if we put our initials and the date in a small heart in the concrete?"

"Why would you want to do *that?*" he said in irritation, shooting me a disdainful look as if I intended to ruin the property. Maybe he was right. It was probably a childish thing to do.

The kitchen was complete with custom granite counters and a matching island. "The kitchen is my domain," he said, "and I know just what I want." I knew how to cook, but nothing I prepared was to his liking, so I just gave up. Captain X took over in the kitchen when he was home, and I took the job of setting the table and doing the cleanup. "You're so lucky! Your husband cooks. My husband can't even boil water," women would say enviously, not realizing that it was a way of controlling me.

The five bedroom house had vaulted ceilings in the formal living area with enormous windows that looked out onto the swimming pool and adjoining hot tub. It was a classic contemporary house, monochromatic, with eggshell-colored walls throughout. Matching carpeting covered the formal living and family room floors. Most of the large windows were fitted with plantation shutters. Two of the three upstairs bedrooms off the huge open loft became our personal offices, while the third was the guest room. My office became my own haven to paint, sew, craft, and restore and sell small antiques for a little profit through eBay. I have fond memories of crafting there.

In my craft room I taught five-year-old Gina to use my sewing machine. Her first project was a green felt eyeglass case; she cautiously pressed her foot on the control pedal to keep the machine from speeding off on its own. She decorated it with a glued-on oval rhinestone. "Here Mommy, I made this for you." I was so proud of her accomplishment and my new gift.

When Gina was 11 we were at a loss for what to give her dad for Father's Day. "Gina, I know, let's sew him a robe!" She agreed so off we

went to the fabric store to pick out fabric and a pattern. She chose a checkered seersucker fabric. "He's going to like this, Mommy," Gina proudly
proclaimed. "Yes, especially since you're making it all by yourself," I added.
Gina learned to pin the tissue pattern to the fabric, cut out the pieces and
sew everything together, while I read the instructions. "Beautiful, baby," I
said, looking at the robe. When Father's Day came she proudly presented
the gift to her dad. He offered simple thanks, never expounding on all the
time and handiwork it took her to produce the gift. He even asked us to
shorten it, which I did. I thought his reaction to the gift was callous. He
wore the robe a few times but never made a big deal out of it.

Gina's bedroom was downstairs on one end of the house. I loved decorating and redecorating my little girl's room when she was old enough to
vocalize what she wanted. The décor changed often as she grew.

Our huge master bedroom was on the other wing of the house. The
spacious master bath had a large whirlpool bathtub, making it my second
favorite room. There I was able to soak my increasingly painful arthritic
body in comfort and style against the jets of hot water in the deep, luxurious tub.

The new Foxhollow neighbors were nice enough; our neighbors in the
cul-de-sac included Don and Lynn, Terry and Tim, Dick and Linda and
David and Katie. I anticipated a close-knit neighborhood and hopefully a
new female friend, since most of the women were stay-at-home mothers
like me. Linda was always planning some neighborhood get-together we
attended when Captain X wasn't flying. Linda started an annual progressive
Christmas dinner that Captain X made an extra special effort to attend. He
took delight in outdoing everyone's food expertise, working at a feverish
pace in the kitchen. Meanwhile I loved the social life with the couples.

Captain X never shared with me how he made these gourmet dinners,
despite my asking to try my hand at it. "The kitchen's my place. I know
what I am doing. We both can't be in here," he said firmly. Cooking seemed
to be his only hobby, so I left him alone in his kitchen. I never questioned
this. Eventually I lost all confidence in preparing food for anyone other
than Gina.

Dining with Gina was fun. When Captain X was flying we made
'sketti,' my homemade spaghetti sauce. "Yummy, Mommy," she would say,

her mouth covered with sauce. "Yummy," I answered back. Captain X hated spaghetti, so when he was flying it became a favorite dinner. Other times we had macaroni and cheese with shredded roasted chicken. Once I surprised her with a "backward dinner" starting with ice cream sundae and then went onto our main course. "Oh Mommy, this is fun!" she said, smiling.

Despite the lavish dinner parties that took Captain X days of preparation, we seldom received return dinner invitations. *Maybe they feel they can't top Captain X's rack of lamb or Beef Wellington*, I told myself. Didn't they like us? Didn't they like him? Maybe they didn't like me. I couldn't understand why the neighbor women never warmed up to me. Maybe it was that I was from New York, wasn't a serial shopper, or because we didn't belong to their church. *You can't win them all*, I thought.

One bright sunny summer day, Captain X and I took Gina to the local McDonald's so our four-year-old could play in the ball pit after eating. There we met Susan and Joel and their four-year-old daughter, Allison. Allison and Gina squealed in delight, playing together as if they were old friends. "It's nice to meet someone with a daughter the same age as Gina," I said. "We just enrolled her in the Montessori school across the street," I added, pointing in the direction of the facility. "No kidding! Allison is starting there next week," Susan said. We finally met another couple. *It's about time*, I thought.

Susan was a gregarious, stay-at-home mom like me. Her husband Joel was an investment banker. Susan and I got together during our daughters play dates. I loved laughing with her, having someone locally as a friend. Captain X and I finally had friends, and our daughters became best friends. We would hire a babysitter for the girls and go out to an upscale restaurant for dinner, where we alternated picking up the check.

Joel and Susan had their life planned well in advance and were very involved in investing for their family's future. They were planning for Allison's education. Allegra and George had established a generous college fund for Gina. Allison and Gina's friendship continued through elementary school. Allison soon was in accelerated classes; meanwhile, eight-year-old Gina's report card was far from impressive. Her reading skills were poor. I had to get to the bottom of this. *Nancy Drew* mysteries came to the rescue. I actually looked forward to reading out loud to Gina after dinner at the kitchen table. I added theatrics to my reading to get her full attention. Before long, Gina's readings scores increased. The only drawback was that Nancy Drew owned a car, introducing Gina to the idea of car ownership at a very young age. *Gina, you have time to think about that*, I smiled to myself.

One evening, after returning home from dinner with Joel and Susan when was our turn to pick up the check, Captain X complained about the high cost of the meal. "Joel makes a hell of a lot of money," he said. "I don't make half of what he does. Do you have any idea what the bill was?" he asked. "Over $175," he complained. I was fuzzy after the dinner wine. I tried to understand why Captain X was complaining about the bill. *We don't frequent fine restaurants more than once every month or two*, I told myself. *What's the big deal?*

I imagined our spacious house would be filled with new people in our life, that we would entertain family and new and exciting friends. We could easily have entertained 40 people in the free-flowing home. This never happened. Other than annual birthday parties for Gina, we only had two big parties: Captain X's 40th birthday Mexican fiesta, and a millennium party. Unfortunately, on both occasions Susan and Joel had prior commitments. We had to scrounge to find anyone, *any* neighbor who could attend. Some neighbors asked if they could bring friends and family. I readily agreed. It was embarrassing how few people we had in our lives. The more I talked to Captain X about this, the more he deflected my questions, somehow avoided answering, or used his flying schedule or another diversionary tactic to keep me off track. "It's hard to meet people in my business," he would say. There was always an excuse for having few people in our lives.

Most of my friends lived in other cities, many in European countries. A handful of my antique or New York friends visited our home, but I preferred visiting them since I could fly to see them, saving them the expense of visiting me. Captain X seemed to have no social life, no one to bring home to entertain.

The huge Captain's House was lonely. It was also way too big for me to care for by myself, especially with my painful arthritis. Our neighbor Terry suggested we hire her cleaning lady, Sue. I had mixed emotions about having help in the house, but Sue did a great job vacuuming and cleaning the floors during her four-hour bi-monthly visit. She was a trustworthy, no-nonsense lady. I liked her. Over time I began to feel there was no sense in having such a big house if no one visited, except an occasional dinner with Susan and Joel. On the other hand, everyone in our upscale neighborhood had big houses *and* cleaning ladies. I was living an upscale life Captain X wanted.

Being extremely creative, I continued to decorate the huge house on a budget. I couldn't find master and guest room bedspreads, so I made them with my trusty sewing machine. The ugly couches Captain X's parents bought for our first house looked cheap and out of place in the house, so I reupholstered them with some help from Captain X in a soft cream-colored fabric that gave the house a lovely monochromatic feel. I even created a bright contemporary painting to adorn the huge, ivory-colored blank walls. I took great pride in being creative and frugally decorating the house.

It was around this period, while I was decorating, that Captain X started to talk about money. "You know, money is getting tight. We spent a lot on infertility treatments, adoption, and buying this house." His words went in one ear and out the other. I knew that I didn't spend much money. I even taught Gina how to shop. At the age of six she darted straight to the sale rack first at any store. "Look Mommy, a SALE!" she shouted.

I knew Captain X's family had helped us with many of our financial needs. Although our house was expensive, he had a good paying job. For some reason he kept saying, "Money is tight." Again, I was confused. I was always organizing garage sales to bring in cash for our travels. Gina had lots of clothes and toys she outgrew quickly, so my garage sales were always successful.

One day as I was working on my small eBay antique sales, Captain X walked into my office and surprised me by saying, "I need to borrow some money from your eBay checking account." I said nothing, looking perplexed. "It's just a loan, for Christ's sake. I'll pay it back. I just ran short this month. I just need cash to get us through a tight time. Come on, you know you can trust me." I relegated all my profits from my little eBay antique business and garage sales to pay for family vacations. "I'm not taking your money. I'm just taking a loan," he pressed. I eventually gave in, giving him a thousand dollars from my small account. A few weeks later he paid it back, just as he'd said. I was totally unaware that this was a tactic to gain my trust. I never asked him why he was short.

When I wanted to sit down with him and talk finances, he had to get ready for a trip. He was too tired from a trip. He had to study for training. He had to enter his flight revisions. He needed to go to a union meeting. We'll do it tomorrow. I wondered why he wasn't willing to sit down and talk about the finances. He *always* had an excuse. I couldn't lasso him down.

After every trip to the ATM he handed me $200, saving me from going to get cash on my own. I always had enough money. Maybe "money was tight" because there were unforeseen expenses like house repairs. Maybe he was embarrassed that he hadn't budgeted for the high energy bills during a prolonged heat wave. He totally skipped over the reasons "money was tight" and went straight to a resolve that things would be much better when his pilots' union signed a new contract. I was completely unaware that airline contract negotiations often took years to settle. He had me utterly confused about our finances. I was starting to become confused about a lot of things.

"They just don't pay us what we are worth. When the union signs our new contract, we'll be just fine. Until then, we just have to cut down." He soon had me convinced we were indeed financial victims of Major Airways. To me, his airline contract signing story seemed entirely plausible. I continued to live my life the way I always did, with no extravagant spending. Our vacations may have appeared extravagant to an outsider, but with my small eBay sales and the deeply discounted travel benefits we received from his airline, none of our trips impacted our finances.

While looking for inexpensive picture frames for Gina's childhood art work at my favorite haunt, a Goodwill Industries resale shop, I bought a cheap $2 frame with a child's drawing under glass. I was going to paint the frame to match others, saving 10 or 15 dollars on new frames. When I opened it to clean it, underneath I found a serigraph by a well-known artist. I sold it for $3,000 to a Santa Fe art gallery. Thrilled, I put this money into my account to be used for family travel expenses.

One day Captain X came out of his office after reviewing the finances and said, "Hey, I have great idea! Why don't we get a divorce and then you can get half of my pension. Then we'd have cash to pay off the bills." He was referring to the now-famous 2009 case in which nine Continental Airlines pilots divorced their spouses and then remarried them, all in an attempt to get a portion of their airline pensions. "Yeah, sure, let's get divorced so we can get your pension," I laughed, thinking he was joking. He probably wasn't.

To economize, rather than using our lawn service every spring I was relegated to planting flowers in our flower beds. Despite my increasingly arthritic body I planted red lantanas in the back of the house by the pool, and in front of the house by a border of jasmine. Although gardening was not my passion, the plants flourished. I never questioned why I was planting flowers with my painful arthritis. If we could afford the house, why couldn't we afford to have the gardener? Oh, yes, I remember: "money was tight" and I was doing my part to keep costs down.

I often drove past the front of our house to admire it. I looked at it in awe before I turned into an alley to park in our three-car rear garage. Since most of the homes had rear entry, the street was almost always empty. I saw nobody. It was hard to believe that I was half-owner of this huge home. *If I own it, why aren't I happy in it?* I asked myself. *Why am I so lonely?* I didn't realize that I was slowly being isolated in the ivory castle, the house at the end of the tree-lined cul-de-sac. I was slowly feeling like a captive in the Captain's House.

Chapter 7: A Hinkey Marriage

SHORTLY AFTER SETTLING into the Captain's House, I began to question my marriage. Things didn't add up. Captain X's lack of friends and our lack of local friends seemed of no concern to him. He was charming and engaging, qualities I thought would draw people into our life, but they didn't. I craved a social life together with Captain X, but he had me convinced his profession was the problem. I couldn't plan anything to meet people. We argued constantly over this. "You fly with people every trip. You mean to tell me all pilots live like this, without friends?" I asked. "Now don't start up again," he warned. An argument would ensue. Any confrontation was soon followed by him firmly placing his hands on my shoulders with intense eye contact, saying "Divorce is *not* an option." In the beginning I felt this was his way of apologizing. As time progressed, this hypnotic make-up ritual, with its eye-to-eye lock, immobilized me, as if I were in a trance. I was frozen, unable to say anything. I mistakenly took this proclamation as a reaffirmation of how, no matter what, we could work out problems. Our marriage would never end in divorce. *He loves me. He'll never divorce me,* I said to myself in confusion, learning only later that this was a method of controlling me.

The most common reason couples argue is money. This fact, oddly enough, comforted me. It made my marriage seem normal in what was beginning to feel like a marriage in disharmony. I had no women friends in the airline industry, and very few friends locally to talk over my concerns. I trusted him implicitly, ignoring the red flags that flashed before me. "Marriage is forever." The phrase was part of my being.

Our first big fight occurred just after we married. I discovered he was sending $200 every month to the son of his former Colorado girlfriend. For some reason he had co-signed a loan for her son's car and was resigned to sending a monthly stipend to the 18-year-old boy to keep up the loan. "What's this?" I said. "Why are you sending money to some kid I don't even know? You have no contact with him. Don't you realize if he gets in an accident and kills someone, we're liable?" I was furious, but he was unyielding. "I'll handle this, stay out of it. This began before we were married. It's my problem and I'll figure it out." The day of that argument we were visiting his parents. I wanted to keep them out of our personal life; Captain X, however, shared everything with his family, so they were soon involved in our marital spat. I never expected their response, nor could I even see the logic in what they said. "Let it go. He knows what he's doing," they said. Again it was three against one. *I must be wrong,* I thought. When we arrived back home, Captain X did get his name off the car loan and stopped sending the monthly check. The situation was dropped.

Before Gina became part of our family, Allegra and George invited us to join them on a short vacation to Santa Fe. We were to leave the day after Captain X returned from a three-day trip. While he was away, American Express Fraud Protection Center phoned asking to speak to him, saying it was important. I replied, "He's away working. Can I take a message? I'm his wife."

"Have him call when he returns," they replied. I confronted him about the American Express phone calls as soon as he returned home. At first he dismissed the calls, saying, "It's nothing, just a computer error. I'll take care of it."

"I want a goddamn answer!" I said. "What's this about?" I kept demanding an explanation. I wouldn't let it go. After my constant prodding, he sheepishly admitted, "I had a slip." His head was low when he confessed he'd used his American Express card for a cash advance during his Dominican Republic layover and lost $5,000 gambling. I was livid! Crocodile tears appeared in his eyes. "I'm begging you, forgive me. I promise you it'll never happen again." He said this with a somewhat sincere look he conjured up, holding me in a strong embrace. How did this happen? How could he do this to us? Before we married he had admitted to a gambling problem, saying it was totally under control, he had not gambled in years, and he vowed never to gamble again—but he did! Here I was, penny pinching, flying to Mexico to get fertility drugs for our costly baby quest and he had gambled money away! I was in such a state of shock and sobbing, I told him I didn't know how I could possibly go on the Santa Fe trip. We were out $5,000 for what he referred to as "a gambling slip."

He took a step back, looked at me and said, "I told you it won't happen again. I said I'm sorry, NOW GET OVER IT," he demanded. I was already in a very stressed and emotional state from infertility. I was lonely. *I need people and his parents are waiting for us*, I consoled myself, as we drove to the airport to catch a flight to Santa Fe, guests of Allegra and George. Once there, we stayed in the best hotel and dined at the best restaurants. The gambling incident was never brought up again.

Simple things continued to confuse me. Captain X provided me with a Neiman Marcus charge card. I can count the handful of times I used it, yet we always had a substantial balance on the Neiman's account from his clothing purchases, even when he started saying "money is tight, we have to cut down." He often said one thing and did the complete opposite.

For his 40th Fiesta birthday party, four-year-old Gina and I planned to surprise him with an expensive watch we had picked from a newspaper ad. I planned on using this secret project to instill my thrifty habit in my daughter, as well teach her gift giving. Together Gina and I started six months before his big day, saving money every way possible to help buy her daddy the watch. We took all her outgrown clothes and toys to a children's consignment shop. "Gina, if your old things sell, these people will give us money for Daddy's present," I said to her, trying to explain how consignment shops operate. I even had her rounding up soda cans for cash. "Come on Gina, we're taking the bag of cans to the recycling machine to get some money." She watched intently as I unloaded the plastic garbage bag filled with cans into the mouth of the big machine. Soon the large machine spit out clinking coins amounting to a just a few dollars for our efforts, making barely a dent in our quest to buy Captain X's gift. "Look Mommy, money!" she said in glee. At least I was providing Gina a learning experience.

Eventually we bought him the watch, primarily with my eBay profits, never tapping into the family joint checking account. At his party, we handed him the surprise watch. "Gina worked hard to buy you this," I whispered into his ear. I don't remember him even thanking her for the watch we scrimped to buy. He acted as if he was entitled to the gift, never expressing surprise or appreciation. I didn't mind him not thanking me, but I felt Gina needed to hear appreciation from her daddy after working so hard in her own way, at such a young age, to help purchase the gift. His sense of entitlement was becoming more and more apparent.

One day when we had been married about seven years, something frightening happened. Captain X was flying international routes so I placed Gina in the hands of a sitter for a few days hoping for a romantic layover. After tossing our rollaboards into his car, we left for the airport, hitting the beginning of the morning rush hour. Suddenly the skies opened up and torrents of rain pelted down on the windshield, hindering visibility. We were in the fast lane, the far left side of the expressway, when a compact car on the far right careened into the right side guardrail and then spun off horizontally, flashing in front of us. I have no idea how he did it, but Captain X managed to veer our car sharply to the right, preventing us from crashing into the out-of-control vehicle. He continued driving towards the airport as if nothing had happened. I turned my head back in shock to look at the results of what had just occurred. The compact car had crashed hard into the guard rail of the left lane, the one we were originally driving in. "Shouldn't we stop?" I asked. I was shaking and crying from the experience. "No, someone will come. I have to get to work," he said in a monotone voice, staring straight ahead with dead eyes.

Maybe this is a pilot thing, to remain cool, calm and in control under pressure, I told myself. Yet something didn't compute. We could have died in that crash. The driver of the careening vehicle might be dead, but Captain X showed no emotion whatsoever. The thought of the near-death experience stayed with me for quite a while. I expected him to say something like "Holy shit," but he said absolutely nothing. I soon noticed he could control his emotions—or lack of them—even under what most people would consider extremely stressful, difficult, or dangerous situations.

Captain X loved to do the marketing alone. "I know what I want and what I need." I stayed home gladly, because huge markets overwhelmed me after years of small New York markets. I was happy he seemed to enjoy the simple, common task of marketing. He would shop for the ingredients for dinners he planned for the few nights he was home, buying the most expensive cuts of meat and ingredients. He also kept our bar stocked with brand name spirits. When I mentioned his spending habits, he always came up with what seemed to be a plausible answer: "We have to eat. I like good quality meats. They don't cost much more. You're blowing this out of proportion." His shopping trips often took many hours. When I asked why he was gone for so long, he'd say, "I went to have my car inspected. Don't you remember?" Other excuses were that they were out of his favorite fish, or cuts of meat, and he had to go to another market to find his culinary ingredients. His being away from home an hour or two longer than I expected seemed to be happening more frequently. I overlooked this because when he returned, along with bags of groceries he would surprise me with a bouquet of cut flowers.

Because of his love of cooking, Captain X mentioned that "someday I want to take cooking classes. Maybe I'll even open a restaurant when I retire." I mentioned his new idea to Allegra, so a few months later at Christmas she gifted him with a $300 gift certificate to the top local culinary school. Captain X placed the certificate on a shelf in his closet where it sat, far exceeding its expiration date. I found it odd that he loved cooking, yet never attended the classes. He would come up with ideas for projects but soon lose all interest.

The only people I can recall Captain X ever having friendships with were three pilots. Lowell was a bachelor captain he often buddy-bid to fly with. Buddy bidding allowed him to specify his preference to fly with a certain pilot. He loved flying with Lowell, often telling me of their antics on layovers. After Lowell retired, their friendship ended. Ben was a fellow Major Airways pilot living in Utah; Captain X knew him from his early days, when they both flew for the same commuter airline. They kept in touch, sharing salty emails. Much later he added Pete, another Major Airways captain. I only met these friends two or three times socially during our entire 22-year marriage. He did get on well with one neighbor, Tim, a Texas transplant. Tim used to refer to Captain X as "you old horndog, you" in his thick Texas drawl. I was so naive at the time I thought this was a term of endearment between men. Later I would pay deeply for not understanding the term. In most every conversation Captain X referred to people as "my good friend so-and-so," but in reality, he had few friends.

I began to question my husband's "wonderful family." When Gina was four years old we planned a three-day visit to Allegra and George in the Bay Area. Gina looked incredibly cute on the airplane, dressed in jeans and a denim jacket which I decorated with glitzy rhinestones. When we arrived at Allegra and George's house, George's brother and his wife, Uncle Kostas and Aunt Helen were there visiting.

We sat in the backyard relaxing over drinks and enjoying the sunny California weather. We hadn't been there more than 20 minutes when I called for Gina. "Gina, where are you?" I yelled through their big two-story house. She knew Grammy and Grampy's house and was probably hiding or playing somewhere in it.

"Gina, come out here *now*," I yelled throughout the house. No answer. I was frantic after 10 minutes. I went back outside to the patio, interrupting their conversation. "I can't find Gina! I've been in every room in the house! Where is she? Help me find her!" I said in an alarmed tone any mother can relate to.

"She's here somewhere, don't get so excited," Allegra answered. "Calm down, what are you getting so upset about?" Captain X said, looking at me, annoyed, as if I was crazy to be upset over my missing child. By now Gina had been gone for 20 minutes. The family had just noticed that Uncle Kostas was missing, too. Forty minutes passed and I had still had no idea where Gina was. I was frantic, yet Captain X and his family continued to tell me to calm down. Just then Uncle Kostas walked into the yard holding Gina's hand.

"Where were you?" I asked Gina, hugging her tightly. "We just walked around the block," Uncle Kostas responded. Uncle Kostas never asked my permission to take Gina for a walk. Gina hardly even knew him! I was furious. Captain X and his family made it quite clear that I was making a big deal out of nothing. Nothing? He takes my four-year-old daughter for a walk without asking me and it's nothing? I was confused, yet I tried to absorb what they said. My daughter's welfare *was* a big deal. Captain X and his family's reaction made no sense to me.

Captain X stressed he was extremely close to his Uncle Kostas. I found this strange since Captain X seldom visited his uncle, and Uncle Kostas and Aunt Helen never once visited us. When Kostas suddenly died, Captain X never shed a tear, nor did he plan to fly attend the funeral service. "Why aren't you going?" I asked him, more than curious. "They're just doing a small service. They don't need me there," he said without a trace of emotion.

Two weeks later, while I was fixing my hair in the master bath, he stormed in to look for something in his closet. "I can't believe it! Helen didn't send me one damn thing of Kostas's. I know Kostas had lots of jewelry. I should have gotten something! Helen should have given me one of his rings! He was my uncle and I deserve something," he said incredulously. I was mystified by his increasing sense of entitlement.

Captain X told me his family was totally supportive of him and his career, so I couldn't understand it when Allegra revealed that neither she nor George had ever flown with Captain X on any of his Major Airways flights. When this came up in conversation, Captain X had already been with Major Airways for nine years. "Oh, we've flown with him before, just not since he got hired by Major Airways," Allegra said. To me it was as if their son played little league baseball, showing up at all his childhood games but they didn't think it important to see him play the World Series! After months of coaxing, they eventually planned to be on a flight with their son, but only after I urged them to join Gina and me on trip to London with Captain X at the controls of a Major Airways flight. Strange.

When cell phones became increasingly common, Captain X purchased two phones. He explained that one phone was for our family, for me to use in contacting him. The other was for company and union business, because "the company is out to get us. The union knows what's best and I'm in the Union Brotherhood." Captain X attended union meetings when his schedule permitted. I continually asked him why he didn't get involved with his union, but he skillfully avoided answering. I still believed every word he said about his job. He continued to call me into his office to read complicated union negation emails, all of which he knew I couldn't understand. I was beginning to feel he was putting on a show to make me feel he was keeping me involved in his work life.

As the world became more computerized, we became a computerized family. In the early days I learned my way around a computer by trial and error, working with a dial-up connection on our one computer in the starter home. Soon after we moved into the Captain's House, each of us had quality computers loaded with the best software. Being an older mother, I justified the expense because I felt I needed to be up-to-date with technology, to be in touch with my daughter's world. Gina used her computer for school and games, and I used mine for buying and selling small antiques and keeping in touch with friends. Captain X used his for Major Airways' union negotiations and keeping track of finances.

Pornography soon proliferated on the Internet. I laughed when Captain X called me into his office to show me a few of the X-rated sites. He even once joked, "I want to make a book of photos of women's faces while they're having an orgasm. I'll call it *Faces of Ecstasy*." He said this with a smile, his eyes gleaming. "Great, you just do that!" I laughed at his outlandish sexual joke.

I considered myself open-minded when I looked at what he showed me on his computer screen. However, as time passed, he was calling me into his office to view videos of sex acts that made me feel uncomfortable, and I resolutely told him so. I easily dismissed his viewing an occasional site as ordinary; he was just like every other man in the country with a computer. His occasional glimpse of pornography didn't seem to affect our sex life, which could only be described as adequate.

Along with an increasing boredom, I noticed he showed little enthusiasm in his voice. As an extravert, when I was happy, the whole world knew it by the tone of my voice. I also showed my anger, lashing out loudly. Captain X's voice seemed to take on a monotone quality devoid of emotion. *When did this start?* I asked myself. One day I yelled back at him, "Stop using that goddamn airplane voice when you talk to me. Don't talk like a PA! I'm your wife!"

I remember the day Captain X came out of his office in a very strange mood after spending hours in his office with the door shut, saying, "You know what? You just don't know what's in my head, all the pressures I have." He looked tormented! *Is he referring to flying?* I asked myself. *Paying bills? What?* What a strange statement for him to make! It caught me off guard. Instead of asking him "What pressures?" I tried to offer suggestions to make his life less stressful. I only wanted to make my husband happy, telling him frequently that I loved him.

Another time he came out of his office and said flatly, "My job is nothing. I'm just a glorified bus driver in the sky." *I thought he loved flying! Where did this come from?* I asked myself. I put my arms around him, telling him "How can you say that? You fly loved ones on their honeymoons, people to their families. You make people happy flying them where they want to go." He didn't reply. He just did not connect with the emotions I was trying to convey. He soon left for his scheduled trip looking lost and distant, leaving me perplexed and confused.

Captain X was privy to all kinds of travel industry discounts, allowing us to frequent our favorite all-inclusive resort in the Caribbean. I could easily rationalize these vacations, since the cost of the three of us at the resort was actually less expensive than maintaining our lifestyle in the Captain's House. I joked that we might consider moving into the resort full-time! Most of the expenses for these trips were paid for from my eBay sales profits or his parents' gifts. Captain X and I had leisure time alone together while Gina busied herself with supervised children's activities. We spent lunches and dinners bolstered with bottles of French wine, feasting on superb cuisine from the long buffet tables. I loved the socializing, something I was sorely lacking at home. When our dining table companions discovered Captain X was a pilot, they were mesmerized. Again, Captain X was the center of attention, keeping the table constantly entertained.

It was on one of these vacations that I said, "You should write a book about flying."

"I can't. Some stories can't be told," he said flatly. I remember that day on the beach. I said, "I know! You can call it *The Secret Life of Captain X*. You can use a pseudonym!" He looked at me with an odd smile. His eyes were twinkling. "Yeah that sounds good, *The Secret Life of Captain X*." He certainly had stories to keep people entertained, so this wasn't a pipe dream.

Months later, at Christmas, I gifted him with an artistic prototype cover for his proposed book, along with books in the same genre. I remember him going to his office where he stayed for a few hours with the door closed. "What are you doing up there?" I yelled from the first floor. "I'm busy working on my book," he shouted. He even purchased a mini-computer to take with him on his flights so he could write on layovers. Soon he was bored with the book project. It was forgotten.

One year during Gina's elementary school spring break, we were at our favorite Caribbean resort. Captain X and I settled into a routine of relaxing under a straw palapa to read. He was not a big reader; he confided then that he had a mild form of dyslexia, making reading difficult. I never thought to ask him how that affected his flying career. To my surprise, he eventually became engrossed in detective novels. Meanwhile I was addicted to true crime books by Ann Rule. Most of her books involved psychopath killers. Rule often used the term "hinkey" in her books, meaning something is not quite right. Her books were my first introduction to psychopaths. I thought psychopaths were all killers, like those she wrote about. Actually, most psy-chopaths are not criminals, but rather socialized individuals and charming manipulators who show no empathy, guilt, remorse or fear.

Since Captain X constantly mentioned that money was tight, we dis-cussed the possibility of him applying for a check airman position. A check airman conducts pilot's flight checks while on scheduled trips or in a flight simulator. Being a check airman would mean a pay increase. This provided a goal for Captain X. He applied for the position. "I'll try for it, but I don't want to be stuck on the ground teaching, not flying all the time," he said resolutely.

Months later he informed me in a voice devoid of emotion, looking straight into my eyes with a predatory stare, "I didn't get the check airman job. To tell you the truth, they didn't say it directly. They're a closed group but when you made that big scene at the Pilots' Wives, when they put the baby in your arms, you were out of control. The guys think you have emo-tional problems. Rumor has it that's why I didn't get the check airman job." I was mortified! I was the cause of my husband not getting the check air-man position! It was my fault! *All my fault?*

This terrible news swirled around in my head and strong waves of guilt crashed against the walls of my skull. It took me years to understand that this was just one of many times Captain X used a gaslighting technique on me in an attempt to make me descend into madness. He almost succeeded. Something was definitely hinkey in our marriage.

Chapter 8: Maladies and Madness

MY MOM INSTILLED in me a fear of doctors. She had health problems her whole adult life, and a terrible fear of cancer. When she died, it was from a stroke, not cancer. I was positive I could face any medical problem of my own with my husband at my side.

I was born with an unusual vein mass on my upper right rib cage, originally considered a birthmark. When I reached my 50s it had grown closer to my breast and became hot to the touch. After a suspicious mammogram, I had a breast biopsy. I was terrified, and thankfully, it was nonmalignant. Captain X showed little reaction to my biopsy, leaving me confused. *Perhaps I made a big deal out of nothing. Breast biopsies are common,* I told myself. A vascular malformation specialist diagnosed the vein mass as a hemangioma, an abnormal buildup of blood vessels. I was relieved. I was footloose and fancy free of health issues.

Four months later we had dinner with Susan and her daughter Allison. Susan's husband was away on business. After placing our orders, Susan leaned over the table and confided, "I have to have a breast biopsy tomorrow and Joel's away."

"Wait a second," Captain X said indignantly. "You mean you're going to be alone for your biopsy? I'll take you. You shouldn't be alone." He offered to take her to her medical procedure? I sat in disbelief. "That's OK, I have a friend taking me," Susan answered. *He offered to help her with her biopsy and he played mine down?* I was speechless and confused. It was unsettling.

After the terrible events of 9/11 the world changed, and so did Captain X's profession. Now Major Airways made it possible for pilots to trip trade, switching monthly assigned trips with another captain. At times Captain X would give me his next month's schedule in the morning, and by the evening he'd changed it three times! With his constant trip trading I was resigned to not being able to plan ahead for anything. I had no control over my life. It was taking a toll on me.

Our family had two local physicians. Captain X chose Dr. Bob. I thought Dr. Bob was a competent GP, but I preferred a female GP from India, Dr. Kaimal. Dr. Kaimal always found time to spend with her patients. I remember well the day I came in for an exam, revealing odd symptoms. "I'm starting to feel really strange. I'm having palpitations and tingling," I told her. Dr. Kaimal was familiar with our family, and taken by Captain X's charm.

Out of nowhere I broke down sobbing. "I'm so lonely and mixed up. I've been feeling strange, weird," I blurted out. My sobbing continued as she checked my vitals. "It seems I'm always out of sorts. My husband is constantly switching his trips. It's making me crazy! I'm so lonely," I confided through my tears. She handed me a tissue. "You're sooooo lucky. You have such a wonderful husband who loves you! You just need to meet people," she said in her thick Indian accent. I couldn't stop crying. My physician was telling me Captain X loved me, how wonderful he was. If I was loved, why did I feel so lonely and unloved? She diagnosed me with high blood pressure and prescribed medication to control it. *She got to the bottom of my problem*, I told myself. She also reinforced how lucky I was to be married to him. I left her office feeling somewhat reassured.

In 2005 I underwent arthroscopic outpatient surgery for a torn meniscus in my right knee. My recovery went well. But with all the stress in my now 17-year marriage, I was concerned about my emotional and physical well-being. Was my body starting to wear out? Were all those years of dancing taking their toll? Captain X was younger than me. He seldom had health issues, while I was having all kinds of health problems. I always seemed to have strep throat or sinus infections and was emotionally drained. I exercised when I felt well enough, either walking or taking a dance/exercise class.

One day, during an exercise class, I heard something in my body pop. I developed terrible pain in both my groin and hip area. To make matters worse, it was accompanied by lower back pain. Soon I was spending three days a week at the neighborhood chiropractor, Dr. Don. His treatments were helpful and relaxing, but his friendship helped me more. We talked mostly about traveling. His wife didn't like to travel and I knew he envied my travels. For the first time in my marriage I found myself attracted to a man, but I put this attraction out of my head. I knew I felt this way because he genuinely seemed to care for me.

I tried again to get to know our finances but Captain X was now adamant that he alone should handle them. "You know damn well I know what I am doing and you can trust me," he said. I had no idea that Captain X had applied for every credit card that came in the mail, using my name on the cards. I should have been involved in the finances, but at the time I had to attend to my body, which was screaming for attention.

The recurring pain in my right hip and lower back was confusing and overwhelming. The chronic pain continued. I kept telling myself I was imagining it, and causing problems in the marriage. *Yes, that's it. I am making up the pain!* When not taking over-the-counter anti-inflammatory medication, I shared many strong pre-dinner drinks with Captain X, the only time he seemed to enjoy being with me other than an occasional dinner. *I don't blame him for being distant*, I thought. *I'm always having health problems.* My hip and back pain didn't help our slowly diminishing sex life. Being an inadequate sex partner fueled my growing list of my insecurities.

Dr. Don said that climbing stairs was bad for my problem back, and my office was upstairs. I told Captain X this. I was in such physical and emotional agony that I broke down crying. I clutched his ankles as he was going up to his office. "Please sell the house! I'm so unhappy," I begged him. "What are we doing in this huge house when you and Gina are out all the time? It's just me alone. The house is too big, too expensive and I'm lonely!" I begged him through my tears.

Surely when you are in a marriage there should be some compromise. He stopped a few steps up the staircase, turned his head, and sneered back angrily, "When you make the fucking money you can tell me what to do with it!" and proceeded up the stairs, leaving me crying in a heap at the landing. If he loved me, as Dr. Kaimal had confirmed, why wouldn't he want me to be happy? If we were in debt as he said, why wouldn't he sell the house? I was in pain. I couldn't sleep. *Why? Why?* I kept asking myself.

I couldn't see I was in an abusive marriage. How could I? I was too physically and emotionally ill, living in a constant state of distortion. The ups and downs and mixed messages in the marriage were as constant as my ills.

In 2006, I was floundering through a medical maze, trying to find someone to diagnose me. As the pain in my hip and back increased, so did my sleep deprivation. An orthopedic physician suggested a hip injection done under fluoroscopy. This procedure involved anesthetic and cortisone targeted into the joint.

The morning of my procedure Captain X was preoccupied in his office. When it was time to leave he was agitated. "What's wrong?" I asked. "What's going on with you? I'm the one having a medical procedure?" I asked. He didn't answer. We were halfway to our destination when he pulled the car into a parking lot. Turning off the engine, he looked at me and said with a blank stare, "We're going to have to file for bankruptcy. There seems no way around it. I can't keep up with the expenses." *What? Bankruptcy? Huh? Why is he telling me this now, before my procedure?* I burst into heavy sobs. Then, in matter of seconds, his attitude changed and he shifted the story. "I can probably avoid it. Don't worry, I'll handle it, I always get things under control," he said, starting the engine up again. I was shocked into silence. I had to focus on my health, since he wasn't. I'd get to the bottom of our finances as soon as I was healthy, wondering if I would ever see a day I *would* be healthy.

The hip injection didn't work. I found another orthopedic specialist and Captain X accompanied me to the office visit. After reviewing my paperwork and my X-rays, the doctor said, "You're definitely going to have to undergo hip replacement surgery." Then, to my shock he quickly added, "But before you do that, you need to go to a neurosurgeon because you have spinal problems due to advanced arthritis." Oh my God, what? I was stunned hearing this news. Captain X said nothing, methodically writing the neurosurgeon's information. I felt like an old woman, damaged goods. Captain X's silence did little to change the way I felt.

In 2007 I underwent a 360° spinal fusion. An incision was made in my abdomen and my back in order to fuse specific vertebra in my spine. I didn't care how invasive the surgery was. I just hoped it would fix me. Fix my body. Fix my mind. Then I could fix my marriage that appeared to be deteriorating before my eyes.

I remember little of my recuperation because I was prescribed Percocet, a narcotic pain reliever. Captain X laid out the Percocet and sedatives on the granite countertop in the kitchen, close to the family room where I recuperated for months. "Here, take this," he said, doling out my pills. "Are you sure I am supposed to take that?" I asked drowsily. "Just take it," he said. I took anything he gave me to feel better.

I remember wearing some sort of body brace that felt like a steel cage, to protect my spine as it healed. I was so drugged I was constantly in an emotional fog. One thing I am positive of: *I can't recall Captain X ever saying one comforting word to me during the long recuperation process.*

I have vivid memories of being constantly cold, shivering. My teeth chattered all the time. I just couldn't get warm, despite layers of clothes and piles of blankets. I couldn't focus on anything. I blindly stared at the flat screen television in the family room.

I had no appetite whatsoever, and was losing weight. Captain X liked trim women. *He's going to love me when I'm thin and beautiful. At least I will be skinny after this,* I thought. I was mad with loneliness and the medical recovery, yet still looking for Captain X's love and approval.

That period in my life was surreal. I was incapable of standing up without an aluminum walker. In my drug-induced foggy way of thinking, I had gone from being a beautiful dancer to a woman who could not move without home medical equipment often used by the elderly.

I remember using the walker, hearing the shuffling sounds of my rubber-soled house slippers against the wood floor as I slowly made my way to the master bath to relieve myself. I parked the walker in front of the elevated toilet seat, pushed down my fleece sweatpants, and eased myself onto the seat. Captain X walked into the room on his way to his closet, glaring at me with an unnerving gaze in his eyes. Or was it disdain? *Why did he look at me that way? Doesn't he love me? Does he think I'm faking this?* I asked myself. *Maybe it's my imagination. It's the drugs, the painkillers. They're making me crazy. I'm going crazy. CRAZY!*

Captain X hired a professional caretaker to help me while he was flying trips. She looked at me with contempt as if I were an ungrateful woman, lucky to be living in a McMansion with such a wonderful husband, the man who hired her. We hardly talked as she bathed, dressed and fed me, helped me to the toilet, and doled out my medications.

After a month of recuperating during the cold Phoenix winter, I was positive I was in hell. I remember trying to get Captain X's attention when he returned from his scheduled trip. "Help me ... please hold me. Hold me, please, I need to be held!" I pleaded softly through my tears. He lightly put his arms on me, not around me. This is the only time I remember him touching me during my entire recuperation period. "What do you want me to do? I don't know what you want me to do," he said in a flat voice. He never once said he loved me or reassured me that I would be all right. I hadn't yet realized that he was incapable of empathy.

Captain X had me on the brink of madness since I couldn't grasp why he showed no love, care, or emotion while I was in such bad physical shape. To all the health professionals, our few friends, acquaintances and family, he appeared to be concerned about my health. In reality he never was. It was almost as if he was happiest when I was unable to move due to my surgeries, or when I was lost in loneliness.

I looked at the amber-colored plastic bottles of Percocet, Vicodin and Ativan lined up on the granite bar and pondered suicide for the first time in my life. I thought I was going mad enduring the pain alone. I'm sure I would have ended my life if it were not for the love I felt for Gina.

Gina, where was Gina all this time? I don't know. Did Captain X tell her to stay away from me? Is that what happened? Teenage Gina had been invited to a high school dance. Captain X was now acting like a single parent, indulging her every whim, helping her pick out an expensive dress for the dance. I was completely left out of parenting Gina. I wanted to help pick out her dress! I wanted to be there for her special days! I couldn't. I was an invalid.

When Captain X came home from a trip he would take Gina out for dinner at a local restaurant, bringing me back a carry-out meal, tossing it on the coffee table before me. *Am I imagining this? Did he really toss the carry-out meal like throwing a bone to a dog? No, it couldn't be! Something is wrong. It's me. It's me and the drugs. It is the drugs. The drugs.*

I have few memories of visitors. I faintly remember going to Susan and Joel's house for a holiday meal. Was it Thanksgiving or Christmas? It's all jumbled. I remember stretching a sparkly knit top over my body brace in hopes the sparkles might brighten my mood. While seated in a comfortable chair in their family room. I remember hearing Susan's high-pitched laughter coming from her kitchen after one of Captain X's jokes. Her house was filled with family and friends enjoying a lively holiday gathering. *This is what I was supposed to have*, I thought. I didn't last long that night. I was in pain. Within a few hours I needed to go home.

Captain X was now sleeping in the guest room upstairs. "Sorry, but your tossing about and writhing keeps me awake," he said. *He's right, of course. He needs his sleep*, I told myself.

Six months after my back surgery I was almost completely healed, but caught in the horrendous cycle of Percocet addiction, with pills easily provided through a Pain Management Center with my physician's prescription. Captain X encouraged me to continue these drugs, and I did. It never occurred to me he wanted to keep me docile. By then, I craved every bit of interest he took in me, like a crumb offered to a starving person. I was bouncing back, like I always did, ready to go forward and forget the back surgery.

As soon as I was mobile enough, I planned a warm weather family vacation. I was beginning to feel normal, whatever that was. My back surgery kept my family grounded in the wrong way. I wanted the three of us back together as a family. My life was a constant cycle of ups and downs, good and bad. I hoped sun would warm my body and soul.

Off we flew to our favorite Caribbean resort. I was trim and bikini-clad, despite being in my late 50s with a body marred by recent surgery scars. Again I hoped for a glimmer of warmth from my husband. I was at a beautiful resort and should have been happy. I was oblivious to my Percocet addiction. I didn't even know why I was taking it except to make the pain go away. But which pain, body or mind?

While Captain X took Gina to check out the resort's activities, I went to the main bar. I sat down next to a male guest and struck up a conversation. I desperately needed to talk to someone! I explained my spinal surgery. What else could I talk about that defined me at the moment? He mentioned he was a dentist. He looked at me inquisitively as I explained I was still taking Percocet. "You've been on that drug far too long. If you continue, you won't see your next birthday," he said.

Later I told Captain X what the dentist said. "What the fuck does he know? He's only a dentist," he replied. I recoiled, saying nothing. I immediately cut my Percocet intake down, substituting it with Tylenol, and was soon off the drug. I never told Captain X. By that time he was nearly ignoring me.

I had warmed my body and soul in the Caribbean, but I had only a short respite. The pain in my arthritic right hip had now become so unbearable I had to undergo yet another surgery, a hip replacement.

I was used to the drill of the pre-operative tests. A few days before I was to enter the hospital I busied myself to keep my mind off it. The house phone rang and Captain X ran to answer it, closing the door. "Who called?" I asked as he came out of his office. "Dr. Bob's office. They got your pre-op blood work back and found a problem. It's OK though, a mix-up. I didn't want to worry you, so I didn't mention it." *Oh, that's nice of him, trying to shield me from unnecessary stress. He does love me despite all the medical stress I'm putting us through*, I thought.

Unlike my spinal fusion, my hip replacement recovery went surprisingly well. I was a star patient, walking in record time due to strong leg muscles from my dancing career. It was still an ordeal, but I knew what to expect, the walker and raised toilet seat. Again there was no empathy from my Captain X. I didn't expect it.

Allegra never visited me during my recoveries. After both surgeries I received short phone calls from her, acting concerned. She started the conversations by asking how I felt, adding, "You're lucky you have Captain X take care of you." No, he wasn't taking care of me, but I didn't tell her that. Then she went into long, self-absorbed tangents about herself, details about her teeth cleaning experience as if she, herself, had undergone major surgery. Soon I avoided her calls. They did little to help my already battered psyche.

By then I could not think straight. Surely the past two surgeries had made me a bit crazy. I tried to not overanalyze my life. *Just keep busy*, I told myself. Five months after my hip replacement, I felt a stabbing pain in my abdomen. I tried to dismiss the pain as indigestion, but the agony increased as the day went on.

"According to the Internet, you're not vomiting so it's not appendicitis," Captain X chided. I was too weak and too shocked by yet another medical dilemma. "Oooooh, hurt. Hurt. Hospital, I need hospital," I moaned. I curled up in a fetal position, hugging my stomach in Captain X's car and we drove to the hospital. There I underwent an emergency appendectomy, my third surgery in 14 months. "Give me a break, God!" I prayed.

Captain X was to pick me up the next morning at 10:30 AM. He arrived an hour and a half late. While waiting for him I tearfully poured out my confusion and medical woes to a kindly nurse, who was at a loss for how to comfort me. Years later I found out why Captain X was late.

After the appendectomy it was obvious that something was wrong with me emotionally. I was in desperate need of someone to talk to. Captain X had done nothing to help me during my surgeries. Now he was expressing concern that I might have a mental illness. It never crossed my mind that I was depressed and had good reason to be.

Captain X consulted with his "good friend Dr. Bob" who suggested I see a psychologist, Dr. Ryan Evans. Evans was soft-spoken and slow-paced, not that I would know how therapy sessions worked. I had never been in therapy. After my initial visit with Dr. Evans, Captain X scheduled a private visit with him. I never understood why, but I granted the necessary approval. The talk therapy sessions seemed robotic and pointless. Dr. Ryan diagnosed me with clinical depression due to three major surgeries in fourteen months and sleep deprivation. After eight visits I stopped seeing him. Nothing was getting better.

Sometime after the appendectomy, Captain X and I planned a dinner date with new friends Nina and her husband Jim Radcliff, a CFO for a national consulting firm. I now had a trim figure, compliments of my

surgeries, and I longed to dress up and be with these nice people, thrilled to
be socializing after undergoing so much.

At the upscale restaurant, Captain X did what he always did when we
were with company, charming Nina and Jim with his stories about flying,
but now his stories included jokes about sex. They were embarrassing.

When we left the restaurant he was cold and indifferent, almost reptil-
ian in his attitude towards them. Captain X was always trying to figure out
Jim. "I don't how he makes all that money. Why the hell is *he* so damn
rich?" he spat. Captain X detested anyone more successful than himself. I
ignored his comment. I loved their company. Despite their enormous
wealth, Nina and Jim were very down-to-earth. Captain X drank his usual
three or so cocktails but was always in control by the time the evening wore
down. While driving the short ride home I made small talk, but Captain X
was in a mercurial mood.

Before reaching our home, we stopped at the local pharmacy to pick
up a prescription for Gina, who was at home with a sinus infection. As he
pulled up at the drive-through pharmacy, the cars ahead were barely moving. I turned to Captain X and said, "You should have phoned in the prescription." *Whackkkkkkk*. I had no sooner said the words when Captain X
punched me in the jaw.

I sat frozen in disbelief, my mind grasping what had just happened. He
had never been physically abusive to me. Well, maybe a few bruises on my
arm early on when grabbed me during the stress of infertility or when he
was angry, but *no, not real abuse,* I told myself, not recognizing I'd hid the
other instances of physical abuse somewhere in the back of my mind. My
body went numb. *What just happened,* I asked myself. *Did that really happen?*

I knew I would bruise and most likely had a minor fracture. I was
shocked and sobbing as we drove home, where a confused Gina saw me
open the freezer to grab an ice pack. Captain X told me early on that "pilots
can't have domestic abuse reports on their records or they lose their license." Now he begged me, "Please, please don't call the police."

What should I do? Go to a women's shelter? No, I couldn't do that.
Gina would never come with me, she'd never leave her adoring dad. My
mind was racing. "If you ever hit me again I'll go straight to the police," I
said. "I'm sorry, *you know I'm sorry.* I just don't know what got into me. I

seem to be a mess these days. I'll do anything to make this up to you. I promise. Please forgive me! You know I love you," he said as he tried to embrace me. I moved away from him, my body frozen, rigid in response. Somehow I had the foresight to demand he take a digital photo of my face. I removed the frigid ice pack from my swollen jaw and he took the photo, softly saying, "I swear I'll never hurt you again, I promise."

The incident got lost in my mind until years later. *After all*, I told myself, *this wasn't spousal abuse. It was an accident. He lost his temper. Spousal abuse happens to other people, not to me, not to Mrs. X!*

Chapter 9: Suddenly Sixty and Strapped

BIRTHDAYS HAVE ALWAYS been important to me. When I worked in the theater, monthly cast parties became shared birthday parties. Since I shared the same birthday as Captain X's mother Allegra, I naturally assumed we would have an annual joint birthday celebration. I actually would have enjoyed it. To my surprise, in 22 years of marriage, she chose to celebrate our special day together only twice: once in our first year when I was 40, and 10 years later on my 50th birthday. This was odd. I could fly virtually for free, and parents of pilots got discount passes. Allegra was affluent. She could well afford an airline ticket. As a result, every year I sent her a present, usually an artistic homemade gift. In return she sent me the standard check.

Early in our marriage, Captain X bought me flowers and small gifts for my birthday. He always gave me an expensive poetic card with scrolled prose professing undying love and affection. Each and every manufactured greeting card or florist's card was signed with an apology: "I'm sorry," or "Things will get better, I promise." I bundled these up in a drawer filled with marital memories, but years later, after rereading the cards and notes, I threw them out. Notes of love should not be filled with apologies.

Captain X appeared to make attempts to show he loved me, that he cared. "I'm making you a special birthday dinner," he'd announce. He always made a special dinner on my birthday, displaying his culinary expertise, but my birthday dinners were no different than any other dinner he might prepare, other than the store-bought birthday cake Gina took delight in selecting. "I love it Gina," I said, making a point to mention how much I appreciated it.

For my 50th birthday, one of the times his family did fly to Phoenix to share our birthdays, Captain X went all out, surprising me with an expensive Louis Vuitton handbag and French lingerie. "I love the handbag! It's perfect and the lingerie is dreamy," I told him, overjoyed. I didn't think milestone birthdays were a time to be frugal. Later I realized the gifts were all a show for his family, to show them he loved me. He never made my birthday feel special.

I didn't expect extravagant birthdays. On one birthday I simply wanted to go on an inexpensive driving trip antiquing. As the day wore on, we found ourselves eating an early dinner at a cheap family-style buffet restaurant. When I returned from the ladies room, a group of wait staff was singing "Happy Birthday," but the song was for another patron, not me. Captain X never even thought to ask them to repeat the celebratory song for me. Other than receiving a mass market birthday card, that was how I spent that birthday.

On occasion Captain X surprised me, out of the blue for no special reason, with jewelry he purchased from his "good friend Pedro," a jeweler in South America. He bought handcrafted jewelry with semi-precious stones from Pedro's shop near his layover hotel. I often wondered if he wanted his crew to witness his generosity, buying jewelry for me.

I didn't like or want the garish jewelry, but I accepted and wore it graciously. I wished he had given them for special occasions, like my birthday, Christmas or Valentine's Day. Pondering this, I told myself I was ungrateful, that the jewelry did show that he loved me. But he told me constantly that money was tight. So why was I getting jewelry for no special reason? More mixed messages. I was confused.

"To tell you the truth, it didn't cost that much," he would say, brushing off my financial concerns. "To tell you the truth" was his favorite expression. In hindsight I should have paid more attention to this, his constant qualifying statement. I wore the jewelry every time we went out. In my mind it was the right thing to do.

The mixed messages about money happened constantly. I had just recovered from three surgeries in 14 months so my health concerns outweighed any financial concerns I had. My blind trust in the marriage continued. I remember him saying, "Just sign this. I need to get it to the mortgage company this afternoon." I didn't realize he was re-financing the house. Dumb, trusting me. I signed everything he instructed me to sign as he placed the papers in front of me. I didn't know that the house was being mortgaged to the hilt. I was so financially naïve, so trusting. I always felt secure knowing he had a good income and besides, I was frugal.

When Captain X turned 50, despite his complaints and incessant mixed messages about money I planned a trip to China so he could celebrate his special day on the Great Wall. Who wouldn't want to spend their special birthday on the Great Wall? The trip was a bargain with Captain X's industry discounts. I would pay for it with my small antique business profits. I had my own Visa Advantage Business Card to which I thankfully never added his name, so I charged the trip. I always made sure Gina was staying with a conscientious caretaker while we were away. Upon our return, I immediately paid it off from my eBay earnings. No family funds were used for the trip.

China was beautiful, but sharing this special exotic Far East trip with Captain X left me emotionally empty. We were on other side of the world, but Captain X took it all in stride. He never once showed appreciation for the hours I worked to pay for the trip. At this time in our marriage I had yet to undergo my back surgery and was hoping for romance in Asia, but there was none. There was no affection, no appreciation. He never once mentioned to our friendly dining mates that I had given him the China trip for his birthday. Instead, he charmed all of them with his airline stories. I consoled myself with the thought that at least I was getting to see the world.

The China trip gave me insight into another side of his personality I hadn't yet been privy to. After cocktails with our dining mates while sailing down the Yangtze River, we retired to our stateroom. Captain X poured us a nightcap and we took our drinks out to our small cabin balcony where I leaned over the railing, feeling the evening breeze in the exotic eastern port where we were docked. Without even a kiss or a word, he approached me sexually from the rear, lifting up my dress in an attempt to have vaginal intercourse while I was leaning over balcony. Normally I'd have no problem with this sexual interlude, but as I gazed out over the railing, another ship was docked parallel to ours, with throngs of people just 30 feet away. The hairs on the back of my neck stood up and chills ran down my spine, sobering me up instantly. He had never shown exhibitionist tendencies before. "Are you crazy? People can see us!" I stammered in surprise. "Fuck 'em, we'll never see them again," he replied. "I'm going to bed," I said, and I did. I totally forgot the China incident, until it came back to me much later in one of hundreds of memories I would spend years trying to sort out.

All the surgeries and confusion in the marriage left me grasping for any happiness I could find. I had the last of my surgeries when I was 59. The thought of turning 60 in a lonely marriage, after enduring so many surgeries, was depressing.

Once again I found solace in travel, my great emotional escape. I told Captain X I wanted to go on a packaged trip to Egypt, on the Nile River, because it was one of my "bucket list" destinations. I was excited. It had a nice ring to it, "turning 60 on the Nile," I told myself. Despite the constant barrage of mixed messages, I was adamant about going to Egypt. I made few personal demands in the marriage. I needed this trip.

"I want to go to Egypt for my 60th birthday. I'll pay for everything. I'll plan the whole trip. I just need you to get the vacation time off. You had a big birthday in China. Now it's my turn," I boldly told him.

He hissed, "Lady, you're out of your fucking mind. We can't afford a big trip like that. You know nothing about planning a big trip like that." I couldn't think of any valid reason I shouldn't be planning my 60th birthday trip. Looking directly into his eyes I mustered up some newfound courage and said, "You may be captain on Major Airways but you're NOT captain of this house or of this marriage! If you don't want to go, I'm going without you. I deserve a special 60th birthday." This was the first time in the marriage I realized I didn't even care if he joined me on the trip. My persistence in planning my 60th birthday trip, getting someone to take care of Gina, and planning the details of this extensive trip gave me a new and unusual feeling of assertiveness and personal accomplishment.

Captain X eventually grudgingly agreed to join me on my Egyptian birthday tour. Major Airways didn't have routes to Africa, so to arrive in Cairo we had to fly Major Airways to Paris and then board a different airline for the Cairo leg. Not only was I excited about spending my special birthday in a dream location, but in a sense, I longed to celebrate my life's milestone in style.

Egypt was unlike any of the destinations I had traveled to. It was exciting, exotic and unknown. While on the Egyptian tour Captain X went through a series of mercurial mood swings. Sometimes he seemed lost or stoic, and other times he was seething, especially after not finding anyone amongst the passengers he could charm and entertain with his stories of flying. I ignored him while I took in the desert sunshine and dry breezes as we cast off from the Cairo dock.

Captain X never held me or kissed me on my special day. I didn't expect him to, and I didn't care. I felt I was a vivacious 60-year-old woman and had somehow found some new inner happiness. I was finally standing up to my husband and all his craziness. It felt good. I was feeling proud of myself, a feeling I hadn't felt in a long time.

No one who saw us together would have assumed I was the older partner in the marriage. Captain X was now balding, with only a c-shaped fringe of nearly all-white hair. He looked old and sullen as he glared at me from under the white canvas tarp sun covers on the cruise ship deck. I sat far from him on the ship's hull where I sunned myself on a lounge deck chair in my sleek black maillot swimsuit, ignoring him and listening to *Beethoven's Fifth Symphony* on my iPod as the ship began its first day down the Nile River. I was the Queen of the Nile on my 60th birthday! For the first time in our marriage, I did something totally for myself. Unfortunately, I did something for myself way too late, and I paid dearly for it.

After returning from Egypt we started receiving odd phone calls on the house line. When I'd pick up the phone, the caller would hang up. These continued for a long time and seemed to progress as Gina's March birthday approached. My immediate thought was that they were from Gina's birth mother, that she had somehow found us and was trying to contact Gina. When I shared my concern with Captain X, he said, "They're nothing, ignore them. Get over it." We were also getting phone calls from credit companies. He said to tell them that he was out on a trip, and he'd get back to them when he returned. These phone hang-ups and the creditor calls were unnerving me.

When the three of us were home dining, seated at the round glass table off the family room, it felt as if we were a normal family. Captain X would whip up dinner while I set the table and called Gina in from her room. "Dinner's ready, Gina," I'd announce. As we started on the meal I would try to make family conversation. "How is high school going, honey?" I would ask. "She's doing great, but needs work on her world history," Captain X would answer. *What,* I asked myself? *Why is he answering for Gina?* I looked at him sternly and said, "I'm not talking to you. I'm asking Gina a question. I'm trying to make conversation with my daughter. Why are you answering for her?" I asked. "Well, you've been sick for so long and you're not up-to-date with her school," he answered defensively. "*Do not* answer for Gina," I said sternly. Poor Gina was in the middle of this and soon left the table. "Don't ever answer a question I am asking Gina," I said angrily. "Why in the hell are you making a big deal out of this?" he asked. He even seemed to be controlling Gina's voice. Something was terribly wrong, but I just couldn't figure it out.

My 60th birthday trip provided me with some long overdue inner strength. A week after returning, I demanded to see everything about our finances. My head was no longer fuzzy from drugs and pain. Walking into his office I said, "Show me everything. I want to see everything *now*," I demanded. "Don't start this again, damn it!" he said, his green eyes raging with anger as he tried to control the situation. "I *said* show it to me *now!*" I steadfastly demanded.

Our eyes never met as he slowly pulled up a financial spreadsheet on his computer. I insisted on a printout with all the debt in red. His printer spit out the pages, each covered in red. "Are you happy now?" he said, angrily. *Oh my God we're broke!* "WHAT HAVE YOU DONE?" I cried. Most every credit card, many I never knew existed, were maxed. I was in shock. I didn't know this man.

"You're a financial fuck-up! You're Captain Stupid and I'm Mrs. Stupid!" I screamed. "You have no idea how I've been juggling the finances since infertility, adoption, your surgeries, the house costs, and my 9/11 pay cut. Then there's the travel and the eating out. You think you can do better, but you can't," he spat at me. He kept directing any accountability away from himself. It was as if I was talking to a 14-year-old boy, not a mature, responsible airline captain with a good income.

Tears flowed but I quickly composed myself. For the next three hours I phoned creditors trying to remove my name from accounts he had listed me on as an authorized, joint, or co-user, all to no avail. I closed unnecessary accounts. I came into the marriage with two credit cards. Now my name was on more than 20, most of which were maxed. Eventually I would discover he had nine American Express accounts, many to which he'd added my name. He also charged $9,806 for property taxes to *my* Visa credit card days after my spinal fusion surgery.

"There's no way you're going to win this argument!" I screamed at him. He had financially duped me. *Where did the money go?* I asked myself. Before I could ask, he started to cry in a strange way. "I'll do anything to make this right. Let's see a financial planner," he said. "I'm not stupid. Financial planners are for people with money to invest. We have debts, not money!" I shouted. "Let's do credit counseling," he said, grasping at anything to take the sting away. "Credit counseling is for people who can't handle money. I'm great with money!"

Suddenly he stopped crying and started pleading in a straightforward voice, "I'll do anything to make this right." He knew I had just discovered his secret. Hours of trying to absorb, understand and fix the financial mess exhausted me.

Months earlier I had made plans to visit my friend Melody in Detroit. My trip was scheduled for the next day. I needed to get away from him to think clearly, consider my options, and most of all, to seek comfort and advice from a true friend.

Our conversation was terse during the 30-minute drive to the airport. Sitting in the boarding lounge waiting for my departure, something in my banter about sorting the finances began to enrage him. His face reddened as he spewed profanities at me. His final words were "Fuck you!" and he left, leaving me sobbing. *What happened? What should I do?* The questions and tears stayed with me throughout the flight.

Hiding my teary eyes behind sunglasses, I arrived in Detroit, welcomed by Melody's warm embrace as I sobbed uncontrollably.

Melody spent the hour drive to her home trying to cheer me up. "It happened to me too," she confided. "During my first marriage I found out my ex-husband ruined us financially. After my divorce I worked three jobs just to get back on my feet. What's worse is that I found out he had a secret life. I don't tell this to many people but I found out he was gay. Now I'm happy and have a wonderful new husband. I still keep separate bank accounts. It took a long time to get over it but I did," she said softly. I listened intently to her story, consoling myself that my husband just mismanaged the finances. At least he didn't have a secret life. Melody had met Captain X several times. "He always seemed nice and competent. This is really hard to believe. I'm so sorry," she said sincerely.

A week after my return, when Captain X was on a trip, he sent me an email suggesting we get tickets to an Andrea Bocelli concert, adding a link to the concert site. Captain X had told me he loved music when we were dating, but we attended only one concert when I surprised him one Christmas with tickets to see his favorite artists, Billy Joel and Elton John. We were broke and he wanted to buy expensive concert tickets? He was continually baiting and switching me.

Captain X shocked me again by announcing, "I'm selling the house. I'm giving you what you wanted. Look, with the money we get from the sale of the house we'll be able to pay off the bills. I promise you, everything will be OK." He had finally decided to put the Captain's House on the market.

I was elated! No more stairs to climb with my bad back. No more money spent for upkeep on the big, empty house we barely lived in, that by then I despised. I took this to mean he was finally listening to me. Captain X was now making a prudent move to alleviate our debt and plan for our future. He even wrote me a letter saying so, saying:

I promise you that I am committed to selling our house to pay off debts. I promise you that the first debts to be paid off will be those for which you are the primary card holder. We will pay off the rest of our debts one by one, from the smallest to the largest until the proceeds from the sale of the house are gone.

I also promise you that in every conversation I have had with anyone at any time related to the financial debt we are in, that I have always said you are not to blame for our debts. I have said time and time again that you are the most frugal, conservative person I have ever known, and that my loss of pay at Major Airways and my desire to maintain the lifestyle we became used to has been the most substantial reason for the position we are currently in.

I have told you this over and over, and now as I write this and sign it I hope you will believe and trust me when I say that I will never go back to the way things are today.

I want you to know that I love you and that you are the only one I have ever loved. That I will do everything in my power to earn your love and try my best to never do anything to lose it again.

Captain X

There it was in writing. He loved me and was trying. I had to forgive him, and so there was nothing to do but look forward.

We sat in his office and looked on his computer at small house rentals in the same school district so Gina wouldn't have to change schools. Captain X made it very clear that he needed his own office. I didn't understand why we couldn't share an office, but I didn't dwell on this, his one minor request. I was in favor of any plan to get us out of the Captain's House. No longer would I put up with his off-the-wall justification for our debt, his constant statements that "it will be better when my union contract is signed," mentioning "I'll be inheriting a lot of money." I didn't know that this confusing talk and mind changing is called "crazy-making" in a relationship.

Captain X was making a responsible move in agreeing to sell the house. His letter showed love and he was taking responsibility for the debt, yet I still had an underlying feeling of doom. I was utterly confused and alone. Again I couldn't think straight.

We selected Tori Smith as our real estate agent. Tori and I had known each other a few years, sharing our passion for antiques and flea markets.

She had a lot of experience in the real estate market, and I was positive she would do her best to sell the house. I was oblivious to the fact that our house went on the market just as the housing crisis was beginning.

Having sold one house with Captain X, I knew the drill. I had to keep the house immaculate for showings, most which occurred while Captain X was flying a trip. I hated having to leave for a showing, but the sale of the house was vital to our future. After a few months, the house showings slowed to a trickle. Captain X was at the controls of this marriage. If something didn't happen soon, we would crash and burn.

In all the years of our marriage, I never once told Allegra my confusion about our finances, nor did I share the recent revelation of the massive debt her son alone had created. I grew up thinking you never complain to your mother-in-law about her son. Meanwhile, Allegra aimed all money-related topics at me. She even sent us books by best-selling financial advisors. I was torn between telling her that her son was a financial fuck-up and protecting her from the truth about him. I just couldn't win.

The confusion never stopped. One day as Captain X was driving home from a trip he called me on his cell phone and sounded excited, as if he had just won the lottery. "Hey, guess what? I just met up with Pete Howard on my layover. He knows a movie producer who will finance my picture book, *Faces of Ecstasy*! Isn't that great? With this project we'll get money to pay the bills." Not believing my ears, dumbfounded, I responded, "You're fucking crazy," and slammed the phone down. A few years later I would discover that Captain X wasn't crazy. He was something far worse, but I wouldn't find out who he *really was* until much later.

PART II

Chapter 10: The Pilot Petitions for Divorce

I RETURNED FROM a loving visit with Melody to the dreaded Captain's House realizing my marriage was in deep trouble. My immediate thought was just to hang on in the marriage for a few more years until Gina went to college. This would give me time to investigate all that was involved in getting a divorce, just in case I had to consider that route. It would also give me time to accumulate some cash. But when I returned from Detroit, Captain X had yet another surprise waiting.

"I made an appointment for us to see a marriage counselor. I think this will help, don't you?" *Maybe he does want to save the marriage. After all, he did put the house on the market,* I thought. But again something didn't feel right. I didn't know where our marriage was going. I was grasping at straws.

Captain X got the name of a marriage counselor from his neighborhood friend Tim. This seemed odd to me, because less than a year earlier Tim and Terry had divorced. "Hello, I'm Liza Thompson," the counselor said, extending her hand. "Have a seat." I remember feeling numb as she asked superficial questions about our marriage, never digging into the dynamics. I was a robot, providing only the basic information, just as I had done with my psychologist.

Captain X controlled each marital therapy session. Soon it was obvious that Liza was enamored with Captain X as he manipulated the conversation, often rattling off some flying stories, so I tuned both of them out. Decades of crazy-making were beginning to take their toll on me. Everything being said was useless. For some reason the family finances never came up. "She seems nice enough. I think this will help us," he said stoically as we got in the car. "Let's go get some lunch." And we so we did, speaking little of the session.

After three sessions with Liza, she was eager to book more. "I don't have my flight schedule yet, so I'll call you when I get it," Captain X said. We never saw her again. Like a war victim, I was in a daze from my marriage battles.

Everything was mixed up in my mind except one thought: Gina would never leave Captain X. She was more attached to him than ever since he had taken over as full-time parent during my many surgeries. She was a wonderful, typical teen. I was no longer dealing with a child, but rather a 16-year-old, a teenager with the independence of a brand new car her daddy had purchased for her with the help of Allegra and George. I was left out of Gina's big 16th birthday and car selection, since it happened during one of my recuperation periods. A few weeks after seeing Liza, Captain X was in his office when I approached him again about his constantly changing work schedule. "Why can't you stop switching your schedule so often? This is weird. I just don't understand. You mean to tell me that all Major Airways pilots switch trips as often as you do? Why does this happen? I just can't believe other pilots' wives stand for this," I said, exasperated.

Captain X quickly got up from his rolling office chair. "You fucking cunt, don't you ever question me again!" he raged, pulling off his wedding band and throwing it straight at my face. "You're a fucking cunt, you know that?" he shouted, exploding in anger, his green serpentine eyes glaring. The ring hit my cheek hard, and then fell softly to the carpeted floor. I stood frozen as waves of shock engulfed my body. Then the tears poured out as I held my cheek.

I didn't know if Gina heard her dad call me "a fucking cunt." She was in her downstairs bedroom so she never saw him hit me in the face with his wedding band. Crying, I ran downstairs to Gina's bedroom looking for comfort from the only person I was positive loved me. "I don't know what Daddy's doing. I don't understand!" I cried in despair. Instantly I knew going to her was a huge mistake, but I didn't know what else to do. "I don't want to get in between this," my teenager said in a matter-of-fact tone.

Parental fights and divorce had affected many of her friends. She took the only measures she knew, staying out of her parents' lives.

She was right. I shouldn't have involved her, but Captain X's frightening, angry rage came out of nowhere and had cut me to the core. I was lost and confused. I went back to the master bathroom and sobbed, noting that Captain X and Gina had left the house together. I wondered again, *what did I do to cause his rage? What did I do?*

When they returned much later, Captain X slept in the upstairs guest bedroom, a room used by guests fewer than 10 times in more than a decade. I walked around in a daze, shell-shocked, without anyone to confide in about the abuse and the latest outburst.

Soon afterwards, on an early March morning two days after Gina's 17th birthday, Captain X returned from a South American trip. There was a stony silence as he went into his closet to hang up his uniform jacket. When he came back he handed me some papers. In a calm and flat tone he said, "I have something I need you to sign." I stood there in shock and disbelief. He had just handed me divorce papers. He's divorcing me! I never dreamed *he* would divorce *me*. Even after he threw his wedding ring at me, I still didn't see it coming. Why would I, when he continually gave me mixed messages? "Divorce is not an option." He had written me a love note just a few months before, saying, "I want you to know that I love you and that you are the only one I have ever loved." He put the house up for sale. We went to a marriage therapist. Then he did the opposite, throwing his wedding band at my face and shouting obscenities. I was utterly lost, confused, and stunned. I was chilled from the shock waves produced by the knowledge that this was really happening to me.

"What did I do wrong except support and love you?" I asked him softly, still in shock. He spoke in a monotone with an empty look in his eyes and said, "It's for the best, it's just not working. Things haven't been going well for a while now." I glanced over the legal papers, documents so foreign to me that the words could have been printed in Chinese. I barely noticed the document attached, signed by Gina, enabling her to live with Captain X. At the time I didn't realize he had told Gina he was divorcing me *before he even told me*. I was too shocked to speak as he started to discard me after 22 years of marriage.

I was totally ignorant about divorce. I somehow had avoided contact with people whose lives were impacted by divorce. I even habitually misspelled the word. Both my spelling and my knowledge of the topic greatly improved from that fateful day on. Again, Captain X had lied. Divorce *was* an option for him; I was the one with no options. I had to get it together quickly and take some action to get some control over my life.

I drove to a local book store to purchase a book on divorce in our state. Wearing sunglasses and holding a wet Kleenex to my puffy tear-streaked face, I purchased the self-help book I never thought I would own.

Arizona is a no-fault divorce state. Captain X, as the party who wanted the divorce, did not have to show a specific reason or misbehavior to get a divorce. If there is no chance the marriage can be saved, that is sufficient grounds for a divorce. All assets and debts are the responsibility of both of parties. My years of frugality meant nothing.

I contacted my friends Susan and Tori, both in "good marriages," for a recommendation of a divorce attorney. I was amazed at how little comfort I received from them. "It's all for the best," they said. They, like Captain X, showed little empathy, something I very much needed. I also wondered if they could be afraid of him. If so, they didn't share that with me.

At that point I was 60 years old with medical problems, few marketable skills, and in a community property state leaving a marriage laden with financial debt that I did not incur. *So much for being so lucky to be married to a charming, successful airline captain*, I told myself, desperately trying to find some humor in this new life crisis.

I phoned to make an appointment with the Weinberg law firm, located nearby. According to the firm's website, they had been "handling complex cases for over 35 years." *That's comforting*, I told myself in a sarcastic tone. The firm specialized in family law, with Marvin Weinberg and Bessie Rolland experienced in divorces. Hiring a divorce attorney after being hypnotized for 22 years, in a marriage that was never supposed to end, was mind boggling.

I opened one of the double glass doors with the firm's name marked on it and approached a young receptionist. I'm sure she saw many tear-streaked faces on new clients approaching her desk. "I'm here for an appointment with Mr. Weinberg," I said. "Have a seat. He'll be with you shortly," she replied, never looking up from her computer as she lifted the phone and said, "Marvin, your ten o'clock is here."

Well over six feet tall, lean with silver hair, dressed in an expensive, well-tailored Italian suit, Howard Weinberg greeted me. "Come in here where we can talk," he said, leading me into a large conference room. I hoped I would like him. Weinberg had a stellar reputation as a divorce attorney. I was well aware that divorce is a business; I hoped I could garner enough confidence from our meeting to ask him to represent me. I was in no state to go attorney shopping.

"So, tell me about your situation," he said as he took off his reading glasses. I handed him the papers Captain X had given me. I agonized as I told him of Captain X's mishandling of our finances and the shock of him divorcing me. During that first meeting I never would have believed that I knew only part of my story.

"Well, it's good that he served you. The petitioner does all the filing, so that saves you money," he replied. "Now the question is do you want to divorce him?"

"God, yes!" I blurted out through my tears. I was tired of walking on eggshells in a marriage filled with mixed messages. "OK, let's get started," he said as he explained his fees.

"I need a $5,000 retainer. My fee is $500 an hour. You'll have to come in tomorrow to fill out forms. Bring all your financial records with you," he said as he led me back to the reception area and shook my hand. To pay the retainer I handed the receptionist my Citibank Advantage Visa Business card, the only card I owned that Captain X had no access to. It had a $20,000 limit with only a $180 balance.

Still never looking at me, the receptionist said, "We'll see you tomorrow at 10:00AM. You'll be meeting with Hanna Bailey, a paralegal." I drove home trying to estimate how many air miles I would receive after charging $5000. Maybe I could get enough to get on a plane and disappear. My mind was wandering.

The next morning, with red-rimmed eyes from an entire night of crying, I went back to the law firm. Hanna looked like a no-nonsense librarian in her late 50s. She extended her hand, greeting me. "Hello, let me take that from you," she said, reaching for the required paperwork I was holding.

Her voice was soft as a marshmallow. I told her the same story I'd told Marvin Weinberg. I was prepared to be perceived as a financial ditz, though surely I couldn't be the first woman who had her head in the sand about marital finances.

"Let's see what you have here," she said, reviewing the spreadsheet. "Oh my, he's pure evil. He's a psychopath," she said softly. *Surely she means he's just a liar, or financially inept*, I told myself. I didn't know what a psychopath was. I never took a psychology course. The only people in my mind who fit that description were murderers; Ted Bundy and Charles Manson came to mind. I should have paid more attention to Hanna's statement, but I was too busy learning about divorce. I filed Hanna's psychopath comment somewhere in the back of my constantly throbbing head.

Afterwards I phoned my friend Nina to tell her my divorce news. Nina insisted on buying lunch the next day. Nina chatters a lot and I loved her for that. She always seemed to have a positive outlook. I knew she could help me get my mind in the right direction. The wine flowed as easily as my tears did. Out of nowhere Nina said, "Did you know that the last time the four of had dinner and you left for the powder room, your husband told us that you're bipolar?"

"I'm not bipolar! What are you talking about? When was that? What did you say?" I answered in a shocked tone. "Jim and I couldn't believe it. Why would anyone say that about his wife? To tell you the truth, I didn't know how to tell you," she confided. *Oh my God,* I wondered, *how many other people did he poison with lies about me?* "Nina, I'm not bipolar. My therapist said I was sleep deprived and suffering from depression after having three major surgeries in 14 months. That's it!" I said, confused. *Why would he say that?* I asked myself.

Nina insisted I read the current bestseller *The Secret*, a self-help book by Rhonda Byrne which claimed that positive thinking will create life-changing results. Positive thinking wasn't going to help me in my horrific situation, but I let her rattle on while I helped myself to another glass of wine.

After lunch with Nina I went back home and phoned Tori and Susan, asking them if Captain X had ever mentioned I was bipolar. Tori said yes and Susan said she didn't recall, clearly indicating she didn't want to get involved. I certainly was learning who my friends were. *Just who did I marry and why did he spread the lie that I was bipolar?*

In a few days Captain X would be off to Chile on his scheduled trip. Gina would be in school and at a sleepover afterwards. As soon as my newly shattered family left the Captain's House, I vowed I would search for answers. I had to make some sense of all this so I could quickly get through the process of divorcing Captain X.

Chapter 11: Computer Shock

AS I CLIMBED the beige carpeted steps leading to Captain X's office, my hand clutched the flat contemporary iron banister. I wished it could provide me with emotional stability along with physical stability as I went in search of answers. Captain X's office was the first room on the left, just off the empty loft area overlooking the downstairs living room and the pool in the back yard. "I want a good look at Gina's bikini-clad girlfriends when they come over for pool parties," he said jokingly. Gina was not yet in grade school when we moved into the Captain's House and he chose that room for his office.

His aviation-themed office décor had a cozy chair facing his desk. When Gina was five I sat in it and she played flight attendant while I was a demanding passenger. "Oh miss, could I have some coffee?" I'd ask. "I'll be right back," she'd say, leaving the room, returning with a pretend cup. Soon she lost interest in the game, leaving me positive she'd never be a flight attendant. I also sat there whenever I came in to talk to Captain X. His modular desk had filing cabinets filled with neatly labeled file folders containing important paperwork. Captain X's office was always meticulously neat. Pens and papers were left facing a certain way when he left the room. For some reason this trait never led me to be suspicious. But this time I was suspicious.

I couldn't leave telltale signs of my sleuthing. Glancing around the room with its bookshelves, file cabinets and desktop, I realized digital photos would be my only recourse to recreate the precision look of his office after I completed my mission. For the first time in a very long time, I was proud of myself for thinking smart. *It's bittersweet to think I'm being smart now, while searching for answers*, I said to myself. I clicked away with my camera, getting shots of the room exactly as it was.

I booted up his computer, remembering back to our early years when we used America Online as our Internet provider. Captain X used a password that was slang for female genitalia. I thought it was funny at the time. I was sure no one would suspect *that* as his login password. I was surprised to see that he was still using it. *Now, where do I start?*

A screensaver photograph of Gina soon popped up on his monitor, surrounded by desktop shortcuts and Word documents. One document titled "Desktop Notes" immediately caught my eye. It contained a list of accounts and passwords, many airline-related, and his AOL, Yahoo, and Hotmail accounts with their passwords. Also listed were passwords for websites I'd never heard of, ASPD.net, Verotel and WSG. In 22 years I had never invaded his privacy. *I have to find answers*, I told myself as I forged on investigating his computer.

As I typed his email address and password into his Hotmail account, I had no idea what I would see.

A list of his emails popped up on the screen; quite a few were from eHarmony, the Internet dating website. My immediate thought was that they were advertisements, but a closer look revealed that they were communications directly from eHarmony! *Why would he be on eHarmony? That's for single people*, I told myself. *This just doesn't fit*, I said to myself in disbelief. The hairs on the nape of my neck started to bristle. *This isn't rational. He would never cheat on me!*

Confusion gave way to shock and then numbness set in as I continued to view his eHarmony matches from women from all over the world. And to think I was never jealous or suspicious! *Twenty-two years of marriage and I hadn't a clue! I hadn't a clue!*

There were a several emails in his Hotmail account from Sonia in Argentina, emails that indicated they'd met through eHarmony. *Well, that answers why he bids to fly South America*, I said to myself. He'd say, "I love to fly South America. That's where pilots get the respect we deserve." Sonia appeared to be shy and sweet in her emails. *My God, he's dating her!* I thought. *I wonder if she knows he's married. I wonder if eHarmony knows he's married!*

I started to print out copies of everything. I didn't realize it at the time, but I had just begun to uncover Captain X's secret life, a secret life I would spend thousands of hours documenting.

Among his Hotmail emails was one from Sexsearch.com adult personals, and there on the email was his handle, "PussELuvR." He also had a friend request from Horney Lila in Scottsdale. eHarmony was a dating website, but sexsearch.com was an adult personal website.

I was confused. Was he dating or looking for sex? *Who is he?* I kept asking myself. I started to feel very uncomfortable sleuthing in his office, so I ran to my office to continue where I left off, and signed into a SexSearch.com account with a pseudonym. After logging in, I entered PussELuvR in the search field. The tears flowed yet I could not stop as my search revealed his bio with an illustration of a silhouetted male in place of his photo:

PussELuvR

"Looking for fun on the side … top … and bottom"
Birthday: May 2, 1956
Age: 53
Zodiac: Taurus
Location: Phoenix AZ, United States
Sexual Orientation: Straight
Marital Status: Married
Height: 6'1"
Body Type: Average
Hair: Black
Eyes: Tell You Later
Circumcised: Cut
Smoker: Tell You Later
Drinker: Tell You Later
Race: Caucasian
Language: English

Man looking for woman for 1-on-1 dating, swingers, online
friends, alternative activities, fetishes.

"That's him! That's his birth date! That is him! The piece of shit," I
screamed loudly, awaiting no response in the empty house. *I hate my life. It
was all a lie. What more can there be?* I had to keep going. *What is ASPD.net?* I
asked myself as I quickly pulled up their website to find even further
shocking revelations. ASPD.net (it's now been taken down) stood for
Amber Systems Posting Directory. The initials ASPD would impact my life
again much later, but in an entirely different context.

I found a website *against* ASPD that summed up what the site
provided:

ASPD (aka RAPS, the Review and Posting Society), available at
aspd.net, is an organization of men dedicated to the promotion
and practice of prostitution. They post graphic accounts of sex
acts between prostitutes and their clients. They practice anilingus
and cunnilingus on prostitutes and require unprotected fellatio of
prostitutes. They delete information regarding the spread of sexually transmitted diseases among its membership. They condone
racism, chauvinism, homophobia and degrading treatment of
women. Moderators of ASPD.net often refuse to wear condoms
when receiving sexual services, even for anal sex, and also demand and accept free and discounted sexual services from prostitutes. In exchange, they keep message boards free of postings
and reviews that would hurt the business of protected prostitutes.
ASPD is a threat to public order and endangers public health.
Please report ASPD activity to law enforcement and help shut
down this immoral site.

Shock, horror, and anger engulfed me as the massive betrayal I had
just uncovered in cyberspace was shattering what remained of my world.

I went downstairs to the granite-topped bar and poured myself a
strong scotch in Captain X's favorite Waterford rocks glasses, trying to absorb the nightmare I was now living. Before I returned upstairs I grabbed a

clump of tissues from the master bath, where I stared in the large mirror at my red eyes.

"Get a grip," I told myself, staring into my reflection. "This is good, this is good. This means you're not crazy, maybe stupid for not knowing, but not crazy!" Reinforced with my new outlook about my mental health, my body and emotions were as icy cold as the drink I clutched in my hand.

I returned to my office upstairs to continue my search, now infiltrating ASPD.net by joining the website pretending to be a "provider," a prostitute. It was the only way I could find out if PussELuvR had a profile on their site. What else would it reveal? I now had to know *everything*. The antique-related websites on my desktop looked senseless compared to what I was now doing, which I can only call pornographic sleuthing, peering over advertisements of prostitutes showing every possible part of their anatomies to procure customers. Finally, I located Captain X's ASPD profile:

Profile For PussELuvR

Date Registered: 11-18-2001
Status: BCD
Handle: PussELuvR
Birthday: 05-2
Gender: Male
Biography: Traveling professional having hobbied around the globe. It's a job and I have to do it!
Location: Phoenix
Occupation: Pilot

The BCD status meant Behind Closed Doors. Captain X—or should I say PussELuvR—received this special BCD status by constantly posting reviews of his encounters with prostitutes. This status makes it easier to get clearance as a client for future encounters with ASPD prostitutes. I looked for his reviews of prostitutes. There he was, as witty and charming as ever on postings, talking about his "all-time favorite!" by the name of Tami. Tears welled in my eyes as I spent the entire night pulling up hundreds of postings made by my charming husband, PussELuvR. His review postings on ASPD.net went back as far as November 2001, when he first registered with the prostitution website. Most of his postings were brief, but the length of his post about a prostitute named Tiffany Sparks left me sickened and incensed:

Date: 2/2/2009
Provider: Tiffany
Phone or Pager: given after screening
City: Phoenix
State: Arizona
Area/Address: Phoenix Suburb
Appointment type: Incall
Provider category: Independent
Activities: BBBJ, DATY, MPCFS
Session length scheduled: 1hr
Fee: $150
Total paid: $150
Was tipping an issue? No
Was the description you were given accurate? Yes
Hair color and length: Blonde
Age: 19
Race: White
Perfume/Fragrance: Fresh and all Natural
Smoking status: Could Not Tell Either Way
What was the provider's attitude like? Warm, friendly and sweet
    as can be
Comments: Tiffany ... WOW!!

I had seen her photos on the Internet but none did her justice. This girl is hot! She is as cute as she is sweet and she is the spitting image as the girl next door. The only difference is that she does not spit.

I saw her posting showing her special available, $150 for the hour. It seemed too good a deal to pass up and believe me it was.

I emailed her my screening info and she responded back within a few minutes. We set the date for that afternoon and it could not have gone smoother.

I showed up at the apartment on time and called her for the gate code and apartment number. She greeted me wearing a black silky thing and sporting an adorable smile. This girl's eyes and smile are enough to make you loose it right there but don't cause there is more to come.

She showed me into her room and I made myself comfortable. After a brief visit I reached her and kissed her. Hands began to roam and the firm wonderful body of this 19 year old woman/girl became mine. I began to let my lips and tongue explore down her frame and found her nipples to resemble fresh erasers from my #2 pencils back from school. She was responsive and relaxed as I enjoyed more and more. Her freshly shaved smooth, young tasty pussy became my home. I could have spent the afternoon there and did linger for a long time enjoying her reaction for a while.

I found myself stiffening and wanted to let Tiffany return my oral activity so I rolled over on my back and enjoyed her talented hand and mouth coordination as she went down on me. Very good but I had to have another taste as I moved her into a 69. This was great. Her marvelous ass in my face, my tongue planted inside of her and her mouth bobbing up and down on me. I had to move on soon or things would have cum to a conclusion.

I suited up and moved into a missionary start only to find that her snug grip on me would have soon been too much for me so I backed off for a bit to extend the experience. I found myself wanting to alter my original plan for this visit. I had thought about doing some hard fast screwing but I was having such a great time I decided I now only wanted to lean in, kiss this sweet woman and grind away into a fantastic conclusion. So I did. Tiffany clearly reached her climax just before mine and we were both satisfied that our first meeting had been a success.

I can honestly tell you that this young lady is a true joy to know. She is bright, cute, sexy and focused on the fact that it is as much of a hobby for her as it is for us. Don't miss the opportunity to go get to know her while you can. Tiffany is a true pleasure to know and play with and I feel certain I will see her again.

PussELuvR
Would you recommend this Provider to others? Yes

I immediately went to Tiffany's website. There she was in photographs, looking a few years older than Gina, posing in sexy lingerie. I could have done without the visuals.

Tiffany listed three abbreviations for sex acts she provided: BBBJ (oral sex without a condom), DATY (performing oral sex on her), and MPCFS (Multiple Positions Covered Full Service) in her profile. The ASPD website provided an abbreviation list allowing providers to feature their specialties as well as to allow clients to make more concise postings. Just some of the abbreviations included:

Agency: A company that manages calls, bookings, and advertising for providers.
BCD: Behind Closed Doors
BDSM: Bondage, Discipline, Sado-Masochism
BBBJ: Bare Back Blow Job (oral sex without condom)
Call Girl: Outcall provider, usually implies agency
CBT: Cock and Ball Torture
DATY: Dining at the Y (Performing oral sex on a woman)
Doubles: A threesome with two girls and you
Hobbyist: A man who patronizes prostitutes
Hooker: Prostitute

Hostess Club: A lower end strip club where bargaining for sex acts with the dancers is acceptable, and some activities may occur on premises

Incall: You meet the girl at her place

Independent, Indie: An escort who works on her own, without an agency affiliation

MPCFS: Multiple Positions Covered Full Service

Outcall: The girl comes to your place

Screening: A provider or agency does a pre-session background check on a new client

SO: Significant Other

Soon I was easily navigating the ASPD.net site, finding Captain X's postings since he had an easily recognizable avatar, a graphic of a woman's body with his handle PussELuvR located above each of his postings. As I continued to pore through hundreds of his postings, they revealed his preference for sexual acts he never ever hinted at, including anal sex, domination, and CBT—cock and ball torture.

I had the proof before me that Captain X paid for threesomes with prostitutes and attended sex parties in back rooms of private sex clubs. *Who is this man?* I asked myself as I went through reams of paper printing his ASPD posts revealing his sexual escapades with "providers," including one he mentioned who was "barely 18." *Now I knew where the money went!* He had been seeing prostitutes for years, skimming funds from our family accounts. I was a victim of both marital deception and embezzlement.

Only a month before he'd said the reason we were in debt was because of our traveling too much, or did he say it was because of all my medical bills? Or his airline contract not being signed or … I screamed loudly as I saw yet more vile pornographic postings of Captain X's secret life. Numbness engulfed me as I printed out everything, documenting years of deception.

I went into my office closet and pulled out a large white plastic binder, placing the ASPD sexual reviews by PussELuvR into chronological order, like a high school project. *I'm not nuts*, I said to myself. *He's nuts. He's sick. I'll be OK!*

The number of sexual postings Captain X put on the Internet as PussELuvR was mindboggling. Another posting captured my eye, with not one but with two prostitutes:

Review: Threesome with Candy and Vicki
Author: PussELuvR
Date: 5/1/07
Provider: Candy and Vicki
City: Phoenix
State: Arizona
Area/Address: City
Appointment type: Incall
Provider category: Spa or Studio
Activities: BBBJ, DATY, MPCFS
Session length scheduled: 1hr, not clock watchers
Was the description you were given accurate? Yes
Hair color and length: Candy Blonde below shoulder—Vicki
    Brunette to middle of back
Age: 3's
Race: White
Perfume/Fragrance: Fresh and all Natural
Smoking status: Could Not Tell Either Way
Where did you hear about this provider? ASPD
Provider's body: Absolutely no bad surprises with these two.
    Vicki a bit rounder and Candy a bit tanner but over all very
    beautiful ladies!
What was the provider's attitude like? Welcome, let's have some
    fun!

Comments:
I had seen Vicki about a month ago and had been teased by reviews of Candy for quite some time. I called to see who was available with the idea of seeing Candy and when she told me both of them were available both my heads began to spin.

I had made an appointment only with Candy but after some more thought I called back and booked the both of them.

When I showed up I was greeted and shown into a room by both of these wonderful ladies. They began to disrobe and I followed their lead. As we got to know each other it became clear they are not bashful with one another as they gently stroked each other and we all began become familiar.

I have always been a fan of double BBBJ and with Candy firmly seated on my face the two girls began to attack. Vicki remembered I sometimes like things a bit rough and she went to work on my balls while Candy took me as well.

Candy has such a wonderful ass that my tongue had to explore and she seemed to enjoy what I was doing. Soon I just needed to get some so I covered up and mounted Candy on top while Vicki made sure my ass and balls were attended to.

Round one came to completion while deep inside of Candy and I believed we both enjoyed ourselves together.

After a brief rest I bent Vicki over the table and went to work on her as Candy played with her nipples. I was a bit worn out to finish the second round but neither of the ladies ever made any move to call an end to things.

These two are wonderful! A great double as they clearly enjoy you and each other. The rate is reasonable and the fun is so grand that it would be tough to see either of them without the other in the future.

Would you recommend this provider to others? Yes

I started looking at old calendars, both months and years, to cross-reference dates of his prostitutes with days in our life. That was a day the house was showing and I was out shopping! I think he told me he was having his car inspected. *How could this happen? "You're so lucky to be married to him. He so wonderful! He loves to cook. You get to travel. He loves you so much."* Everything everyone said about Captain X was running through my mind. *No one will believe what I found*, I told myself. I could hardly believe it myself, but there it was right in front of me. I had proof Captain X had a secret life.

By 4:00 in the morning my eyes were dry and stinging. I had long since switched from scotch to coffee, which slightly cleared my head but added acid to my already-sick stomach. While printing everything I could find relating to Captain X, I delved deeper into the ASPD.net website to learn more about it.

The men on ASPD considered themselves a "brotherhood," a secret society of men who participate in the "hobby." When posters on ASPD talked about the costs of a prostitute's services, they used dollar signs: $ for $100, $$ for $200 and $$$ for $300. They also used the code word "roses." My husband, PussELuvR, usually paid two or three roses (two or three hundred dollars) for his prostitutes. I was too exhausted to do the math, but it all added up to why we were so unbelievably in debt. I kept wiping away tears as I read. Some prostitutes gave discounts to veterans and had rainy day specials! The brotherhood of ASPD had well over 5,000 members. One of the members of the brotherhood even posted his expertise in a manual on how to keep the hobby from your SO (significant other), wife:

1) Stay two steps ahead of your SO. Physical evidence is the enemy. Shower and smell like you did when you left home, using the same soap, deodorant, shampoo, hairspray and cologne. If you smell differently wives notice. If you have an All-Time Favorite, give them a bag of your toiletries. Don't leave these items in your car unless you have a good explanation.

   Make sure your provider does a once-over! Most don't wear perfume. If for some reason you come home with makeup on the collar, lipstick or strange scent, break down and tell her you went to a strip joint and you're sorry. You had no idea how aggressive those woman are. Mention you are mad that so-and-so talked you into going.

Always be on guard. Expect the unexpected. Have excuses and explanations for your whereabouts. Lie quickly. What are you going to do when your kid needs you and your wife can't find you? You need preplanned plausible explanations. Be ready to explain everything; phone calls, phone numbers, computer data, phone bills, credit card receipts, bank statements, unusual cash withdrawals, etc. Be ready for this shit because when confronted, if you can't quickly explain it away, all hell will break loose.

Hopefully your wife has no suspicions. If something happens to make her wonder, her antenna will go up. A married woman with her antenna up is dangerous. She will notice things and look for evidence everywhere. At first she will suspect an affair. This is major hiatus time from the hobby. You haven't been busted but she thinks something isn't right. This isn't good but you're not caught yet.

2) Don't vary your life patterns. Depending on how long you have been married, you have established patterns the wife is familiar with. The longer you have been married, the more ingrained these patterns are. Build your hobby time around these life patterns. If you don't go out on weeknights with the buddies, then you can't hobby then. If you start changing the way you do things for the hobby, you're going have trouble.

If you don't give your wife gifts and flowers, don't start now because of a hobby guilt trip. She'll know something is up. On the other hand if you become distant, cold, quiet or angry this will make her wonder. Keep your normal demeanor.

Absolutely do not start having less sex at home. She will be thinking "He's needed it two or three times a week for the past 10 years. Last month we went two weeks without and it's happened again this month … he's f--king someone!"

3) If you don't already have a beard, then get one. He's the guy you
blame everything on. Have a close friend who beards for you and
vice versa. A beard covers for you and you can blame everything
on him.

4) Deny! Deny! Deny! Unless your wife walks in and sees you in the
act she doesn't know for certain what you have done. Some
hobbyists get so guilt ridden they subconsciously want to get
caught. They are good husbands, fathers and wage earners but
they have this "dark side" and it eats at them. If confronted by
your wife of sleeping with someone else, these are the first guys
to fess up. If this even remotely describes you, then I strongly
urge you to reconsider your participation in the hobby. The married guys that last in the hobby can totally separate their two lives.

Captain X separated his two lives for years. He was a pro. I hadn't a
clue.

Some of the postings were almost funny. One hobbyist suggested
spraying your crotch with Febreze air freshener to prevent your dog from
jumping all over you after visiting a provider, deterring the pet from zeroing
in on any tell-tale scent of sex. The majority of the postings were from edu-
cated professionals, including lawyers, doctors, and law enforcement officials. There were numerous postings about designating an extra cell phone
for the hobby. *I actually believed Captain X when he said his extra cell phone was for
being on call for flights and pilot union negotiations!* I never questioned this. I felt
so stupid, so humiliated, so used.

To be cleared for clients and have a Behind Closed Doors (BCD) rating, Captain X had to pay a fee to Amber Data Systems to be cleared for
ASPD prostitutes. He paid the prostitutes by cash, PayPal and Verotel, a
payment service provider for "high risk services."

Sunlight peeked through the plantation shutters in my office as I
switched off the overhead lights. I glanced out the window at the street. I
wondered if any of our neighbors in this idyllic suburban neighborhood
ever faced deception in their lives of the magnitude I'd just uncovered.

I never did look at the digital photos I took of Captain X's office, photos I had taken in what seemed like a lifetime ago. I was too exhausted, so I just put everything back to the best of my recollection. Stumbling around in a sleepless stupor, I gathered up my notebook packed with evidence and went downstairs to my closet, where I carefully hid it.

I'd found what I was looking for. As soon as I had some sleep I would call Dr. Evans, my former psychologist, and tell him what I'd uncovered. I wanted to show him proof something was actually terribly wrong in our marriage. Then I would share this new revelation with my divorce attorney.

My mind was racing when yet another potentially life-shattering thought entered my mind. I'd have to be tested for HIV. I felt like I had been shot in the head.

I fell into bed fully clothed and somehow managed to fall asleep sobbing, only to wake up in a start. Was Captain X's infertility problem, his low sperm volume, the result of his using up his semen in sexual encounters with prostitutes? No, I only had proof of his infidelity back to 2001. I felt so lost and confused, but positive of one thing: Captain X was not charming. He was just plain evil.

Chapter 12: The Captain Commandeers Gina

I WOKE UP with a throbbing headache, hoping all I had discovered the night before was just a horrible nightmare. It wasn't. My feelings of confusion in my marriage were now replaced with shock and desperation to figure out what to do next. Somehow adrenaline was rushing through my body. I had to take full advantage of it.

Gina would be home from school that afternoon so I had to use my time wisely. Armed with my binder of evidence of Captain X's infidelity, I had to see both my lawyer and therapist as soon as possible. I have no idea how I showered and dressed.

When I arrived at my lawyer's office, paralegal Hanna guided me into the conference room where I showed her the binder. "Oh, my!" she said as she slowly paged through it, digesting the material, absorbing the impact it would have in my divorce. "We'll need copies of everything. Have you told Captain X you know about this?" she asked. "No, he's flying," I responded. "Good. Don't. We don't want him to know that we know until later. Just avoid him," she said. Less than a week ago I was a married woman. Now I had to act as though I was going through an amicable divorce.

I could only hope that I was in capable hands with the Weinberg law firm, that they would help me as best they could in my divorce. It was another case of blind trust. I gathered up my binder, drained from the raw emotions I was constantly feeling.

I couldn't see Dr. Ryan until 2:00PM, so I drove home and turned on my computer. I couldn't rest until I learned everything I could about

Captain X. His accounts and computer continued to present a treasure trove of endless emails, Word documents, and other painful reminders that my marriage had been a sham. There were even responses from Craigslist, where he sought sexual partners.

A few months earlier news broke about the Craigslist murderer, a killer who met his prostitute victims through Craigslist. Captain X had just returned home. Our routine was that while he unpacked I would get him up to date on current events he might have missed. "Honey, do you believe people actually use Craigslist to get prostitutes?" I asked him incredulously. "No kidding, *really?*" he answered. *I gave him the idea,* I told myself. Again I was blaming myself. *No, no,* I corrected my thoughts. *You didn't give him the idea. He was getting prostitutes from Craigslist before that conversation.*

I was driven to find more information, anything to help me understand what had happened, who Captain X really was. As I delved deeper into his accounts, each email revealed more shocking revelations. From his America Online account I found old emails he had written to my therapist. They were long-winded and strange to read. He wrote, "This past Mother's Day I just returned from flying a four day trip. Out of nowhere she was out of control and cried all the time." Captain X liked to say "you're out of control" when there was any conflict between us. I had been crying and very upset that Mother's Day. I couldn't believe I didn't receive a gift. I don't remember even a card. Nothing special was planned that day, just his usual dinner. Gina was off to her part-time job and Captain X was busy cleaning the pool. "Jesus, what in the hell is wrong with you?" Captain X asked. "Gina's getting cake for you. I'm making a special dinner tonight. What in the hell do you want?" he asked in a sharp biting tone.

I lost my temper with him. I wasn't mad at Gina, I was mad at him. He was the parent and could have suggested something to Gina to make the day special. I wanted to feel appreciated but I didn't. I felt abandoned. It didn't help that I'd just had my third surgery three months before, when he was late to pick me up. After cross-referencing the date he was to pick me up from my appendectomy, I discovered he was on his computer at 7:00 that morning joining SexSearch.com, an adult personal website. I put the proof in my binder. I could only assume he was late to pick me up from the hospital because he'd found the sex he was searching for. *His session must have run late*, I said to myself, crying.

As I read further I was dumbfounded to read emails Captain X had written to Dr. Evans. "What do you see as a future for her? I've been putting up with her totally unbelievable behavior for years. This is not just the result of her surgeries. I want her healthy, but she keeps destroying everything that was ever good about us. Does she need to be hospitalized?" *What? He wants me hospitalized? He wants to commit me!* Dr. Evans responded that I couldn't be hospitalized unless I was a danger to myself. He suggested that Captain X get counseling. Captain X responded, saying he'd been "concerned about the marriage for a long time" and that "as she has gotten older, she lives in this marriage as though she was single." *I live in this marriage as though I am single?* I quickly cross-referenced the dates on these emails with my calendar and found he was confirming a date with a prostitute named Raven two days prior to his email to Dr. Evans. I copied the emails and grabbed my binder as I set off for my ex-therapist's office.

I hadn't seen Dr. Evans in a year. Now I could see that he had been incapable of helping me fix my problems when I hadn't even known what they were! I was filled with a sense of urgency as I rushed to his office. Without greeting him properly, I blurted out, "Look, I'm not crazy!" as I slammed the binder and printed emails on his desk. "My charming husband has been seeing prostitutes for years and here's the proof! Now he's divorcing *me!* Take a look at the emails you shared! Oh, and on top of that, he has us more than $200,000 in debt!" I immediately burst into tears.

Dr. Evans handed me tissues and looked over my evidence. After absorbing what was before him, he said softly, "I'm really sorry. He's a psychopath. He fooled me too." There it was again, the psychopath moniker.

As expected, Dr. Evans inquired if I wanted to schedule sessions again. "No, I just want to get divorced and get him out of my life," I replied. My entire marriage was one big puzzle. I had just uncovered another huge piece. I needed to find all the pieces, something only I could do.

I had to get home to Gina. I knew she was avoiding me. When we did talk our conversations were brief, about where she was going and when she would be home. Gina was constantly busy with school, her part-time job, or friends, so I wasn't overly concerned. I was in such bad shape absorbing all that I had uncovered I was actually glad she was out of the house so often. I couldn't think straight to talk to her. I didn't know what was happening to me. I felt as if I were in a drug-induced nightmare.

Two days later Captain X returned from his trip early in the morning, around 8:00AM. I was now giving the performance of a lifetime, acting as if I was fully resigned to an amicable divorce. I avoided him. That was easy to do in the huge Captain's House.

When he arrived home from a trip, he had a routine. He changed out of his uniform, showered, then walked up to his office wearing just his navy briefs, and closed the door. I knew he would be sitting at his computer checking his emails and making calls before he caught up on his sleep in the guest room. I could hear him on the phone talking to his parents. He must have told them about the divorce before he told me. I overheard him saying, "Yeah Mom, she's really taking it surprisingly well. OK, talk to you later." After the phone conversation he went into the guest room and closed the door behind him. We had almost no interaction over the next three days.

I didn't realize I was in a state of shock; I had never experienced psychological shock at this level. It started the day I found out about the debt, then grew the day Captain X handed me divorce papers. The trauma of discovering his prostitution habit shocked me yet again. Like military shell-shock casualties, my behavior was unpredictable. I was totally unstable and yet somehow I was supposed to continue with the ruse of an amicable divorce. This was crazy.

Captain X left for his scheduled trip and Gina passed in and out of the house, saying little. I didn't know where I was, other than being in hell once again.

When Captain X returned in the morning from his second South American trip that month, I had just showered and was still in the master bath. For some reason I just couldn't budge from the room. I sat silently on the closed commode wearing a worn terrycloth robe, just staring at him. I could see he was visibly uncomfortable with me in his presence.

When we built the Captain's House, we never wanted a door to the commode. It would just take up space. Instead we chose for it to be inset into a small cubicle, but it was still in full view of what was going on in the huge master bath. Bodily functions were normal in each other's presence, we were *that* intimate with each other—or so I'd thought. Our realtor mentioned the lack of a door to the commode cubicle was often brought up by potential buyers. That was the least of my concerns.

The silence was deafening as I watched my husband of 22 years open the sliding mirrored door that led into his closet on one side of the huge master bath. As always, upon returning from a trip, he removed his uniform jacket and hung it up. Next he removed his tie and his epaulets, putting them on the exact same shelf he had assigned them to for years. Then he took off his uniform shirt and pants and tossed them in the basket designated for the dry cleaners. His briefs were last, and he tossed them into a basket for household laundry. My mind wandered. Captain X always chose his own clothing. His choice in underwear wasn't flattering. I recalled reading an article stating that signs your husband is having an affair are when he gets his body toned and purchases attractive underwear. Captain X had done neither.

He went into the large glass block shower stall and proceeded to take a long steamy shower. I had spent many years sitting on the closed commode, talking to him over the shower noise, making small talk as wives often do when their husbands return from business-related travel. Captain X spent a long time showering, always generously lathering and vigorously scrubbing his body. Then he would towel dry himself hard, rubbing his skin briskly with a terrycloth towel. "You're going to wear out your skin taking such long showers and rubbing yourself dry so hard," I'd joke. Now I fully understood his lengthy showers.

I looked at his naked body through the clear glass shower door. The steam couldn't hide the image of the man who had deceived me for so many years. His balding head sported a few strands of faded black and gray hair, and his chest hair was completely gray. His paunch and flaccid penis all were in clear view for me to see. I had seen enough. I left the room.

I went up to my office to think, but it was impossible. I couldn't focus on anything. Half an hour later he went into his office and closed the door. I didn't know what he was doing and didn't care. Then he went into the guest room to sleep. I left my office as soon as I heard the latch on the guest room door close. I could no longer stand to be physically near him.

Something was happening to me. I was going insane in the absurdity of my situation. I tried to live each day cautiously, minute by minute, hour by hour, day by day, pretending I had no knowledge he deceived me.

I went into the family room and turned on the TV, hoping to find something to focus on. I played with the remote. I must have sat there staring at the screen for hours. It provided me with no diversion, no help. My life was out of my control and in the hands of my attorney.

I wandered around the house, looking at how I had tried to make it a home, my artwork, my decorator touches, the framed photographs of our wedding day and of Gina growing up. In reality, the Captain's House was never a home, just a house where people lived.

I finally went into the master bath and entered my closet to select clothes for the new me, a soon-to-be divorced 60-year-old woman. As I slipped on underwear and comfortable jeans and a t-shirt I realized *I didn't do this! I didn't do anything wrong. I am tired of being controlled. Fuck the attorneys! Fuck everyone.* My anger was mounting. FUCK HIM!

Captain X had been sleeping for four hours. I walked into the seldom-used formal living room and sat on one of the couches just looking around the massive room with its high vaulted ceiling. I looked up to the loft and then towards the guest room where Captain X was sleeping. I couldn't keep it in any longer. It was a volcanic rage. I went crazy and just started screaming. "I know who you are, you're a fucking whore! So you like it in the ass, do you? Wonderful Captain X, the loving husband and father FUCKS WHORES with OUR MONEY and WE'RE BROKE! You've been going to whores for years in Phoenix and all over the world. I KNOW *EVERYTHING*, you piece of shit! You're a worthless piece of crap. Do you know that?" I was positive my screaming had woken him. I continued my rant, aiming it up towards the room he was in. "And *YOU'RE* divorcing me? What a laugh! You pay women to fuck you in the ass and then come home and tell me we're broke because of *me*? You piece of shit! You're not human. You sick fuck!" I screamed at the top of my lungs. "I know all about Tiffany Sparks and the others. I know *everything!*" In my rage I grasped for every obscenity I could think of. I didn't know where it was coming from but I couldn't stop. "How many roses a week did you spend during our marriage, you miserable freak?" I shouted, knowing he would get the ASPD.net reference. I didn't expect an answer. "You tell people that I'm sick! I'M NOT THE SICK ONE, YOU ARE! *YOU MISERABLE FUCK!*"

My body was shaking and my voice was hoarse from screaming at him. I noticed he'd left the guest bedroom and went into his office around the corner, slamming the door loudly behind him. He said absolutely nothing in response to my rage.

I heard jostling at the front door. It was Gina was returning from school. I knew my face was red and puffy and wet from tears, but I fought hard for control, to greet her. "Hi honey," my hoarse voiced croaked while my acting expertise kicked in. "Mom and Dad are having a bad day. Could you please go to your room?" I asked her in a hoarse voice. Not saying a word she obediently went to her room, closing the door behind her. Meanwhile Captain X ran furiously down the stairs past me to his closet, where he quickly dressed.

Everything was happening so fast. He was in Gina's room. Then said, "Gina, come with me *now!*" Before I knew it they had left the Captain's House carrying a few packed bags which I assumed were overnight items.

I had no idea my explosive outburst would cause him to take Gina away. Their sudden exit left me stunned. I knew I shouldn't fight him to keep Gina at home with me. You should never fight with a child between you. Gina loved her daddy too much. She would do anything he said. They were both gone and I was alone again in the Captain's House. Captain X had succeeded. I felt crazy.

I sobbed uncontrollably for hours, rehashing what had just happened, my rant about the prostitutes and their sudden exit. Captain X had me so emotionally ill that I didn't realize that I was still controlled by him. I didn't confront him face-to-face about his massive infidelities. I only had the courage to shout up to him from the first floor while he was in the guest room above. Suddenly I felt frightened of him because after 22 years, I didn't know him.

I ate very little that evening but succeeded in drowning my sorrows in Captain X's expensive scotch to try to numb my feelings, eventually falling to sleep in a drunken stupor.

After many cups of coffee the next day, I called my attorney. I admitted confronting Captain X. I told them he had taken Gina away with him. "Find out where my daughter is!" I demanded. They said they would call when they contacted his attorney and had some news to share. Their cold unconcerned attitude angered me.

Within a few days, Hanna phoned. "Gina's OK. She's with her father. They moved into an apartment in Gina's school district. Just give us some time to sort this out with joint custody paperwork," she said. *Gina's OK. She's with my sicko husband*, I said to myself.

As the days passed slowly, the silence in the big Captain's House was deafening. I walked into Gina's pink bedroom. It looked ransacked. I had never pushed her to keep her room clean as long as she maintained good grades, helped around the house, or worked part-time jobs. She kept the bargain.

Signs of her were everywhere. Her Hong Kong dolly smiled down on me from a built-in shelf high above. I went through Gina's drawers, uncovering old letters to boyfriends and teenage camp keepsakes.

I went into her adjacent bathroom. There on the vanity was her hairbrush filled her long brunette hair, reminding me of the day I first felt her infant hair against my cheek. I found her passport and the expensive jewelry her godmother had given her. I grabbed these valuables and left her bedroom. I couldn't bear spending one more minute in her room. It was in shambles, just like my life.

My time now was filled with endless phone calls and emails with PDF files from my attorney. As the days passed, the pain of having no contact from Gina filled me with grief. I prepared myself to be calm when I talked to her. I fully understood that I could never say anything against her father, that you don't use a child as a pawn in a divorce. I constantly dialed her cell phone, but she never answered.

Marvin Weinberg's office emailed me legal documents indicating that Judge Bales, the judge assigned to our case, mandated that Gina attend counseling with each of her parents separately.

I set up a counseling session with a child psychologist, and then sent an email to Gina with the appointment information. I eagerly awaited my daughter's arrival at the psychologist's office after not having seen her in the week since Captain X had taken her from the house.

A half hour after our appointed time I realized Gina was not going to show up for the appointment. I kept phoning her. When she finally answered my call she sounded angry and defiant, like a different person. "I'm not coming. Dad says I don't have to go." I burst into tears. My only conversation with my daughter in a week was for her to tell me that she would only do what Captain X said. I was overwhelmed that my marriage was a sham, and now Captain X had taken my daughter from me.

I went directly to my attorney's office, telling them what had happened. As I stated the facts of Gina's refusal to go to counseling, Hanna looked at me incredulously and said, "I don't understand why Gina won't go."

"I told you Hanna, Gina said her dad said she didn't have to go. Her father is controlling her. As my attorney, isn't it your job to fix this?" I asked, frustrated. Hanna didn't answer.

Marvin Weinberg said that when Gina turned 18 in a year she would be an emancipated minor, free to choose what she wanted to do. He concluded that "it was senseless to spend time and money in the divorce to enforce the judge's ruling for counseling and shared custody of Gina." I was devastated.

As the days went on, Hanna and a handful of friends said, "She'll come back to you later, you'll see," as if that statement was any consolation. I would hear this same statement for years to come.

In our state divorcing couples must take a mandatory parenting class before their divorce can be finalized. I wanted to get it over with as soon as possible. Hanna gave me my assigned day and time to show up. I entered the state office where the class was held, taking a seat in the back of the room among 40 participants at various stages of their divorces. The class consisted of watching a two-hour movie with a question and answer session afterward. I stared at the screen where actors said, "Mommy and Daddy both love you, and it's not your fault but we decided it's best that we get a divorce."

I glanced at the pamphlet I was handed with a list of "Parental Behaviors That Destroy Children." It mentioned that "children need to be free to love both parents. Unfortunately the best of parents may develop destructive patterns." Captain X had already demonstrated these destructive patterns, and there was nothing in the world I could do to remedy this.

While surfing the Internet I came across a blog about cheating husbands that categorized them by profession. I looked under the heading for pilots. There I found postings from wives and girlfriends of pilots worldwide, all going through similar experiences.

I immediately made a posting, looking for a woman divorcing a pilot with Major Airways. I desperately needed to learn about Major Airways' retirement plan and its QDRO, Qualified Domestic Relations Order. My attorney had been asking me about it, assuming I knew the ins and outs of divorcing a pilot. Wasn't that why I'd hired them? I'd never heard of a QDRO. I didn't know it entitled me to receive a percentage of Captain X's retirement funds.

Within days I received an email from a woman named Betsy. We quickly exchanged phone numbers and soon shared our stories over the phone. "So, you're married to a fucktard flyboy, too!" she said, matter-of-factly. Like me, Betsy was in the throes of divorce. She had been married for 20 years and had two little boys. She discovered her husband, a Major Airways captain, was sleeping with a Major Airways gate agent in the Dominican Republic after finding a compromising photo of them on Facebook.

"Do you believe the asshole would call in sick with Major Airways and then *pay* to fly JetBlue to go meet up with her? He also has a huge gambling problem so we're broke. Once Crew Scheduling called the house to assign him a trip and he was out on a trip. He was out all right, fucking!" She finished her story the way I felt. "I hate him."

I had forgotten that Major Airways Crew Scheduling once called our house, too, looking for Captain X. I answered, "Don't you know where he is? He's flying." When he returned from his "trip" I asked him about the call. His explanation sounded reasonable and logical. I was so stupidly trusting.

Betsy listened attentively while I told her about Captain X's prostitution habit. Then I told her about him taking Gina. She listened as my voice cracked with emotion. I could hear the plunking sounds of her computer keyboard during our call. "It's called PAS, parental alienation syndrome. Look into it. Maybe someone can help. I'm sending you a link." Betsy knew her way around a computer. She seemed always to be on it when we talked. I didn't realize Betsy would provide emotional support for years to come.

I found only one parental alienation support group in my area and made plans to attend their next meeting. The group met in a local church hall once a month. As I signed in, sticking an adhesive name tag to my blouse, I scanned the room looking at the other women who were alienated from their children. Two of us were new attendees. We were asked to share a brief description of our child alienation.

I was handed a box of tissues as I told my story. The mention of Captain X's prostitution habit brought looks of disbelief from the group. The other new attendee was a woman alienated from her three small children. Her ex-husband had the courts convinced she was mentally ill. I passed her the tissue box. We shared the same pain.

The members of the group seemed to know each other, reporting on progress they might have made in contacting their children. Except for the other new attendee and me, the members all had older children who left home on their own because they refused to follow their parent's strict religious teachings. These people were hell-bent on cramming their religious beliefs down their teenage children's throats. As the meeting concluded, I waved goodbye to the other new attendee, knowing neither of us would be returning.

Driving back to the lonely Captain's House I realized I was useless to Gina in the condition I was in. I couldn't tell her about her father. I didn't even understand what kind of person he was. An analogy popped into my head; I was similar to a mother flying with a small child during a flight emergency. I had to grab my oxygen mask first and breathe into it to get stable before I could even think of helping Gina.

Chapter 13: He Never Kissed You

DR. KAIMAL WAS out of town, so I called Dr. Bob to make an appointment for an HIV test. There was no way I was going to tell Dr. Bob's receptionist the purpose of my visit. I just said firmly, "I need to see him about a private matter," setting an appointment for later that day.

I was disappointed. I really wanted to see Dr. Kaimal. I wanted to tell her about Captain X's secret life, since she was so charmed by him. I wondered how she would have responded when I told her the reason I needed an HIV test. I wondered if she would have had answers for me. I would never find out; I never saw her again.

Dr. Bob's office manager was usually so overtly cheerful that I could barely put up with her on what I considered a normal day, let alone now with all the pain I was going through. I felt there was a chance I might go ballistic if she greeted me saying, "And how are you doing today?" stretching out the words like a southern drawl.

I arrived with my red-rimmed eyes hidden behind large sunglasses as I wrote my name on the sign-in sheet. I was led into a small, sterile examination room where I sat on the paper-covered examination table. I was instantly reminded of all the sad, lonely medical procedures I endured with no empathy from my husband. I wept softly. Dr. Bob knocked and entered, smiling while he asked, "What can I help you with today?"

I struggled to control my tears as I spewed out my horrific story to Dr. Bob. "He's been going to prostitutes and I have proof. Now he's divorcing me! He's ruined my life. I need to be tested for HIV, *now!*" I said firmly, trying to regain my composure from my painful diatribe. *Dr. Bob probably thinks I'm crazy. What do I care?* After all I had been through, anyone would be crazy. At least my story and mental state got me a prescription for Valium.

"I'm so sorry," he said softly as he took my blood. Realizing there was a possibility Dr. Bob might have actually listened to me and understood my despair, I found enough clarity to ask a question. "Did Captain X ever see you for any sexually transmitted diseases?" I asked. Dr. Bob paused a long time before he answered my question. "You know I can't answer that. Medical records are confidential, even between married couples." Actually I hadn't known that! Later I would find out I could be told if my husband had been treated for a communicable disease if, in fact, Dr. Bob had treated him for a communicable disease and recorded my husband's diagnosis as such, as he was legally bound to do. "What I can tell you is that your husband is two months overdue on his payment to us for his last physical. I'd appreciate it if you would pass that information on." I looked him straight in the eyes with disbelief. "You can tell him that yourself, if you can find him. And when you do, you'd better get in line. He has creditors calling us constantly."

Dr. Bob looked a bit alarmed over my statement, but soon he was back in his physician mode. "I'm sure the test is fine, but we'll call if there's anything to be concerned about. Again, I'm really sorry," he said softly as he quickly left the room. As I drove home, an ominous feeling came over me. I thought about the way Captain X often referred to Dr. Bob as his "good buddy." Many physicians were members of ASPD. I wondered if Dr. Bob was in the brotherhood.

I drove home, stopping on the way at our neighborhood pharmacy drive-through to get the Valium prescription filled. As I waited in the car, my mind wandered. Never in my life would I have dreamed I'd be taking an HIV test at 60. I was overwhelmed once again.

Once home I was drawn to my computer where I looked up a Word document where I kept my personal medical information. In the document I had noted five months earlier, in January, Dr. Bob had treated me for an "undefined vaginal discharge." I remember him handing me a prescription for azithromycin, an antibiotic used to treat common bacterial infections including the sexually transmitted diseases gonorrhea and chlamydia.

My mind was going crazy. Had Dr. Bob treated me that day for an STD Captain X had given me, never telling me my true diagnosis? I felt I couldn't trust anyone. I was alone in this horror, not caring if I was infected with the HIV virus. I was already dying of despair. That night, with the help of the Valium, I fell into a deep, sorely needed sleep.

I woke up the next morning feeling a bit better. I knew I had to get some control over my life. I remained glued to my computer, searching everywhere to find the extent of Captain X's secret life, and why I hadn't a clue. It was heartbreaking to cross-reference my calendar with his ASPD dated posts or emails indicating he was with prostitutes. Not only did he visit prostitutes when he was out of the country flying, but also while he was home when I was seeing friends, seeing doctors, or visiting my antique or New York friends. He visited prostitutes around special days, like his birthday, my birthday, our anniversary and holidays. Captain X frequented a local prostitute named Christie, paying $200 plus a tip towards "Christie's college fund." I cried when I read that. Gina would soon be entering college.

Somehow I just couldn't wrap my head around the fact that he also frequented a prostitute named Allegra, the same name as his mother! *What kind of man does that?*

The Internet is filled with stories of people who had been in deceptive marriages. Most I read were posted by women who came to the conclusion their spouse was a sex addict. *Maybe that's what he is,* I thought. *Maybe he's a sex addict. Maybe that's just another piece of the puzzle that will help me understand who Captain X really is.*

I researched sexual addiction on the Internet, trying to find a support group for spouses so I could learn more about sexual addiction. I located a local chapter of COSA (Co-Dependents of Sex Addicts), based on the Alcoholics Anonymous twelve-step program. I wanted to attend a meeting to better understand sexual addiction.

Not only did I assume Captain X was a sex addict because of the evidence I had uncovered, but also because he seldom kissed me. When he did, his kisses were not passionate. They lacked intimacy. In the beginning of our marriage I assumed that in time more passion and kissing would evolve. Now I thought he didn't kiss me because he had been with so many prostitutes. I had heard that most prostitutes don't kiss their clients. This thought stayed with me as I parked my car to attend the COSA meeting, another support group held in a church annex.

At the COSA meeting I was greeted by a sympathetic group of women, all in relationships affected by sex addiction. Again, the 18 women sat in a semi-circle on metal folding chairs. After the moderator read the group's mission statement and prayer, each attendee briefly shared updates about her life with a sexual addict. I was in the company of women who understood my pain. The majority of these women chose to try to salvage their relationships, if their partners would undergo therapy and join a sexual addiction support group. No story was the same, but all were equally devastating and heartbreaking.

I was the only new attendee. Again, I tearfully told my story as I talked between gulps of air and stopping to blow my nose. As painful as it was to share my story, it felt good to share it with women who could relate to my experience. I did notice their looks of disbelief when I told them of the child alienation.

My story of the sexual infidelity in my marriage was out of place with the parental alienation support group I previously attended. Here, my story of being alienated from my daughter was out of place with the COSA group. I wondered if there was a support group for women experiencing both.

After the meeting, the group invited me to join them for a bite to eat. Once outside, a woman embraced me and said, "You and I have something in common."

"What's that?" I replied.

"We both have husbands who are in professions that seem to have many sex addicts."

"Your husband is a pilot?" I asked.

"No," she said softly, "he's an ordained minister."

Despite being informative and understanding, COSA was not for me. These women loved their husbands and wanted to stay with them. I had no intention of staying with Captain X after learning his sexual secret life. I was a victim of it, and a victim of so much more.

I knew I needed to pull myself together and get out of the house. I had fallen into the habit of not showering, and wearing the same sweat suit for days. I knew I had to get back into the habit of dressing, going out for dinner or drinks, just to feel alive. I tried to do this at least once a week, despite the expense. My attorney obtained court-ordered funds of $200 a week for me to live on, so I had to be frugal. *I was always frugal. Look where it got me*, I thought.

When I went out for dinner, I ordered one or two drinks, but no more. I never drove unless I was sober. One evening I treated myself to a night out at a restaurant that catered to an older crowd. I easily found an empty bar chair in the corner where I placed my order with the bartender, ordering the least expensive meal on the menu and a glass of house wine. The wine quickly relaxed me but altered my mood. Soon I was feeling sorry for myself. My eyes started to moisten.

Seated a few chairs away was a woman alone nursing a drink. She could see the pain on my face, my eyes starting to tear up. As she moved closer to me I wanted to bolt. I didn't want to share my painful story, revealing I was an emotional mess. She moved in quickly, giving me a strong hug. "Whatever it is, it'll be all right," she said soothingly. I broke down and spewed out my whole story, punctuating every sentence with tears. She opened her purse and handed me tissues.

"Look honey, I know exactly what you're talking about. I bet he never kissed you," she said. "How did you know that?" I asked, amazed she had such insight into my personal life. "Mine never did. Kissing is way too intimate," she said. "Consider yourself lucky. Mine had me doing all kinds of kinky shit. It started with computer porn, and then escalated to bondage. Then one day he asked me to piss on him. I'm pretty liberal, but I just wasn't ready for *that*. I have two great kids and didn't want a divorce. Believe it or not I loved him, so I did what he wanted. It was sick. I did it because I wanted to stay married. I could only take his kink for so long. I had to divorce him, so here I am going through a divorce, too. He just never kissed me, and I knew from what you told me about yours, he didn't either. Now I'm involved with a normal man who really kisses me, and it's wonderful. The only problem is I have shared custody of the kids with my ex, so I still have to see him."

Her shocking story of kinky sex and no kissing was an earful. "You'll be OK," she said after embracing me when we parted company. I drove home, repeating to myself over and over her words "he never kissed you." I had no idea kissing habits could reveal so much about a person.

While computer sleuthing I came across a posting from 2006 by a prostitute named Provider 88. It was a tell-all about ASPD, the prostitution website Captain X frequented. The posting provided me with some odd humor in a time I had nothing to laugh about:

ASPD.net is a place for hookers (called "providers") to post free ads about what they do and what those services cost. The men on ASPD.net read those ads and choose the "provider" they wish to see, based on her ad and/or review. ASPD.net as well does "reviews" on "providers." These reviews consist of a description of the "provider" and what was done at the appointment and what it costs. This entire thing is called "hobbying" by the men on ASPD.net.

Most (not all, but most) are older married men looking for sex. Most of the men are not anything you'd want to date outside of the "hobby" or even want to be seen with. Many have bad teeth and breath and can't even get it up.

I personally choose to remain anonymous to keep the lucrative business I already have. There is not one person on ASPD.net who will know who I am. If they knew I would lose a lot of business, anonymity is a good thing.

What is so bad about ASPD.net is the men put down the girls. If they don't get what they want, or don't get what they think they should get, then they'll write a bad "review" on you, and that hurts your business.

Yes the "hooker" business has long been on the web. It's a lucrative business many know nothing about. Am I worried about getting busted? Hardly, the majority of the girls there know how to screen and check for references and if you are smart you don't share much information.

ASPD.net is the scumbag of the forums. Nothing but a bunch of older, lonely, smelly men who don't want or don't care about themselves and surely not their other half.

When I leave the business, I'll be calling all their wives and letting them know what's going on. Are you scared? You should be. This is a place that needs to be shut down. I'm on my way out, and when I leave I'll leave no tracks and no goodbyes. Am I doing anything wrong? Well, yes, prostitution is against the law, that's why I've made my money and am on my way out while I am still young. But these guys need a wake-up call. Nothing but a bunch of lying horny ass old men.

I laughed and cried at the same time as I read her insightful post. I phoned Betsy and said, "You are not going to believe what I just found! A prostitute posted on the Internet what the men who go to her are really like. You're gonna love this!" I said, laughing, trying to find any humor for us to share. I immediately emailed her a copy of the posting. I had cried so often over the phone to Betsy. The posting provided us with some much-needed comic relief while we were both going through divorces involving infidelity.

I stopped to think about other wives who might have discovered their husbands were cheating on them with prostitutes. If I met one, I'd say, "He never kissed you," and they would probably answer the same as I did, "How did you know?"

Chapter 14: The Cowgirl from Craiglist

I SAT IN the family room, staring at the flat screen TV, not having the faintest idea what to do next. The house was for sale but there was no interest. The market had crashed and I couldn't care less. I hated the house. It was my jail. Why was I in jail if I had done nothing wrong? I was surrounded by moving boxes filled with my past life, my part of the community property items. I had little recollection of the day Captain X came through the house with an air of diplomacy, going through each room dividing our marital possessions.

We owned two pieces of quality art, oil paintings of the same value, so that division was easy. "I want the dining room painting so you get the living room painting," he said indignantly, as if he was in charge of the separation of our marital goods. "OK," I said, stunned, as he rushed taking items. My mind flashed back to when we bought the art, investments for the future, paintings that would help make the house a home, I thought. It never worked. That was the past. I had to stay focused on the present, watching what he was taking. I didn't care about the furniture. I didn't care much about anything we had shared together. Wherever my future life would be, I didn't want reminders from this marriage, just my photographs of Gina, my antiques, books, clothing and jewelry.

Captain X took his precious Waterford highball glasses, leaving me the matching water goblets and champagne flutes. I was pleased to get the champagne flutes. I thought they might signify a sliver of hope for my future. *Maybe someday I'll have a need to celebrate*, I told myself. My life was crumbling before me but I still had hope for some future celebration. *Where did this optimism come from?*

I was plagued by memories from my life with Captain X. Some went back decades, and others were as recent as six months ago. Each one was like a movie reel in my mind that I had viewed before, but when it came back, I noticed things I hadn't noticed before. "Oh, that's why he did that! *Now* I know what happened! That's why he couldn't join me on that trip. *Now* I know where the money went!" These memories left me drained. I was suffering from post-traumatic stress disorder, but I wouldn't be diagnosed until years later.

He was gone. The house was bleak and silent, so television was my constant company. Tabloid shows aired Tiger Woods' infidelities and Bernie Madoff's Ponzi schemes. I stared in awe. I could relate to Madoff's victims and to the heartbreak of Elin Nordegren, Tiger Woods' wife. Captain X's deviant personality was a combination of both of those not-ables and worse: he alienated me from Gina.

I glanced at the clock and noticed CNN had repeated the same video feeds of Woods and Madoff six times in the last two hours. I had been wearing the same worn grey fleece sweat suit for two days straight, not showering. I was a mess.

Alone and with no one to share my misery, I lived constantly on the Internet learning computer forensics. Captain X wasn't exactly meticulous in covering his tracks. I continued sleuthing, hoping to find anything I'd missed.

One evening I poured myself a drink and sat before the computer with TV for company. For some reason I was drawn back to Craigslist. All of a sudden an idea popped into my head. Maybe I could use Craigslist for *my* purposes.

I looked under the Craigslist heading for roommates and thought, why not? I could post an ambiguous advertisement and if I got an answer, I'd explain to the applicant that I really needed company and that the rent would be free. My attorney advised me not to show any income during this period. A roommate would only have to pay for our food. I would get the benefit of companionship, even if for a short time. I pondered this as care-fully as I could, analyzing whether this plan could backfire. It seemed like a win-win situation, so I carefully created my ad. Then I went back to Craigslist and posted it using a new email address from an account I had just opened:

Looking for a short term roommate,
mature woman or gay man. Huge house
to share. More info when we talk.

Within a few hours of posting the 'roommate wanted' notice on Craigslist, I received an email reply from Jill, who asked a few pertinent questions. I sent her my cell phone number, mentioning in my email that my situation was way too complicated to write about. That was an understatement!

Later that day Jill called. "Hello," she said in the thickest southern accent I had ever heard. "What's the story, honey?" she asked. I had no idea if this would work but I would give it a try. I had to soften the divorce story; no one wants to move in with a crazy person. "I'm in the middle of a horrific divorce. My husband left and took my 17-year-old daughter. He cheated and left me in debt. I'm trying my best to move on but I am in limbo in this house that's for sale. I need someone to keep me company for a few months. Why don't you come over so we can meet?" I said as straightforwardly as possible and paused, waiting for her to answer. "Honey, when's a good time?" she asked. "Tonight if that's OK with you," I said. She agreed. I gave her directions and we set a time for later that evening. I felt a tiny twinge of optimism for the first time since my life with Captain X started spiraling out of control.

I finally I had a reason to get out of my sweats and take a shower. Anyone who saw me in the physical state I was in would have bolted. I peeled off the clothes I had been wearing and entered the glass shower. The hot steamy water sprayed down on me. I felt a glimmer of hope.

I finally took on the appearance of a normal housewife, or whatever I remembered that to be. I tried to keep in mind I had to act the part of "divorcing housewife" too. My costume was clean jeans and an attractive t-shirt. Again my acting ability would be useful.

The doorbell rang. "Howdy! I'm Jill," she said, thrusting out her hand to shake. There she stood: a tall lanky woman topped with a mass of kinky-curly brown and gray hair that cascaded over her shoulders. She wore a leather biker jacket over jeans and shirt. My eyes immediately went down to her black clunky cowboy boots.

Her eyes widened as she looked over the spacious modern Captain's House that gave the appearance we had money, which we should have had. "Y'all have a nice place here," she said. I led her to the family room, where my life's belongings were stacked in cardboard boxes, leaning against the large glass windows partially hiding the view of the pool. We seated ourselves on the black leather recliners. I took a deep breath and repeated a brief version of my story. "I need someone here to keep me company until the house sells or the divorce is final," I repeated.

"Oh, honey, bless your heart! I'm so sorry. That's awful," she replied in a heavy drawl. "Well, my story is that I had to retire early from an IT job to take care of my husband Bobby. He died three months ago of pancreatic cancer back in Flagstaff, where my house is. I was just called back to work on a big IT project in Phoenix for a few months. It's just too far to commute, so I need a place here to live for a few months."

Jill was in her late 50s. I tried to avoid any preconceived ideas about the cowgirl-biker look. She was obviously intelligent and well-traveled. The added plus was that she was compassionate. I took her on a tour of the empty house, leading her to the seldom-used guest room with adjoining bath, which I told her would be her room. I felt good about her. I don't know where this positive feeling came from; it had been a long time since I felt positive about anything.

"Jill, I really don't want any money, any payment for rent. I'm not supposed to show any income during the divorce. I just need you to pay for our food," I explained. Her eyes lit up, realizing that I was offering a pretty good deal. "I do have some rules though. No visitors, pets, or drugs," I said firmly. "I told you I have been through a lot, but so have you, after losing Bobby. I'm sorry for your loss," I said sincerely. "Girly-girl," she answered, "I think this might work out for both of us. Sounds good to me."

"Me too," I said. "I just need a copy of your driver's license, just for my own information." She opened her wallet and handed over her driver's license with no reservations. I scanned a copy of it, trying to appear businesslike, and handed back her license. She had no idea I was so desperate for companionship I would have let the first homeless person who appeared at my door move in if I hadn't thought of Craigslist. I was that lonely.

A few days later Jill moved in with a few boxes, an inflatable bed, and an eight by ten inch framed photograph of Bobby, which she clutched in her arms. She moved through the house clutching the framed photo of Bobby as if it were a moveable shrine. I'd been through a lot, but my mind could not wrap itself around mourning a spouse, a loved one. My husband was a fraud. She had no idea how much I envied her love for Bobby.

Jill told me more about her house. "It's just beautiful! It's out in the country where everybody knows everybody. They were really nice to me when Bobby died. I'll be going there on weekends. That's where I've got our Harleys," she told me proudly. *Well, this is certainly going to be interesting*, I thought.

As roommates we were an odd but compatible couple. During the day Jill went off to work at her eight-to-five job. I spent my time straightening out piles of legal papers, the credit card mess, trying to learn about Major Airways' retirement benefit package, and searching for answers to who or what Captain X was. It was a full-time job I never imagined I would be doing.

Jill brightened my afternoons with phone calls telling me what time to expect her home, and asking me what she should get for dinner. She either shopped for food at the market, brought home take-out, or we ordered a pizza. Sometimes we'd go out to dinner at a local restaurant. After dinner we curled up on the recliners watching sit-coms. She went to bed around 10:00PM and got up around 7:00AM. Quickly we became comfortable roommates.

One evening Jill walked in with a bag of groceries and with a portable charcoal grill in tow. "I'm fixin' to grill us some ribeyes," she announced. She added a salad and baked potatoes, all washed down with red wine. It was wonderful. I hated how Captain X took over the kitchen to make dinner. Somehow I didn't mind one bit when Jill tended to our evening meals.

Something was different when Jill cooked. We really enjoyed each other's company.

Later that evening I caught Jill outside on the patio smoking marijuana. She sheepishly offered me a puff. I declined, thanking her anyway. I really didn't care if she occasionally indulged. Her presence in the lonely Captain's House was keeping me sane, something far more important than her occasional marijuana habit. Our roommate arrangement was going much better than I had ever anticipated. She even made me laugh with her girly-girl talk.

Jill was a seasoned world traveler. Her IT position had sent her to places even I had never been to. I envied her, a woman with career. I had no job to fall back on and was in financial ruin with an uncertain future, all because of my stupid blind trust in Captain X. If my life looked foolish to her, she certainly never judged me. "Girly-girl," she said, "you're gonna do OK, don't you worry."

One weekend she invited me to see her house. Because she drove a worn-out Impala she asked if she could drive my luxury car. I knew how much she wanted to drive it but I didn't know if my insurance covered her, so I didn't feel comfortable letting her drive. The previous year Captain X had traded in my SUV for a luxury sedan. The SUV was high off the ground, and it became difficult for me to get into after my hip and back surgeries. I knew little about cars. He was in charge of the cars. He was in charge of everything.

Jill had no idea how much I looked forward to getting out of the Captain's House. I picked her up at her office at 2:00PM on a Friday, avoiding the evening rush hour traffic. She was in charge of the route, carefully giving me directions. We finally reached her home by dusk.

Driving down a gravel road at sunset she said, "My house is just three-quarters of a mile further down this road." I could finally see the one-story dwelling she called home. The white frame house was surrounded by tall pine and aspen trees. Vehicles in various states of disrepair filled one side of the property. She told me Bobby had been working on them before he got sick.

Jill gave me a tour of her house which was filled with cozy quilts, antiques, memorabilia from her travels, and Bobby's things she had not yet touched. Jill and I were living much the same life, part in the painful past and part in present. We didn't know our futures. She showed me to her guest room where I tossed my weekend bag.

"Wanna beer?" she asked. I nodded and she tossed me a cold one from her fridge. "I'm going to make a few calls and tell my friends I'm home. First I have to call Tony." She had filled me in about Tony. He was a bigwig in the area, owning a local hauling company. Tony wanted a personal relationship with Jill but she wasn't interested, just happy to be friends.

Before we settled in the house Jill took me back to her barn. It wasn't really a barn but rather a large steel building housing two Harley Davidson motorcycles, Bobby's auto body accessories, and hundreds of tools and pieces of machinery. "And here it is, what I call my honky-tonk," she said proudly. She had equipped the building with a bar, dance floor and neon lighting, mimicking a beer hall. "Isn't this special?" She glowed, grinning ear-to-ear as she showed off her pride and joy. "Wow, this is something!" was all I could muster. "Tony and a few friends are coming over tomorrow. We'll party and dance a bit."

"Sounds good," I said. I fell fast asleep that evening. I needed this diversion.

The next morning we drove to the nearby diner called Lynn's. The second we entered, heads turned. A booming male voice said, "Hey, Jill, you're back! Who's that there with the fancy wheels?"

Most of Jill's friends dined at Lynn's. The diner had Naugahyde-covered swiveling stools, Formica tables and a chalkboard listing the days special. Jill introduced me to everyone. "This here is my friend I'm staying with in Phoenix," she said proudly, her arm draped around my back. The men wore jeans, work shirts, cowboy hats and boots. The mature women were a bit on the heavy side. They certainly were not the upscale crowd I was used to, but everyone was warm and welcoming, something I longed for.

Jill and I ate a huge breakfast. When we finished, we drove back to her house where I read while she puttered around the house. Later we drove off to visit Bobby's' parents, Patti Sue and Ray, who she was very close to. They lived in a mobile home about ten miles away. When we arrived I was in culture shock. Bobby's overweight parents were on disability. The crowded mobile home was filled to the brim with belongings, nothing worth keeping as far as I saw, but then again, who was I to say how people live? They instantly made me feel at home. Soon the feeling of being in a cramped mobile home left my mind as we chatted during the short visit. Patti Sue gave Jill a homemade pie she'd just baked as we said our good-byes. "You be sure and visit us again," Patti said to me, hugging me earnestly.

That Saturday night Jill's honky-tonk was filled with people. Sandwiches and beer were in abundance. Jill introduced me to her friends, a pleasant group. Although I was never a beer drinker, I found myself starting to enjoy one cold beer after another. The country and western music blaring from a boom-box soon became pleasant to my ears. I looked around. Everyone had left the honky-tonk to join Jill in the house to indulge in marijuana.

Alone in the honky-tonk and bolstered by beer, I suddenly felt free to dance by myself. I felt a tinge of happiness washing over me, being away from the source of my pain. I have no idea why, but I started to remember dance steps from far back in my past, my ballet chaînés turns. I was off to a good start, twirling in the open space towards an open area when I fell down hard, my right hand smacking the cement floor first, breaking my fall. The pain was instantaneous. I ran to the house for ice. "Jill," I said, "I did a dumb thing. I fell down and need ice for my hand." She quickly handed me an ice pack and some ibuprofen. Embarrassed, I bid everyone goodnight, holding the ice pack on my wounded wrist as I settled into the guest room.

The next morning Tony came over to visit. The three of us discussed my injury, hoping it was a sprain. Tony went to the store and bought me a wrist support bandage while I kept taking ibuprofen, hoping it would alleviate the pain. I tried to ignore my injured wrist, which now felt like a deep and constant throbbing burn.

"Well, girly-girl," I said to Jill later that day, "you got your wish. You're driving us back home." My right hand was swollen. I couldn't drive in such bad shape. Jill's eyes lit up as she started the ignition. Enjoying driving the luxury auto, Jill skillfully drove us back to Phoenix. From the look on her face, I knew that if I owned the car, I probably would have given it to her then and there. It had never brought me pleasure. "These are great wheels," she said as we pulled into the garage.

That night I winced in pain trying to fall asleep. Jill had to get up at seven and I knew she had a busy day. By 3AM I couldn't take the pain any longer. Somehow I managed to get dressed and carefully drove myself to the hospital. I was seen by a doctor immediately, x-rays revealing I had broken my wrist. *Great! I break my wrist dancing alone in a honky-tonk!*

"Why didn't tell me you were going to the hospital? I would have taken you!" Jill said early the next morning. "Look, you needed your sleep for work. I get a cast put on later today. I'll be OK. Just promise me you'll *never* mention I was dancing drunk when this happened," I said. "I promise," she said with a smile as she left for her job.

When Jill had moved in, we moved my computer, personal files, and all my belongings down to the kitchen area. I no longer wanted to climb those stairs. I was now working from the kitchen table near the long granite counter.

Later that evening after Jill went to bed, I immediately went back to my computer sleuthing, printing every posting made by PussELuvR that was still floating in cyberspace. Although I was sporting a cast, I still had use of my fingers. I looked at this work as a way to secure my future, and I tried to keep my emotions out of it.

In the wee morning hours, I lined up Captain X's PussELuvR postings in chronological order, edge to edge on the long granite countertop. It was past 3:00AM when I grabbed one of the ASPD postings spitting out of the printer. I looked down and noticed the number 30 printed in a post Captain X had reviewed of a provider named Lacey, in February of 2006:

> "Lacey is one of the best I and many others
> have seen in my 30+ years in the hobby"

"Nonononononononoooooooo," I screamed at the top of my lungs. Was I reading this right? *This is not happening to me. Am I imagining this? Does this really mean what I think it does?* "Nononooo," I kept screaming. Captain X had been seeing prostitutes for 30 years, *throughout our entire marriage!* His deception was of epic proportions. Just how much more could I take?

I had awakened Jill, who came running down the stairs to find me collapsed and crying on the kitchen floor, the Internet posting in my hand. By now she knew my full story. Handing her the paper, I said, "Look, it says 30 years! Thirty years! He's been fucking whores for 30 years! My marriage was a joke, the fucking bastard has been seeing hookers our entire marriage!" I shrieked.

Mournful sobs racked my body while Jill held me tight, softly reassuring me, "Girly-girl, you're going to be OK," as she stroked my hair. My body heaved from the hurt and pain, while my mind was trying to assimilate what I had just uncovered.

She must have held me for quite some time. The shock of this new evidence had me shaking and gulping for air. My face was smeared with tears and snot. Jill turned off the computer and led me to my bed, tucking me underneath a soft down comforter, my body shaking uncontrollably.

If I had discovered this new revelation without Jill to comfort me, I might not have survived the night. *Will this nightmare ever end? Can I get any help?* I knew I had to find some professional help.

Before she left the master bedroom, Jill said softly, "Darlin', you OK? Need anything?"

"I just need some good professional help," I answered, sniffling into a wet tissue. "You get that, girly-girl. You'll figure it out," she said softly as she left the room.

All of a sudden my mind flashed back to our infertility. "The urologist says I have a low sperm volume," Captain X had said. Prostitutes for 30 years. *I figured it out.*

Chapter 15: Counseled by Queen Latifah

JILL'S COMPANY WAS a ray of sunshine in the Captain's House, but despite her upbeat personality and genuine warmth, I was deeply troubled. I desperately needed mental health counseling.

Getting good professional counseling is easier said than done. I wouldn't go back to Dr. Evans. I was now armed with the entire sordid story of my 22-year deceptive marriage and needed someone new to help put my puzzling and shattered life together. At least now I knew I wasn't crazy. Surely there was someone somewhere who was equipped to help me.

I was putting on a good front for Jill, but in truth I was spiraling fast into depression. A few friends urged me to get on antidepressants—people who had been taking them for years for chronic depression. When I mindlessly watched television, the screen was constantly filled with advertisements for antidepressants, showing people who had no zest for life. Soon after taking the miracle drug advertised, they'd become happy, functioning people. *But I have a zest for life. Captain X didn't succeed in taking that away from me.* Right or wrong, I felt certain that no drug could fix my situation. I just didn't know enough about antidepressants, and I was already confused enough. I was frightened that antidepressants would numb my emotions, muddle my thoughts, and further confuse me. I found another physician willing to prescribe Ativan, a drug often given for short-term treatment of anxiety and insomnia. I certainly had both of those symptoms. I used it sparingly, mostly to help me sleep. The last thing in the world I needed was to acquire a drug habit.

I desperately needed a clear head to understand my past and to assimilate the information I'd acquired. More than anything, I had to find someone who would listen to me, someone who could understand what I went
through, and someone who could help me sort out the mess.

During the divorce proceeding, Captain X was required to maintain
my health insurance. A mental health professional would require me to pay
money upfront for the co-pay. The $200 a week I received from Captain X
for living expenses was barely enough to pay for household, automobile
and personal needs, let alone medical help. I was skeptical that I could afford therapy, but this was an emergency.

After increasingly desperate Internet searches, I found a webpage for
Welcoming Arms Women's Shelter, a not-for-profit agency offering services to individuals and families going through domestic abuse. Maybe they
could help me.

With shaking hands I called their hotline. "Hello, Welcoming Arms.
How can I help you?" a woman's voice answered. "I need help," my voice
quavered in reply. "Are you in any danger?" she asked. My immediate
thought was that I was reaching out to the wrong people. How could I be
in danger when I was living in the massive Captain's House, with a swimming pool, and driving a luxury car? I'd traveled the world; I had a life people envied. *Of course I'm safe.* "No, but I need help," I replied. Then I briefly
blurted out everything that had happened to me to the faceless person on
the other end of the phone. "Are you afraid of your ex-husband?" she
asked. "No, errrrr ... yes, but he's not here. I'm worried about me."

Since I was not in immediate danger, the sympathetic voice on the
phone suggested I call their main number. I made an appointment with a
counselor for later that afternoon. I tried to be as optimistic as I could be,
despite feeling like the walking wounded.

Welcoming Arms was a 25-minute drive away, in an industrial park. A
small brick sign displayed their name and address in front of the nondescript office building. I pulled into the parking lot, wondering what in the
hell I was doing there. Their parking lot held a few Lexuses, BMWs and one
Mercedes. Obviously I wasn't alone. The well-heeled needed counseling
too.

The mauve reception area held a couch and three wicker chairs with floral cushions. A large glass coffee table was strewn with outdated magazines and worn children's books. Two silk ficus trees in brass pots did nothing to brighten the maudlin décor. A woman busied herself with two toddlers as I approached the small receptionist window and gave my name.

"I'm here to see someone about counseling," I said in a low voice. "Have a seat," she replied. After ten minutes, a full-figured, tall, stately black woman introduced herself as Vanessa Jones and led me into a room which looked much like a fourth grade classroom. Vanessa was nothing like I had expected, but then again, just what *was* I expecting? If I were to cast a film of my life story, Vanessa would be played by Queen Latifah: a confident woman of color with a very comforting smile. Vanessa was not a licensed psychologist, but rather a counselor donating her time as she worked towards her degree.

Vanessa closed the door and we sat opposite each other at a long industrial folding table, where she plopped down her huge fake designer handbag. Flashing me a big smile she asked me to tell her about myself. Again, I had to tell the story of Captain X's deception, which now defined me. I showed her my evidence books and financial proof. Tears flowed but I didn't care. Vanessa inspected them as she listened intently, carefully taking notes.

"I think we can help you. First I have to know if you are safe. Is he physically abusive to you?" she asked. I couldn't answer that yet, so I didn't answer.

"Does he have any firearms?" she asked. "Well, yes," I answered. After 9/11, Captain X became an FFDO, a Federal Flight Deck Officer, a pilot permitted to carry a firearm on board international flights. As soon as he got certified in the FFDO program, he'd walk around the house flashing his badge-like credentials like a kid who'd won a medal. "Wanna see my creds?" he'd ask. "I bet I can get out of speeding tickets just by flashing my creds." The pacifist I married had become a gun-toting loony. I had forgotten all about the gun which was supposed to be locked up when he wasn't carrying it. *How could I have forgotten about the gun*, I wondered?

I explained that my lifestyle appeared as though I lived in the lap of luxury, but I didn't. Now I was in jail in the house, with no one to talk to

except Jill. I needed a safe place to talk and cry. I desperately needed to figure out what had happened to me.

"People from all walks of life come through our doors. Now don't
worry. First I want you to fill out these forms. Then I want you to come
back for weekly counseling sessions. I have an opening Thursdays at
3:00PM, would that be good for you?" she asked. "Yes, great. How do I pay
you?" I inquired. "We don't charge for counseling. This is a not-for-profit
organization, helping the community. You can make a donation later if you
want. Right now we just want to help you get through this the best you can.
Fill out the forms and leave them for me with the receptionist. I'll see you
Thursday," she said, shaking my hand and flashing yet another comforting,
warm smile. I walked out of Welcoming Arms feeling welcomed, just as
their name said.

I was filled with anticipation driving to Welcoming Arms that
Thursday. There I was, a 60-year-old woman seeing a counselor, a body
double for Queen Latifah, barely in her late 20s. I was revealing my odd
lonely life in a McMansion, shaded with stories of jet setting and luxury,
with wealthy in-laws, along with the horrors of a financial mess, 22 years of
marital deception with prostitutes, and worst of all, child alienation.

Vanessa let me do all the talking. She listened, occasionally writing
notes on her clipboard. "How could I be so stupid?" I asked her. "How
could I not know he cheated the entire marriage? I feel so dumb, so stupid!" I asked while tears trickled down my cheeks.

Vanessa listened intently and waited for me to answer my own questions. Did she believe me? Even I was having problems believing what had
happened to me! I told her about the medical procedures I had endured
without any empathy from Captain X. I told her that he'd repeatedly said
"divorce is not an option." I told her of the emptiness I felt in the marriage
and how hard I'd tried to make the marriage work. I poured out my heart to
her. For the first time I felt comfortable revealing my true feelings of being
lost in what appeared like a perfect marriage.

I mentioned the constant fights Captain X and I had when I questioned him about money or his work schedule. I mentioned things I had
forgotten, situations I had buried way back in my mind that I never shared
with anyone. Fights over confusing remote controls for TVs and gadgets he

constantly purchased. In his explosive anger, Captain X would kick in a wall, punch a hole in the plasterboard. Once he slammed a cabinet door so hard he broke it off its hinge. His reaction was always the same: looking at me with a clenched jaw he would yell, "Look what you made me do! You made me so fucking angry!" The next day he would repair the damage, as if nothing had happened.

One session she asked, "Did he physically abuse you?" I avoided looking in her eyes. "Well, once, a couple of years back he did." She could see I didn't want to reveal the story, a story I never told anyone—the story of Captain X punching me, a story that would reveal that my perfect life was far from perfect. *My God, do I have Battered Women's Syndrome, too?* I asked myself.

Soon I found myself telling her anything and everything that popped into my head about my marriage. I mentioned how Captain X insisted on doing the marketing and food preparation. I confided this silly tidbit, "No matter how many times I told him I didn't like green beans, he'd still prepare them. So I ate the green beans. I hated them. God, he even dictated what I ate!" *Jesus*, I thought, *I'm crying because I don't like green beans? I'm so screwed up!*

Vanessa may have been a student, but she was already adept in her chosen profession. From her I learned how triangulation played a huge part in my marriage. Triangulation occurs in an unstable two-person emotional system, when a three-person system or triangle is formed. When we adopted Gina, I was so happy that Captain X, a man who said he didn't want to adopt, had built a strong bond with Gina, making her a daddy's girl. What I hadn't realized was that over time he had strengthened their bond to a point where it was destructive. Triangulation is often used in dysfunctional families as a substitute for direct communication. Captain X controlled Gina as a way of controlling me. Never had I anticipated that the bond he had with Gina would be used against me, to alienate her from me. When their bond was strong enough, I was eliminated from the marriage.

My appointments with Vanessa fell into a pattern where I unloaded all the grief, emptiness and anger over my marital deception, jamming as much as I could into each one-hour session. It was during our fifth or sixth session, while I paused to sob into tissues, that Vanessa looked straight into my face and said, "You know that abuse in a marriage does not have to be just physical. It can be emotional, too. Do you realize you were abused? Anyone who has been deceived as much as you have was abused. Do you understand that?" she asked. *What? Was she trying to pigeonhole my 22-year marriage under marital abuse?* The reality of her words chilled me, yet brought an instant clarity.

Yes, I was abused, I told myself. I had been lied to by Captain X so often I didn't know what was real. You forget about the arguments, inaccuracies in stories, fights that increased in frequency, and even physical abuse when everyone tells you "you are so lucky to be married to him." You also hide the abuse in the back of your mind when you are at 35,000 feet, seated on an airplane, traveling around the world. He had belittled me to the point that I had no self-confidence. I was overcome with rage, and so I raged in tears with Vanessa during most every session we shared.

I finally told her about the ring incident, the time he called me a fucking cunt and said not to ever question him again as he threw his wedding band at my face. "Honey, you have to face it, you were physically, emotionally, and psychologically abused," Vanessa said softly. That's why I forgot about the physical abuse, putting it way back in my mind. The psychological abuse from Captain X was so much more damaging.

So there I was, letting it sink in that I had been abused. I was tingling with disbelief that a smart woman like me could not see she was in an abusive marriage. *How did this happen to me?*

I was informed by my attorney that Captain X had taken Gina to Disneyland within a month of moving out of the Captain's House. He became the proverbial "Disneyland Dad," a term used for divorced fathers who treat their kids like they're on the ultimate vacation every time they're with them but do little actual parenting. His behavior was so predictable.

Just a few months later I received word from my attorney that Captain X wanted to take Gina to our favorite resort in the Dominican Republic, where they would share a room together. My attorney instructed me to relinquish Gina's passport so she could go on the trip. I didn't want to return her passport, hoping I could hold on to it and have some control over the way Captain X was buying her love. My attorney was adamant I had to relinquish the passport.

I told Vanessa about the passport request. After months of reviewing my case, Vanessa had good insight into Captain X's sexual proclivities. During this session Vanessa asked me, "Didn't you say you have proof that Captain X likes girls who are barely 18? You said Gina was adopted, right? She's now 17, right? I have to ask you this ... Do you think he ever did anything sexual to Gina?" she asked me in a careful tone. "No, not him," I immediately responded. "No, no, no way," I said softly. Then I paused. *Had anyone told me a year ago that my husband had even one affair, let alone had spent our entire marriage with prostitutes, I would have thought they were crazy.*

After reading his endless PussELuvR sexual postings mentioning young women, I had to weigh this line of Vanessa's questioning as best I could. Could I trust Captain X as a father, or was he even more evil than I could ever imagine, worse than the evidence I had collected revealed?

One of his ASPD postings had a link to an online video he wanted to share with his fellow hobbyists titled "This teen slut loves to lick and stick her tongue in an asshole." I cringed when I found it; the depth of his depravity was endless.

Vanessa noticed her question had put me at a loss for words. "I have to ask you again, are you *positive* that he has never made any sexual advances to Gina?" she asked. "I just don't know. I don't know anything about him anymore. I don't know who he really is," I said, realizing just how honest my words were. "If you're not sure, it's my job to call Child Protective Services and alert them that he may be a danger to Gina."

No, I thought, *he couldn't be. Surely he couldn't be. But what if he is? He's deceived me for such a long time, what if he is a far worse person than I thought?* "I'll try and call Gina and tell her I'll give her back her passport. When I get her on the phone I'll gently tell her to watch out for herself, that her dad may have a problem," I told Vanessa. She looked at me as she led me to the door, "You have to promise me that you'll do this. If you think there's even the slightest possibility he might be worse than you thought, you *must* alert your daughter to the possibility." "I promise, I'll warn her," I said softly, as I left the session.

When I got home I called my attorney's office and told them I would return Gina's passport but only if she called me, that I had to talk to her. I made that stipulation quite clear. They said they would call Captain X's attorney.

Gina phoned me later that evening. I did everything in my power to stay in control while I listened to my teenage daughter's voice. I wanted to talk about anything else in the world than what I had promised Vanessa I would be telling her.

"Mom, are you gonna give me back my passport? I need my passport," Gina demanded in a hard-edged voice. My heart was breaking. *What did he do to poison her against me, to treat me like I don't exist?* I asked myself. "Gina, honey, I've got your passport. I'll have my attorney send it to Dad. Gina, honey, I have to tell you something. After Dad filed for divorce, I found out he has a problem and it has to do with ladies ... Dad seems to like young ladies and I ... I just want you to look out for yourself and be smart and ... I want you to have a good trip. I miss you and I love you so much."

That's all I could say, all I could get out before my tears and anguish got the best of me. Gina responded in a bored teenage voice, "Yeah, whatever, OK, bye," and quickly hung up. I knew I would remember this phone conversation with my daughter for as long as I lived.

Had I made a mistake? Was my mind playing tricks on me? Was I making his secret life out to be more than it really is? Was I trying to use Gina as a pawn? I asked myself over and over. I immediately went to my piles of evidence to make sure I was not imagining it. There it was, on an ASPD site, PussELuvR's review of a provider named Tammy Lynn in which he said, "This one is barely 18."

I kept my promise to Vanessa. I gave Gina a heads-up, just in case Captain X had another secret life, or was yet to cross the line into another secret life. I knew my phone conversation with Gina would build an even bigger wall between us, but I had to say what I said out of my love and concern for her. Captain X tried to take away my role as her mother, but I couldn't, I just wouldn't let him succeed. I said to my daughter what any good mother would say in order to protect her child. I would rather lose Gina forever than take the chance that her vacation with Captain X would lead to more evil than I could even imagine.

One day while driving to my Welcoming Arms appointment, I glanced in my rear view mirror and was shocked to see Captain X's vanity license plates. *Oh my God, he's following me! What kind of mind games is he playing?* I nearly ran a stop light as I quickly pulled into a strip mall store, suddenly feeling terrorized. "Help me! My ex-husband is following me!" I screamed. I gave them a description of Captain X's car and license plates. A sales clerk comforted me while the manager went outside to look for any signs of Captain X's vehicle. He was gone. Fifteen minutes later I regained my composure and thanked them for their kindness. Captain X *was* following me, but I had no proof. I only shared this with Vanessa, because I was positive no one else would believe Captain X was now terrorizing me.

I gladly attended my weekly sessions with Vanessa for about four months. One day I confessed that I would be writing a book about what happened to me. "Honey, that's good, really good for you to write it all out and get it all down. You go do that, for sure," she said with a big smile. Then she took a deep breath and paused. "I've got news for you, too. I'm leaving Welcoming Arms. I have to go back and finish my studies full-time. I'm no longer going to be your counselor."

"Oh no," I said, trying not to show my disappointment. But it was time for us to part. "Thank you for being here for me. I'll never forget you and all you've done to help me." I said it with all the sincerity I could muster, hugging her tightly. Our warm goodbye embrace felt so good I didn't want it to end.

I never returned to Welcoming Arms. I felt I'd gotten all I could through my sessions with Vanessa. It was time for me to work on my own, to delve deeper into how and why I lived in a deceptive, abusive marriage. I had to find out just who Captain X really was. I would keep searching for answers, but this time on my own, without the help of a Queen Latifah look-alike.

Chapter 16: New Digs But Missing Gina

I JUST COULDN'T stand one more day in the Captain's House. I simply had to get out of there, away from the constant memories of my past life.

Jill understood my need to move, offering to help me look for an apartment. I welcomed her help since I hadn't searched for an apartment in decades. I needed a place that was inexpensive and close to shops and restaurants. I wanted to feel alive again, in new surroundings where I could plan my future. Most important, I had to get Gina back in my life.

I chose an apartment close to where Captain X and Gina had moved, in hopes of seeing her. My $800 a month one bedroom apartment on the 5th floor was walking distance to restaurants and shops. A huge shopping center with leading retail stores was just a few miles away. The complex had a small park providing shade on hot sunny days. I envisioned myself sitting there gathering my thoughts. It also had a swimming pool, gym, and party room. I wouldn't have to drive much, other than to my lawyer's office and an occasional doctor visit.

The complex was mostly filled with young singles, but there was a smattering of mature divorced singles like me, so I'd fit in. Jill helped me load my boxed belongings into our two cars. It took two exhausting days to bring what was left of my lifetime of belongings into my new apartment. I took the full bed from Gina's room and added to it a chest of drawers, the kitchen dining table and chairs, two leather recliners, and my bicycle. I had the large items professionally moved.

As we packed the last boxes into our cars, I reminded myself that everything that had happened in the Captain's House had been a lie. *He was in the brotherhood for 30 years*, I told myself as I drove away. The only memories I wanted to keep alive were memories of Gina.

I hoped my new environment might help me think more clearly. The faux "loft apartment" somewhat reminded me of New York. As much as I tried to trick my mind, though, I definitely was not young, and the trendy housing was not New York. The only link was enjoying an occasional copy of the Sunday *New York Times* I shamefully pilfered very early Sunday mornings from a pile in front of a bookstore that had yet to open.

The first week in the apartment I filled my time nesting, making a home for myself. My tiny balcony, more like a New York fire escape, faced west allowing me a glimpse of the sunset. I kept reminding myself that any place away from the Captain's House was a step in the right direction.

The move had been costly and I needed cash fast. The quickest way was to sell my jewelry. I made a list of three jewelers who bought gold and silver. I packed up my engagement ring, wedding band, and assorted rings Captain X bought me. Along with the jewelry I threw in six silver napkin rings we had purchased on our honeymoon. *Good thing we never paid to have them monogrammed*, I thought.

The third jeweler gave me the highest quote for my jewelry. As I handed over my wedding band and engagement ring, the owner handed me a coarse brown paper towel to wipe my eyes. I'm sure he thought I was crying over a love lost. I wasn't. Those days I only shed tears of frustration over the arduous divorce process and Gina. I received $1,200 in cash, which I needed to pay towards the move and living expenses.

I kept emailing and phoning Gina hoping she would answer. I carefully labored over each communication, being as upbeat as I could possibly muster. "Hey, Gina," I said, using the popular teen salutation. "It's Mom. I got a new place to live. I want you to see it. Give me a call. Love you!" Nothing. *Give her space*, I told myself. *She's as confused as I am.*

I tried to focus on myself. Lacking a social life, I joined a Meetup group for Over Fifties Singles. A Meetup group is a local community of people who share a common interest. I was fortunate that the Over Fifties

Singles Meetup met every two weeks at a restaurant within walking distance of my apartment.

I was hopeful about the Meetup group. I worked hard at figuring out how not to spill out my sordid story. *After all, I'm not the only one who with a bad divorce,* I reminded myself. On the other hand, it wasn't just a bad divorce. With the enormity of the infidelity, financial ruin and child alienation, my situation was horrific. Again I would use my acting skills to appear as if I had my life under control.

I carefully selected what I hoped was a perfect outfit to wear the evening of the first Meetup. This was my first social as a single. I lightly applied some makeup. I no longer wore mascara; I broke into tears way too often to wear it. It's bad enough to feel like crap, let alone look like crap with mascara "owl eyes" after crying.

The upscale restaurant where the Meetup cocktail hour was held was the very same restaurant where Captain X and I had shared drinks together less than a year ago. I remembered how he'd complained that it was expensive. I guess it was, if you had a costly secret habit. The restaurant looked totally different to me in my new life. Upon entering I was given an adhesive name tag and I mingled among the mature singles.

At this first Meetup I met Joan, a computer systems analyst. Joan revealed that she, too, had gone through a similarly ugly divorce. She was compassionate, with a wonderful upbeat outlook on life. I could only hope to come through my divorce as emotionally healthy as she had. We soon became good friends. My ongoing computer sleuthing for evidence against Captain X often led to pornographic websites infecting my computer with hidden viruses. With Joan's computer expertise, she removed these damaging viruses from my computer. I was extremely grateful for her help.

Through Joan and the Meetup, I met her boyfriend Mick and a retired banker named Larry. I immediately liked Larry, a born and bred Texan with a great sense of humor and the manners of an absolute gentleman. I found myself enjoying his company and sharing a few dinners, a respite from my problems.

I was making more acquaintances at the Meetups, looking forward to each of their socials, and seeing more clearly just how isolated I had been in my married life. One Meetup gathering took place at a Korean market, where we toured the huge store and then dined on Korean cuisine in one of the many restaurants within the store. I remember having fun. I hadn't had fun for such a long time that the feeling was totally foreign to me.

I tried to keep my personal problems at bay at the Meetups, but I couldn't always control my emotions. At one function a woman asked me if I had children. Tears welled in my eyes and I bolted for the restroom. After regaining my composure, I took a deep breath and rejoined the group.

"I'm sorry," I said to the woman I'd been talking to. "I'm going through a horrible divorce. My husband alienated me from my daughter," I said as straightforwardly as possible. "Oh honey, that happened to me, too," she answered. "You'll be OK. It just takes time. Right now you have to focus on yourself." That was easier said than done.

Soon after I moved into my new digs, I stopped driving my car, parking it in the apartment's underground lot. The luxury auto was a constant reminder of my past life and just how phony it really had been. The car made me look prosperous. In reality I was far from it. Credit card companies constantly phoned me. I wasn't avoiding them, but rather trying to get my name off the accounts that Captain X had fraudulently opened in my name.

While untangling the financial mess, I was constantly being put on hold, subjected to instrumental versions of "Memories," from the Broadway show *Cats*. Then Captain X cancelled my medical insurance, totally against the rules of the divorce. This entailed lengthy phone calls and being put on hold by Major Airways' insurance provider where *they* subjected me to an instrumental version of "My Heart Will Go On" from the movie *Titanic*. I came to despise both of those tunes.

I did add music to my life when I asked Joan to change my generic cell phone ring tone to the 1978 disco tune "I Will Survive," made famous by Gloria Gaynor. Each time my cell rang I heard the inspirational disco tune which became my daily affirmation. It helped.

While living in my new apartment I either walked or biked everywhere. I soon came to the conclusion that there was no place for the luxury auto in my future. On the Internet I located a map for the seldom-used city bus routes. I began to use public transportation to get back and forth to my lawyer's office. I was finding a way to live without a car, its expensive monthly payment, insurance premiums, and fuel and maintenance costs. My car was in Captain X's name and I no longer wanted it.

I phoned my paralegal, Hanna, and told her I was returning the car to Captain X. Being without a car is mindboggling to many, but not to me. After living in Chicago and New York without a car, I could do it again, navigating around by bike, bus or car rental.

"How are you going to get around?" Hanna asked incredulously. "I'm already doing it, Hanna," I responded. "I don't want the damn car. It's just too expensive. I want to simplify my life. Just tell Captain X I'm leaving the keys at my apartment building management's office in an envelope with his name on it." I told her where it was parked.

The day Captain X picked up the auto I parked it in full view of my balcony. I was able to peek down and see him walking in an agitated state, seething as he opened the driver's door. As he drove it away, I was proud of myself. I was cutting costs and giving Captain X the problem of selling the car. *Not my problem*, I told myself. *Not my problem at all.*

It was summer in Phoenix and by ten in the morning the sun beat down on the roads with temperatures reaching in the 85 degree range. In order to shop I'd leave the apartment around eight in the morning. Dressed in shorts, a T-shirt and a baseball hat with cash in my pocket, I'd cycle the few miles to Walmart to purchase as many necessities as my bike's wire basket could hold. Lightweight items like toilet paper and paper towels were slung in plastic bags looped over the bike's handlebars.

Once, when locking my bike up around a steel post in the Walmart parking lot, an affluent-looking woman got out of a current model Mercedes and approached me. "You're so smart to get your exercise and shopping done at the same time! I sure wish I could do that," she said. I worked hard not to cry. "Yes, I *am* smart. That's what divorce does to some of us," I said indignantly as I quickly peddled off to my apartment complex, leaving her standing there confused and my shopping undone.

My favorite place to go was a bookstore in a nearby shopping center. I searched for self-help books, or books on the topics of divorce, debt reduction, or retirement, or anything to take my mind off my life's daily dilemmas. One day I read Elizabeth Gilbert's literary hit *Eat, Pray Love* cover to cover while curled up in a comfortable plush reading chair. I desperately wished someone would pay *me* to travel to Italy, India and Bali. My present exotic locations were bookstores and Walmart.

I justified using the bookstore as a library because the library was too far to bike, and they had current bestsellers in stock. Their air conditioning helped me keep my apartment energy costs down. I was constantly trying to figure out how to save money because I knew I would be liable for half the debt Captain X had put us in. My share of the debt would be well over $100,000.

It was during one of my many bike excursions that I came to the realization that if Gina did not come back to me soon, after the divorce was final, I could move away from Phoenix. Maybe I'd move to a consistently warm climate, to help my arthritis. Everyone seemed to think Phoenix was always warm, but it could have cold winters. I remembered back to when I talked to the American ex-pat in Mexico on a trip with Captain X. I began scouring bookstores and the Internet for information on foreign retirement, since I'd soon be approaching retirement age. Costa Rica appealed to me. I now had a somewhat feasible long-term goal.

My lifelines during this period were Joan and Betsy, women who both had some personal insight into what I was going through. Betsy and I shared almost daily phone conversations, a two-person support group. "Your ex is a fucktard wanker," Betsy exclaimed. She made me laugh, sending me links to humorous YouTube videos about infidelity. Betsy said our exes made us "batshit crazy." Her humor was such a comfort and she was always there when I really needed her.

By now I had not had any contact from Gina for six months. The pain of losing her was unbearable. I could only bear to display one photograph of her in my new apartment. I was thankful my apartment complex had few children.

As the months went on, living my life without Gina continued to be painful and sad. Other than the social life I had with the Meetup singles group, occasional outings with Joan, Mick and Larry, and phone calls from Betsy, I had few people in my life, which was on hold until the divorce was finalized.

My neighbors included a hyper bachelor in his 50s across the hall, and a young newlywed couple next door who, after I revealed a bit of my painful situation, continually grabbed my hands and bowed their heads in prayer. "Lord Jesus, please help her in her time of need," they said every time I saw them. I gave up trying to avoid them. Perhaps they had some spiritual connections that could help me.

As fall approached, Gina never contacted me. I was heartbroken. I had filled her childhood with clever birthday surprises and yet she ignored my birthday. While my heart ached, I told myself Gina needed time to work it all out, according to my research on parental alienation. That was easier said than done, especially during birthdays and holidays.

With Thanksgiving approaching and no contact from Gina, Joan invited me to spend the holiday with her family and friends. I readily accepted since the only child at the table was her grandson, who didn't remind me one bit of Gina.

Soon it was the Christmas season. I pulled the small traveling Christmas tree out of a box I'd rescued from the garage of the Captain's House in hopes that Gina might decorate it with me. Gina still refused to answer my calls or emails. This was one of the darkest periods of my life. The only solace I could find that bleak Christmas Eve was in the company of a 24-year-old woman named Stacey who had just moved into my apartment building. Stacey's marriage had just ended because of her ex-husband's physical abuse. I was sympathetic to her pain. After recognizing that she, too, would be alone for Christmas, I invited her to my apartment for drinks and pizza.

"Do you like the TV show *Sex in the City*?" she asked. "Love it," I said. "Well, I've got the entire series as a Christmas gift so we can watch it," she said, happy to be able to provide our holiday entertainment.

It was a Christmas I never anticipated. Despite the generation gap between us, we shared the commonality of our painful marriages. Together we decorated my faux little tree with a cheap strand of miniature lights, glass balls and candy canes. We ordered pizza, washing it down with beers until we reached a level of inebriation we felt appropriate for our holiday party. Both of us were in states of despair; there was no need to rehash those feelings in conversation.

In the glow of my little Christmas tree, we watched endless episodes of *Sex in the City*, watching Carrie Bradshaw, Amanda Hobbes, Charlotte York and Samantha Jones as singles in Manhattan. Not one episode broached the abuse, deception, financial ruin or loneliness that we newly single women faced that Christmas.

There was simply no reason to celebrate. The past year had been the worst year of my life. I could only face 2010 with the thought that things could not get any worse. Was it really 10 years ago that Captain X and I had the millennium party with no friends to invite? *Look where I am now*, I said to myself. *I still have few people in my life.* I was fast asleep before holiday revelers counted down the hours and minutes to the New Year.

I needed exercise for my physical health and mental health. As the months passed and the weather became colder, I'd walk on the treadmill at the apartment's gym. One day I found myself next to a tall thin woman in her 40s, her head wrapped tightly in a turban. It was obvious she was going through chemotherapy. We introduced ourselves on our neighboring treadmills. Laura was divorced and had custody of her 12-year-old son. She filled me in on her breast cancer. She was upbeat and optimistic when she told me she was approaching her last chemo treatment.

Laura had a new boyfriend. She was going shopping for a dress for an out-of-town wedding she was attending with him. Her son would stay with friends. As I kept up the pace on the treadmill, my mind was going faster than my feet. *Oh my God*, I realized, *I envied her, a woman with the big C, cancer*, I told myself. She had her son, friends, a lover, and people in her life that really cared for her, not just acquaintances. My life was empty compared to this woman battling cancer. Bitterness engulfed me as I realized just how mentally ill I had become. *Snap out of it. You can do it. You'll make it*, I told myself.

In the early months of 2010, I continued to try to take care of myself mentally and physically. I walked and biked constantly when I was not doing computer research about my problems. Vanessa, my Welcoming Arms counselor, had told me that I needed to cry. "Crying is important, but try to limit it to a few times a day," she said. I tried. Every pair of reading glasses I picked up needed cleaning; they were always water spotted from tears.

As spring approached, my feelings about losing Gina had put me in such a state of despair I was beginning to fear for my own life. *What good is my life without Gina?* I asked myself. Everything I believed in was gone. My child was taken from me by a monster. I was so confused that even if I had found help, I doubt I could articulate what I was going through.

I fumbled with my cell phone and dialed the local Crisis Hotline, realizing I was close to a breaking point. Mary, the woman on the other end, asked me if I was in danger of taking my own life. I was crying too hard to answer. She skillfully guided me back to reality and I said, "I'm OK now, really I'm OK." I knew she had my cell phone number through the automated tracking system in her phone bank. Mary helped me by showing compassion during the call. I still remained in a very dark place for weeks afterward. Suicidal thoughts were slowly closing in on me.

Early one morning I sat on a secluded park bench at the park on the apartment property wondering what would happen if I ran in front of a car. "Stop it, stop it," a voice came into my head. "You'd ruin both Gina's and the driver's life. You can get through this." I repeated this to myself, mopping my runny nose and wet eyes with tissues.

I didn't berate myself for the suicidal thoughts. I was longing to end my pain. But suicide was not the answer, I told myself as I walked into the elevator that took me up to my small apartment.

Once there I tried for what seemed like the millionth time to pull myself together, turning on my computer to check my email. As I waited for it to boot up, I was startled by the ring of my cell phone. "Hey Mom, I'm coming over." It was Gina calling, the voice I had hungered to hear for the past seven months, through my birthday, Thanksgiving, Christmas, New Year, and every second in between. "Hi baby, what's up?" I asked. "I'm coming over," she said. "Great!" I responded, trying to hide my shock. I couldn't get in another word. She hung up.

An hour later I buzzed Gina up. There she was, disheveled in a sloppy sweat suit, wearing flip flops despite the chilly weather. Her hair was stringy and dirty and her face was tear-streaked. I hugged her hard. "Hi baby, what happened?" I asked as carefully as I could. My whole body tingled with love.

"Dad took away my car. I walked here. He found out I was smoking. I had some kids over who were drinking. Dad hates my boyfriend Chad and he won't let me see him. He got real mad," she rambled through her tears.

"Oh Gina, honey, it'll be OK. I miss you and love you," I replied. Drawing on everything I had learned about parental alienation and my gut mothering instinct, I carefully chose my words. "I'm sorry baby. I guess it was one hell of a party and you were bound to get caught. It happens. I'm sorry you're upset but I'm really happy to see you. Look, why don't you take a hot shower and then let's go to lunch and talk about it."

After she showered, I handed her one of my sweat suits to change into. I longed to hug her tightly again, but I didn't dare show any deep emotion. Dressed and clean she now looked like the teenager I remembered.

We walked towards a neighborhood restaurant, making small talk along the way. After unloading our trays of salads and seating ourselves at a table, I looked straight into my daughter's eyes and said softly, "You're having sex with Chad, aren't you?" Her face registered disbelief. "How did you know?" she asked, her wide eyes showing her surprise. "I'm your mother, Gina. Moms know everything," I said quietly, with a slight smile on my face.

"It's OK honey, it's OK. It's normal. I was your age once too, you know. I just want you to be safe and use protection." Gina picked at her salad, pondering the fact that I had figured out she'd lost her virginity. Captain X left our 17-year-old daughter alone in his apartment for three days at a time, four weeks each month while he flew trips and visited prostitutes. This was crazy! What the hell did he think would happen? How stupid is he? I worked hard to keep my anger at Captain X buried while talking to Gina.

Easter was approaching. "Hey Gina, do you want to come over and dye Easter eggs on Friday?" I asked. Dyeing Easter eggs was a family custom. "I guess so," she said. The lack of enthusiasm in her voice about seeing me again was not what I had hoped for, but at least I had a glimmer of hope that I would see her again. "Good, I'll see you on Friday then," I said as I hugged and kissed her goodbye as she left my apartment.

I went out on my balcony and watched her enter Chad's car. She had called him to take her back to the condo she shared with Captain X. I had spent barely two hours with my daughter in seven months.

That Friday, Good Friday, was the day we traditionally colored Easter eggs. I had everything ready. I bought two Easter baskets with green paper grass, Easter candy, traditional PAAS Easter egg dye tablets, eggs, sausage, and horseradish. The doorbell rang and I nervously buzzed Gina up.

This time she was neatly dressed, taking a seat on the leather recliner, glancing around my small apartment taking in all the furnishings I'd salvaged from the Captain's House. I avoided any conversation about Captain X. We talked about my new friends in the Meetup group. I also told her I no longer had a car, which clearly shocked her, so I quickly changed the topic to Easter and our holiday task at hand. We boiled the eggs, prepared the dyes, and decorated the eggs. We ate diagonally sliced sausage and the rejected decorated eggs with horseradish from toothpicks. I could see from her expression the smells and tastes reminded her of the past, when our lives were not in turmoil. I fought hard to hold back tears as Gina used a clear crayon to write "Mom" on an egg, dipping it into a vinegar-infused cup of brightly colored dye. After drying it, she handed it to me. My stomach was in knots as I said "Thank you, baby," placing it in my basket. I wondered if she would ever know how much that day meant to me.

I hoped that those two meetings would mean I had my daughter back in my life. It was not to be. Gina once again stopped taking my calls, never answering any emails.

The following month I received a florist delivery, a beautiful bouquet of irises for Mother's Day from Gina. I was thrilled and called her. She didn't answer so I left a voice message, thanking her. Soon afterwards she went back to having no contact with me. From all I had read on child alienation, I knew that Gina was in a horrible state of confusion, just as I was. I had to be patient and plan my future.

People constantly said, "You're strong. You'll get through this." I hated hearing those words, but somehow I found myself repeating them to comfort myself, along with the words Gloria Gaynor sang. I will survive.

Chapter 17: I Married a Psychopath

AS THE DIVORCE dragged on, my confusion over just who Captain X *really was* continued to loom in my mind. I was in a constant state of frustration. My reality had been fractured.

I formulated a phrase to use when dealing with people. When I was on the phone with creditors, I was always emotional, constantly being put on hold with music. When a human voice finally answered, I'd say through my tears, "I'm sorry, bear with me. I'm stressed. I'm going through a horrific divorce from a man who's both Barry Madoff and Tiger Woods." That would ensure a sympathetic reply, "Gee, I'm sorry, that bad, huh?" The phrase also placated those I met in person.

I had recently discovered a new bookstore within bicycling distance where I could buy used books. Now I was looking for self-help books and memoirs about overcoming adversity (I certainly needed those!), as well as books offering me a brief escape from my situation.

I still maintained my interest in Ann Rule's books and other true crime books. My mind wandered. True crime books were about criminals. Captain X was not a criminal, I assured myself. There was nothing criminal about mismanaging finances and leading a secret life, I told myself, ignoring the fact that Captain X had engaged in prostitution, which *is* illegal in the state of Arizona. He also illegally used my credit cards.

While browsing the true crime section I came upon *A Dance with the Devil: A True Story of Marriage to a Psychopath*. There was that word again, psychopath. Barbara Bentley's exposé tells the story of how an intelligent woman was enchanted by an impostor retired rear admiral who drained her financially and emotionally and then attempted to kill her.

This looks interesting, I told myself as I carried it to the checkout, plopped it in my bicycle basket, and peddled back to my apartment. I was happy I had a free morning to read.

Immediately upon reading Bentley's book, clusters of goose bumps ran up my arms while cold chills went up and down my spine. In the second paragraph of her introduction, Bentley writes, "My Prince Charming swept me off my feet, but the euphoria was short-lived. Once the honeymoon was over, he quickly learned how to manipulate my insecurities with his skillful lies."

I quickly grabbed a yellow highlighting pen and ran its fluorescent ink over the paragraph. The words jumped off the page. I read the book cover to cover in one sitting, highlighting sentences, stopping only to grab tissues to dry my tears. When I finished reading, most pages were covered with fluorescent yellow ink. Was Captain X a psychopath like Bentley's husband?

When I first met Hanna, my paralegal at the Weinberg law firm, she'd referred to Captain X as a psychopath. I paid little attention to her statement. At the time I was too deep in shock over the divorce, the massive financial debt, and my shocking discovery of Captain X's secret life. What Hanna said went in one ear and out the other. I had also heard the word psychopath from my psychologist, Dr. Evans. Again, I paid little attention. I was in a state of shock.

Like most people, I thought the term psychopath was synonymous with serial killers, or slang for someone who is crazy. I had no idea a person could have no conscience. I always believed there is good in everyone.

Bentley's book mentioned that her husband tried to kill her, but she made it clear that not all psychopaths are killers. I finally had a name for Captain X, and a name for myself. *Captain X is a psychopath and I am his victim*, I told myself, slowly trying to wrap my mind around my armchair diagnosis.

In *A Dance with the Devil*, Bentley mentioned Dr. Robert Hare's book *Without Conscience: The Disturbing World of the Psychopaths Among Us*. Dr. Hare is the world's leading authority on psychopathy. I immediately purchased *Without Conscience*. Dr. Hare developed the world-renowned Hare Psychopathy Checklist-Revised (PCL-R), a diagnostic tool measuring 20 traits to determine the degree of a person's psychopathic or antisocial tendencies. A person needs high enough scores on enough of the traits to meet the threshold of psychopathy.

As my neon yellow highlighter glided over paragraphs on nearly every page of Dr. Hare's book, a remarkable wave of clarity washed over me. Memories of Captain X's psychopathic personality filled my head as I turned the pages. I didn't have an *a-ha* moment, but rather a complete *a-ha* read. I had the validation I needed. I had no doubt whatsoever that Captain X was a psychopath. I didn't need a clinical psychologist to diagnose him. My 22-year marriage characterized by mixed messages, a stunning lack of empathy, and massive deceptive was just too compelling.

Dr. Hare is adamant that his test should be administered by a qualified clinician under controlled and licensed conditions. Nonetheless, on the Internet I found numerous websites—not affiliated with Dr. Hare—that presented a "psychopath checklist." I wanted to see how Captain X ranked. To score the test, each trait is given a score of 0, 1, or 2, depending on how well it applies to the subject. A typical psychopath receives a maximum score of 40, while someone without any psychopathic traits would score a zero. A score of 30 or more qualifies a person to be diagnosed as a psychopath (although definitive diagnosis should be made by a trained clinician). The 20 psychopathic traits I found on the Internet were similar to these, which I paraphrased:

- Lies constantly
- Lives off other's money or success
- Is overtly charming and smooth
- Is extremely grandiose and thinks highly of themselves
- Is constantly in need of stimulation
- Is extremely sly and manipulative
- Shows no remorse
- Responds with fake or no emotion
- Lacks empathy or mirrors it
- Seldom controls his or her behavior
- Is sexually promiscuous

- Lacks positive goals
- Is impulsive
- Is irresponsible
- Does not accept responsibility for personal problems
- Has many brief personal relationships
- Exhibits early childhood behavior problems
- Was a juvenile delinquent
- Has criminal involvement
- Repeats criminal behavior after release

Without any knowledge of Captain X's childhood, he scored 30 on the informal list of psychopathic traits I found around the Internet.

I found comfort in finding a name for Captain X's behavior. Tears of happiness flowed while I danced around my small apartment repeating out loud for no one but myself to hear: "He's a psychopath, the bastard's a psychopath! Now I know, now I know! He's a psychopath!"

I had to share the news. "Betsy, I just figured it out! Captain X is a psychopath! I mean it, really, he's a psychopath! I just applied a psychopath test I found on the Internet to him and he's definitely a psychopath! It all makes sense to me now. I finally found the answer!" I gushed excitedly into the phone. "Now I understand everything! Oh my God, I'm not crazy. He tried to make me think I'm crazy!"

"I knew he was a fucktard wanker," Betsy said, making me laugh.

My jubilant mood was brief. I had finally come up with the last puzzle piece. Now I could fully understand my confusing marriage. Accepting that I had spent decades married to a psychopath was chilling. Suddenly a wave of paranoia washed over me. I was beginning to get frightened about my future, about the unknown. *After all he's done to me, what is he capable of doing next?* I asked myself. He had controlled me in the past. Now I had to make sure he would never control me again. But he was still controlling me through my biggest weakness and vulnerability, Gina. That's why he alienated her from me. *Would she ever understand who he really is?* I wondered.

From what I had just learned, psychopaths are scary social predators who emotionally and financially destroy the lives of those who cross their paths. If psychologists are right, everyone will encounter or be impacted by a psychopath during their lifetimes. Why isn't there more information available to educate the public about these evil people? *Why? Why?* I asked myself.

I had to get an accurate understanding of how psychopaths function. I began to study everything I could find about psychopaths. I read clinical psychology books, scholarly papers, victim's memoirs, websites, blogs and web boards, and watched documentaries. I even rented films about psychopaths, fully realizing the motion picture industry exaggerates and distorts their fictionalized depiction of psychopath villains.

I thought I was responsible for my own life and had control over my own destiny. I soon learned that when you're involved with a psychopath, the playing field is far from level. Everything I thought I knew about human behavior had changed.

As my knowledge of psychopathy increased, a non-stop stream of memories and even flashbacks popped into my head. They'd started the day Captain X handed me the divorce papers. Now the streams of memories continued with a vengeance. They were both comforting and disconcerting. I would remember something Captain X had done or said that seemed odd or unusual and compare it to all the indicators of psychopathy. *Oh, THAT'S why he did that! That's why that happened!*

One memory frightened me, the one where Captain X pushed me to take Percocet, the drug I had been prescribed after my back surgery. Why was he always pushing me to take the drug? Was it because he wanted me docile, in a perpetual drug-induced state, or was it something more sinister?

These memories and dreams I was suffering were a symptom of PTSD, post-traumatic stress disorder, a psychological disorder I developed as a result of 22 years of crazy-making and trauma that Captain X had put me through. Many think PTSD only affects those in the military, but it can happen to anyone who has been traumatized. I was traumatized after being trapped, like a captive; in a marriage my husband and others had convinced me was normal. Now that I was positive he's a psychopath, my memories were on overdrive. I actually felt the sensation of reliving all the uncomfortable and questionable experiences during my marriage over and over again.

Sometimes the memories came during the day but they invaded my sleep too, in the form of nightmares.

I had many sleepless nights. When I did sleep, I would wake up with my heart racing after a strange dream or nightmare, in sweat-tangled sheets. In one recurring dream I calmly confronted Captain X, whispering in his ear, "It's OK, I know you're a psychopath. I know what it means. I know how empty your life must be. I'm not going to do what you want. I don't need to follow you." Allegra was there, nodding in agreement. Captain X kept trying to make up reasons for his behavior, which of course, made no sense. I was void of emotion in the dream, but always woke up with an overwhelming feeling that the dream meant I was beginning to accept that I had married a profoundly flawed human being.

Once I dreamt of Allegra, except her head was tiny, like a little balloon, and her hair was flat, not the poufy blonde bouffant she always wore. She was looking at my computer, reading my email out loud. I kept trying to tell her that her son was a psychopath, that he abused me for years. But when I tried to speak, the words couldn't come out. Big marbles covered with cloth filled my mouth, preventing me from talking. The dream left me frustrated, feeling as if I were forced into silence, that no one would believe or care that I was married to a psychopath.

Sometimes the nightmares were terrifying. I dreamt Captain X was using a potato peeler on my arm, peeling away at my flesh. I woke up screaming. This nightmare reinforced my newfound knowledge that I had to be careful. I didn't know what Captain X was capable of doing next.

The new clarity of knowing Captain X was a psychopath made me recall an old acquaintance from New York, Martha Siebert, who was a clinical psychologist. I thought I'd give her a call and run my diagnosis of Captain X's psychopathy by her.

Martha had known me for years and had even met Captain X. She had heard about my divorce, but not the ugly details. Over a lengthy phone conversation I told her the facts as clearly as I could and explained why I concluded my husband was a psychopath. Martha agreed. "Psychopaths are dangerous. Even when they go on to new victims, they often will not leave their past victims alone," she said, ending our conversation with a warning. "Get as far away from him as you can," she said. "Well, I was thinking about retiring in Costa Rica when the divorce is over," I said. "Go! Get far away from him!" she said with a tone of urgency in her voice. As I hung up the phone, I was positive Costa Rica would be in my future. But I couldn't move yet; I still was in the process of divorcing Captain X, the psychopath pilot.

Chapter 18: The Daunting Divorce

NOTHING COULD HAVE prepared me for my long, difficult and high-conflict divorce. Captain X filed for the divorce in April of 2009. It continued on through the following year. In the beginning I printed out every legal paper my lawyers emailed me. Eventually I was so worn down I barely glanced at them. With all the stress I was under I just couldn't keep track of anything. I was living on autopilot.

I had lost my faith in the legal system since Captain X took Gina and the Weinberg law firm did nothing to help me get her back into my life. My supposedly capable lawyers cared little about the parental alienation. I could only hope they would find a way to leave me with little marital debt, and as much financial security as possible.

My attorney advised me that if my case went to court and we brought up the prostitutes, the best I could get would be a 60/40 property division of the assets, which included his retirement funds, and a 40/60 split of the debts. I was more than willing to go to court to get this favorable division.

I would soon be on my own, a woman approaching 61 years of age, with health concerns and possessing no marketable job skills in a bad economy. My future would be greatly affected by the outcome of the divorce. Surely a judge would be sympathetic to my proof of Captain X's marital misconduct, fraud, and economic fault.

I now understood the reason Captain X filed for divorce. I was no longer of value to him since I had uncovered his financial deception. Filing for divorce was his way of discarding me, the act of a psychopath. He had no idea his filing would spur me on to uncover his secret life.

One day my friend Melody in Detroit phoned me. "Did you check your email yet?" she asked. "No, I'm on my way home. Why?" I asked curiously. "Captain X just emailed me. I forwarded it to you." I thanked her for calling and quickly took a bus home, curious why he would contact my friends, people he had met only a few times.

I booted up my computer and went into the email she forwarded to me. He told Melody that there are two sides to every story, no truth to anything I say, just hurtful lies about both him and Gina. He said I was a sick and demented woman, angry all the time and unable to see reality. He mentioned he'd spent 22 years trying to make me happy and healthy, and that he never told Gina anything bad about me. He ended by saying he was sincere and that I was a wonderful woman but he didn't know if I would ever be right again.

I couldn't believe his email! He said he'd "spent almost 22 years of [his] life trying to make [me] happy, healthy and content." Did he forget he spent our entire marriage in "the brotherhood"?

A week later I was contacted again, this time by Susan, who forwarded a similar email Captain X had written her. This one was longwinded. He asked her and Joel to pick sides in the divorce, saying he respected their friendship but that I was filling their heads with lies. He called me disturbed. He said he was worried about me but more worried about himself and Gina. He mentioned he never hid our finances from me. He said I yelled at Gina and called her a loser and a fool. I broke down and cried hard when I read that part. He said that all he ever told Gina is that I love her but I need to get help to work through my problems. Then he asked Susan if she believed any of my lies and twisted truths. He said I was a mean, angry, nasty and sick woman. He wondered if I was trying to goad him into taking a swing at me so I could call the cops and ruin him some more. He even complained about burning his sick time during my surgeries! He ended by saying that Gina asks him when they are leaving so they can have a normal life on their own. More tears flowed.

I loved the line about me trying goad him into taking a swing at me so I could call the cops and ruin him more. His psychopathic ramblings and need for control were clearly displayed in the emails. Apparently Captain X was concerned my friends might be my character witnesses. Surely he must have known I shared my knowledge of his secret life with them.

Shortly after Susan forwarded Captain X's email I asked her to be a character witness in the event we went to court. "I don't want to get involved," she answered flatly. I'd known her ten years. I was shocked! Did she fear repercussions from Captain X if she testified on my behalf? Susan had looked ill the day I showed her my binder filled with prostitution evidence. Soon she distanced herself from me and the friendship ended.

In the middle of the divorce proceedings I was called into a conference with Marvin Weinberg and lawyer Bessie Rolland. Paralegal Hanna entered the conference room, her arms filled with piles of heavy, thick plastic binders filled with evidence of Captain X engaging in prostitution. "Here it is. I think I got it all," she said as she placed the heavy binders with a loud thunk in front of us on the massive conference room table. As the meeting went on, Hanna said, "Marvin, what about this, when are we going to get to this?" indicating the law firm's copies of Captain X's secret life.

"We're not going there," Marvin Weinberg answered. "We don't need to add the sex stuff. We have enough of a case already."

I shot a look of disbelief at Hanna and she shot one right back. Hanna turned to Marvin and said, "Marvin, have you even looked at this? Do you know what's in here?"

"I don't think it will help much," he replied. Instantly I thought Marvin Weinberg might be a member of ASPD. Is that why he didn't want to use my evidence?

"Really Marvin, you don't think that hundreds of pages of proof that Captain X solicited and engaged in prostitution and caused financial ruin won't help my case?" I asked. "I'm sorry, but you're dead wrong. I scoured the Internet for this evidence. I am ready, willing and able to go to court and show it to the judge," I said in a clear voice, not knowing where I got the strength to say this.

Later that day I was about to shop for a new attorney when the phone rang. It was Hanna. "Marvin said to keep bringing in evidence."

"Thanks, I'll do that," I replied. I had crazy-making in my marriage. *Why wouldn't my divorce entail even more crazy-making*, I asked myself?

A few weeks later, I heard from Hanna that Captain X had fired his high-powered attorney and hired another, one of the city's most expensive attorneys. Psychopaths enjoy chaos. I could just envision Captain X saying, "That bitch wants all my money. Well she's not going to get it," pointing his finger in the air.

By then I was confident that my searches for evidence of Captain X's secret sex life would pay off. If I hadn't found out about his secret life, I would have been looking at a 50/50 settlement.

In the event we went to court, the Weinberg law firm was going to subpoena Tiffany Sparks, one of Captain X's local prostitutes. Later I uncovered their court preparation paper titled "Notes for Examination of Plaintiff Captain X:"

On 8/16/02 Captain X, did you not write a review of Mina at Apple Bath, $40 for 30 minutes? Did you not participate in a table shower, BBBJ, CFS (bare back blow job, covered full service)? *Would you please tell the court what a table shower, BBBJ and CFS are?*

On 2/24/04 Captain X, did you not write, "Saw Mina myself yesterday and had almost the identical experience. Found her to be very sweet and fun and very attentive. She is Korean, and speaks very little English but is well in other foreign languages. She kissed and smiled the entire time I was with her and wanted me to stay longer but had to run. Another jewel in the queens treasure chest and a must see."

On 11/15/06 Captain X, did you not write, "thanks for the excellent feedback. Your post is exactly what I have been posting in the Locker Room about honest and informative sharing among the brotherhood of the members of ASPD."

On 2/14/07 Captain X, did you not write, "Just saw Jodi yesterday and she is worth it at all rates discussed? This young lady is much fun in bed as out and is bright, articulate and simply a love to be with. Do not miss ..."

On 5/6/08 Captain X, did you not write, "Tami is an addiction of mine. I have had to force myself to stay away for a while because I begin to forget this is a business. Spending time with her is the total package, from her beauty to her sexiness, to her maturity, to her compassion. Tami has it all and I miss her. Wonderful woman and probably my ATF (all time favorite) Go see her!"

On 5/1/07, did you not write another review of a threesome with Candy and Vicki: "I have seen Candy alone (about a month ago), Candy with Vicki and have yet to see Nicole ..."

One day while I was at the Weinberg office sorting through the evidence of Captain X's "hobby," Marvin Weinberg walked in. He finally had taken a look at it. "Well, at least your husband thinks you're good in bed," he said flippantly, referring to a post Captain X made on ASPD.net dated 4/31/03:

"I love my SO (significant other) no matter how screwed up she may be. I just like recreational sex. I never feel guilty. I feel great. I often wonder who and when will be next. Sex with my SO is terrific."

I was shocked! My attorney was making a joke about my sex life! I tried to muster up an appropriate comment but nothing came to mind. I felt as if I had been kicked in the face and I couldn't protest.

Weinberg held the keys to divorcing me from Captain X. If I said anything in anger I might not get the firm's full attention handling my divorce. I bit my tongue to avoid any show of emotion and fled the law office. I probably could have sued him for his sexist, unprofessional statement.

I made it very clear I didn't want the Captain's House. Let Captain X rot in that mausoleum as far as I was concerned. This wasn't a problem; Captain X desperately wanted to get back into the Captain's House. As a psychopath I'm sure he thought it would show the world I ran out on him and that he was the mentally stable one.

As the court date neared I received an email from Captain X. Reading it, I knew he was squirming:

From: Captain X
To: MrsXNomore
Date: Sep 26, 2009

Settle this divorce case and you can go live anywhere you choose. Stop costing me/us money that we don't have. You forced me to move out, doubling our living expenses and I cannot pay for the bills you are running up by delaying to settle this case.

You drove me to file this case and now you seem to not want to finish it. Wake up and get this over or the money you are causing us to spend on lawyers and expenses will leave us very little when this is over.

You think you are screwing me by dragging this out? Look around at how happy you are. Get this over now and move on or I will ride this to trial with you and fight it out to the end. The choice is clearly yours. I am trying to be fair and settle this case. My life will go on after this period. When yours starts over is up to you.

Captain X

I forced him to move out? He walked out of the house with Gina the day I confronted him about his "hobby." *I drove him to file this case?* I was a loving, trusting woman who did nothing wrong except marry a psychopath. I was certainly paying dearly for that.

My attorney determined that when I accessed the home networked computer system, I was not in violation of any federal laws. My actions could not be considered trespassing because I was married to Captain X at the time, which constituted a contractual relationship. On the other hand, Captain X did break the law by engaging in prostitution.

My attorneys prepared a two-page document titled "Prostitutes Identified by Captain X as Sex Partners." It included the names of 50 prostitutes identified by Captain X in his Internet postings, including the dates and the amount of money he spent on them. The document was prepared in the event we went to court. It was just part of what I'd found on the Internet; I am positive there were hundreds or maybe even thousands more, since he was in the "hobby" our entire marriage.

In mid-December 2009 I got a call from Hanna saying, "Marvin wants you in the office *now!*" Captain X and his attorney had proposed a settlement agreement.

I walked into the conference room where Hanna and attorney Bessie Rolland were sitting. Three copies of the proposed divorce settlement papers were placed on the conference table, along with a speakerphone set in the middle. "Marvin wants you to look these over and then he wants to talk to you."

"So, they came up with a settlement?" I asked, carefully forming my words. Hanna and Bessie nodded.

I sat down and looked through the papers. "What would you do if this were your divorce?" I asked. I didn't want them to know I had no strength to stay in divorce hell any longer.

"Well, this is just about a 60/40 split of the assets in your favor and a 40/60 split of the debt, again in your favor. You don't see this often; I'd take it. If you go to court, you'd probably get the same thing, but spend more money to get it. This is about the best settlement you could expect."

I agreed to the settlement, but only if they added I was to get four Major Airways passes a year until Captain X retired. Marvin soon called in on the speakerphone and said he got the airline pass requirement added to the settlement. I was on my way to getting divorced from Captain X.

Days later I realized Captain X had the court records sealed. In the final decree both Captain X and I were permanently enjoined from:

1) Disparaging the other party to anyone including the parties' child and anyone employed by or associated in a formal capacity with Major Airways.

2) Discussing the facts of this divorce suit with anyone including the parties' child or anyone employed by or associated in a formal capacity with Major Airways Company.

I was in such a confused state of mind I didn't realize I had been court ordered not to discuss the case with anyone. When I approached Marvin about this, he said it was a common phrase in divorce settlements.

"Sign here, and here, and here," Hanna instructed, pointing to the 33-page document. My hands trembled as I signed the papers.

When I got home I needed fresh air. The temperature was falling that crisp December day. Christmas was approaching and the shops around the apartment complex were all decorated for the holiday. I decided to take a walk around the area to take it all in while sorting out my thoughts of the surreal day.

My walk was interrupted by a call on my cell phone. It was my sister Margo calling to wish me a Merry Christmas. I was thrilled since she'd remained distant throughout the divorce. I longed for any family contact. I talked to her once when the divorce began, but at the time I was in no shape to go into details, especially since I was terribly confused by everything. I did tell her about the prostitutes, crying hard during our conversation. How do you explain that what looked like a perfect marriage had become a nightmare, and you don't know why?

"Wow, Margo, what a coincidence! I just signed my divorce settlement today. Your timing is incredible," I said. "So, how did it go?" she asked. "How much did you get? What are your plans?" I was shocked that she showed interest and concern about what I had been through. "Well, I believe I got a decent split. I'm trying to feel optimistic." Margo chatted about financial planners and her divorce 25 years earlier. I didn't care, I was happy to hear from her.

During the phone conversation I realized I was sharing way too much information with her. I felt I was being pumped for information instead of getting a call of concern. I switched the topic to her holiday plans because I was starting to feel uncomfortable. "Well, I've got to go. Keep in touch, I'm glad you called," I said and ended the call.

I returned to my apartment and phoned my real estate friend Tori to fill her in on the divorce settlement.

"Tori, it looks like it's over. I got a decent settlement, and guess what? I even heard from my sister Margo," I said excitedly. "Don't you know why? Your sister has been talking to Captain X all through your divorce," Tori stated. *What? Margo was talking* to *Captain X?* Shock waves went through me. My sister had been conversing with the enemy! "Why didn't you tell me this, Tori?" I asked. "Well, while I was trying to sell your house I talked to your husband. I didn't think I should get between you two while I was working." I was furious and hung up.

As soon as I got off the phone with Tori I called Margo. "Margo, have you been in touch with Captain X during our divorce?" I asked. "Yeah, why?" she said. "Why?" I asked. When I first told her of the divorce I'd told her never to speak with him. "How many times?" I asked. "I don't have to tell you that," she answered curtly. I said in shock, "No, you *don't* have to answer me. You don't have to answer anything again. Goodbye." I ended the call and broke into sobs. Psychopath Captain X had charmed both Margo and Tori.

In January of 2010 I was summoned to appear at the County Courthouse to finalize the divorce. *This is it, this is the end,* I thought. Joan's boyfriend, Mick drove me. I welcomed his emotional support, something I'd had so little of during my prolonged nightmare.

I was led into a small windowless office in the courthouse by Marvin Weinberg. Captain X and his attorney were already there. Marvin cracked inappropriate jokes, asking, "Are you two sure you want to do this?" Captain X stared at me like a reptile, unflinching, unwavering and cold. *I'm fine,* I told myself, *just fine.* I had subdued myself with the help of an Ativan. I knew I couldn't face this last leg of my divorce, facing Captain X, without the aid of an anxiolytic to calm me.

Gazing around the court setting, at the attorneys and judge, I felt as if I were in a movie. I wanted to scream, "Get me out of here!" I wanted it to be over. The Ativan was working; I didn't scream.

Captain X's face was flushed red in anger. His green soulless eyes peered into me with a look of contempt as if *I* were the one who ruined the marriage. I reminded myself that my ex-husband, the man signing our final decree of divorce was a psychopath, a man without a conscience.

It was over. I was now divorced from the man who did nothing but lie every day of our 22-year marriage. Now I could continue my life's journey without Captain X at the controls.

Chapter 19: Milestones With Gina

I WAS OFFICIALLY divorced but in limbo, waiting for Major Airways to disburse my part of the retirement funds. That would happen six months after the final decree was signed. My only money was a $20,000 loan from Captain X to live on, and it had to be paid back when my settlement arrived. I was constantly hounded by creditors, now owing well over $100,000. I could do nothing but wait and try to get Gina back in my life.

I thought constantly about Gina. The alienation was destroying me. People said "She'll come back," as if those were words of comfort. They didn't know I was dealing with a psychopathic alienator.

I constantly searched for any information about divorcing a psychopath and how it affects a child, but found little. Books on parental alienation did not mention psychopathy. Books on psychopaths seldom mentioned child alienation. Most memoirs by victims of psychopaths mentioned they either had no children or their relationship ended early on. None mentioned child alienation.

One thing I was sure of—psychopaths do not make good parents. They view their children as possessions. Psychopaths parent in one of two ways: they either target their children, blaming them for everything that goes wrong, or they manipulate them for their personal needs, making them a "golden child." I believe Captain X recognized early on he needed to have Gina on his side as a cover, in order to appear normal. Gina was a daddy's girl. That would have been perfectly fine if I were married to a *normal* person, but he was not normal. Captain X not only love bombed me, he love bombed Gina.

Being a mother was the best part of my life. I loved Gina from the second I held her. Like the 22 years of marriage to Captain X, my 17 years as Gina's mother went through my head like a constant slideshow of events.

I remember a day Gina came home from school crying, six months before Captain X handed me the divorce papers. Gina's closest friend had become severely anorexic. Gina had been keeping to herself during this period so I was happy she came to me for motherly advice. "Mom, Katie is in the hospital for eating disorders. She won't answer my calls. Her mom says she won't eat. She could die," she said, sobbing. I had never seen my daughter so distraught.

"Oh honey, that's horrible," I said, hugging her, comforting my teenager from the terrible pain and helplessness she was feeling. "Gina, we've got to do something special for Katie. Think hard what we can do that will get to her, something that will shake her up and make her know she's important," I said as we huddled in thought in front of my computer. "What does Katie like? What's special to her?" I asked. "Tell me anything that pops in your head."

After wiping her tears Gina became quiet in thought. "She loves swimming, she was on the swim team." I could think of nothing about swimming that we could use to help her friend. "Oh yeah, and she loves Brad Pitt," Gina added.

"Brad Pitt? Brad Pitt is perfect!" I exclaimed. "We'll get Brad Pitt to send a signed picture to Katie telling her to get well. That would work. What do you think, honey?" I asked, hoping she liked the idea. "Can we do that?" she asked timidly. "We can try, baby. Let's do it now," I said. "OK, Gina, this is *your* project. First we go on the Internet and find Brad Pitt's mailing address. Then you have to write a letter telling him who you are, explaining how important Katie is to you, and that you want him to send her a signed photo telling her to get well. I've heard he's a nice guy. I bet this will work," I said convincingly.

Gina and I found two publically available addresses for Brad Pitt. We decided to write to both, requesting Pitt send the photo to Katie at the hospital. With each of Gina's letters we enclosed stamped Priority Mail envelopes addressed to Katie at the hospital.

"This is going to work Gina. You're getting Brad Pitt to write Katie to help her get well," I said. I watched my teenager's face flash a faint smile.

After the project was completed we drove to the post office. We kissed the envelopes for luck. "Brad, do your stuff!" I said loudly. "Yeah, Brad, do your stuff," Gina repeated as she pushed the Priority Mail envelopes into the mail slot.

I hadn't the faintest idea if Pitt's offices would reply. I could only hope Gina's sincere request would not be ignored.

I waited daily for news about Katie's condition, and whether she received mail from Brad Pitt. After two weeks I couldn't wait any longer. I phoned Brad Pitt's contact number and told them the story. "I don't care who signs the darn photo, just send one, *please!*" I begged. I never told Gina of the call.

Weeks later Gina flew into the house. "Mom, *it worked!* Katie texted me! She got a photo signed by Brad Pitt!"

"Wow Gina, I'm proud of you!" I said, enjoying her happy face.

The evening Gina got the Pitt news, Captain X was in a bad mood. I remember him saying, "You only had the Brad Pitt photo sent to make yourself look important. That's all you do, try to make yourself important." It's hard to believe I lived in such craziness.

I continually emailed and phoned Gina. She would only answer once a month or so, and each contact was brief, with guarded answers. I savored every contact she made with me.

Gina's 18th birthday was soon approaching. She was no longer a child. At 18 she could make her own decisions, but she relied heavily on Captain X to guide her. I felt helpless.

Her birthday gave me a good reason to contact her. I hoped she wouldn't ignore me. I called and left a voice message. "It's Mom. My big girl is going to be 18! I can't believe it! I want to see you and give you a present. Love you, call me!"

A week before her March birthday, my cell phone burst forth with its "I Will Survive" ring tone. "Hey Mom," her simple salutation warmed my soul. "Hi Gina! How are you? I am so happy to hear from you," trying to keep the overwhelming emotions I was feeling out of my voice. "I want to see you for your birthday. I have a present for you!"

"Yeah, well, I'm kind of busy," she answered.

"Please honey, can we at least meet for a birthday lunch?"

"Uhhhhh, I guess so. I've been kinda busy with school and my job," she answered. It was nearly a year since Captain X had taken her from me. "What if we meet at Larson's for lunch at noon on Saturday?" I said. Larson's was a nearby restaurant with a sidewalk café. "Yeah, fine I guess so," she replied. "Love ya baby, see you then," I said, ending the call.

Does she have any idea what this lunch date means to me? I wondered. I finally had a date to meet my daughter. Tears of happiness welled in my eyes. I quickly tried to clear my head and think of a clever gift for her special day. I'd grown to be repulsed by Captain X's family's emotionless check-giving habit. Gina knew that I always put thought into gifts. Her 18th birthday was important.

I remembered Grampy's 80th birthday and the carton Gina and I had filled with 80 inexpensive wrapped gifts. Gina thought it was "really cool" so I decided to do the same for her. I spent the next few days buying eighteen simple gifts to individually wrap, including a candy bar, chewing gum, a package of microwave popcorn, a fashion magazine, a note pad, a pair of inexpensive earrings, lacy panties, bubble bath, and a disposable camera, along with gift cards to McDonald's, the local multiplex movie theater, Target, and Mobil Oil. I added two books on the topic of searching for your birthparents, including my copy of *The Family Nobody Wanted*, a 1954 memoir by Helen Doss about a family who adopted 12 children, a book I'd read as a child. The final gift was a little box containing eighteen ten dollar bills, one for each year of her life.

On Saturday morning I was as excited as I had been 18 years earlier when I first held her. I tried not to think of the alienation. I had to focus on the present, our mother-daughter relationship. I carefully dressed in anticipation of our meeting, choosing a young sporty outfit in an attempt to let the colorful clothing put me in a cheery mood. I reminded myself over and over to hide how much I agonized over missing her.

It was a beautiful sunny March day when the hostess led me to an outdoor table covered with a tablecloth. I hid my gift bag underneath. My
emotions were all over the place. *Just remember this is her day*, I told myself.

Gina arrived with a smile on her face. She was dressed in a soft silk
dress, looking like a woman. "Happy birthday, Gina," I said as I hugged
her. We placed our orders and chatted about her latest boyfriend and part-
time jobs. Since I only was privy to tiny segments of her life, I hung on to
her every word.

After we finished our meal I placed the gift bag in front of her. She
unwrapped the little packages with the same expression I remembered from
her past 17 birthdays. I brought my digital camera to capture her special
day. One photo became my all-time favorite. I carried it everywhere.

All too soon it was time for her to leave. "Thanks Mom, this was fun.
I have to leave but I'll talk to you later," she said, hugging me, grabbing the
gift bag. "I love you baby. Have a great birthday," I said as I watched her
walk to her car, not knowing when I would talk to her or see her again.

Gina's high school graduation was two months away. I kept sending
her emails telling her I wanted to attend her graduation. Never in my life
would I have thought I'd have to beg for tickets to my own daughter's high
school graduation!

Her school's website indicated the graduation would be held in a local
amphitheater. A week before the function she finally answered my call.

"Gina, I want to go to your graduation. How can I get a ticket?" I
asked.

"Well, Dad is going to be there … and I … I'm going to be with
Dad," she said.

"Well, sure, I know that. I mean, of course you are," I said.

"We could have dinner before and I could drive you, but you would
have to get home on your own," she offered.

"Oh, that would be great! Just so I can see my baby graduate," I said.

"OK, I'll pick you up on Thursday at 6:00PM," she said and hung up.

I had already given her a graduation gift, a Barbie-like doll that looked
just like her, which I dressed up in a handmade graduation cap and gown,
the same colors she would wear. I fastened a tiny diploma to the doll's hand
and included two one hundred dollar bills rolled up in it. Since her part-

time job was delivering pizzas, the doll's other hand held a miniature pizza box with a crisp twenty dollar bill. I'd dropped off the graduation gift where she worked earlier in the week. Maybe this *was* silly, but it was all I could think of and afford.

My cell rang at 6:00PM that Thursday. "I'm downstairs Mom," she announced. "I'm running late," she said, "so we'll have to grab some fast food." *So much for a formal graduation day dinner with my daughter*, I thought. It didn't matter. I was happy as we gobbled down burgers from a drive-through.

She parked in the underground parking at the amphitheater, preoccupied with the graduation, so I said little to her. As I got out of her car I grabbed her and hugged her. "Thank you for inviting me. I love you. I'm proud of you!" I said, kissing her on the cheek. I never got a photo of us together in her cap and gown. At least I would be able to see her walk across the stage to receive her diploma.

The amphitheater was huge and it was open seating. Everyone came with large families to support their graduates on their special day. As I sat in my seat, I gazed around the crowd.

There he was. Captain X was seated alone just 30 seats to my left, and four rows down. We were just separated by an aisle. He hadn't looked behind so he never noticed me.

I sat in my seat not knowing what to do, how to feel. Suddenly a thought flashed through my head. I walked across and down to approach him. I hadn't seen him since the day we signed our final divorce decree.

"Hi! I just wanted to come over and thank you for divorcing me. It's the nicest thing you ever did for me!" I said in a loud strong voice everyone around could hear. His face was blank as he tried to absorb where I had come from and what I had just said. I then swiftly returned to my seat.

I took him by surprise. There was no benefit in what I said other than it felt incredibly satisfying! I could see his ears and sides of his face turn beet red. I, on the other hand, was smiling, a proud divorced mother of a high school graduate.

Families of three to thirty yelled out whoops and hollers as their graduate's name was called. When Gina's name was called, I stood up and yelled loudly, "Yeahhhhhhh Gina!" Captain X was silent. Gina's graduation cheer came from one person, me.

After Gina received her diploma I left the amphitheater. I had already planned my public transportation route home. The amphitheater area was considered unsafe so I rushed to catch a series of buses to get home. When the bus stopped near my apartment complex, it was 10:00PM. I was dressed for my daughter's graduation with no celebration party to attend, so I decided to go to one of the bars still open. I ordered a drink, making a silent toast to my daughter. I indulged myself with one more cocktail, but soon after, I walked the few well-lit security-patrolled blocks to my apartment. I was in bed by 11:30.

I was dozing off to sleep when the phone rang. It was Gina. "Mom, are you OK? I was worried about you. The graduation was in a bad neighborhood. I was wondering if you are OK," she said with a voice of concern. I melted.

"Oh, Gina, baby, thanks for calling and thinking of me! I got home just fine. I just went out and celebrated your graduation myself. You looked wonderful and I'm so proud of you. Did you hear me yell when your name was called? Were you embarrassed? I hope not," I asked, concerned. "No Mom, that was cool," she said. *Yes it was*, I thought. *I am cool and my daughter was worried about me!* I had lost some ground in the past years but I was still a cool mother. "I love you Gina, congratulations and goodnight." I said. "Love ya too," she said. Our call ended. I smiled, eventually falling into a happy sleep.

I had to keep learning how to handle my relationship with Gina. It was a constant challenge since she allowed me into her life so infrequently. I knew this was happening because psychopath Captain X still controlled her life. Deep down Gina must be in a terrible state of confusion over what had happened to our family. My heart ached for her.

Decades earlier, I had seen a piece of graffiti at my local New York hangout that said, "If you love someone, let them go. If they return to you, it was meant to be. If they don't, their love was never yours to begin with." I never dreamed I'd be applying this quote to my relationship with my own daughter.

I had to let go of constantly worrying about Gina. I was positive that she knew I loved her. I was positive that she loved me. I just had to keep in touch with her the best I could, always reminding her of my love and concern for her. I hoped her psychopathic father's mask would drop someday and she would begin to question her relationship with him. I think deep down inside Gina already had some idea of Captain X's true nature, but she wanted to overlook it, to believe she was truly daddy's girl, and loved by him. I can't blame her. I overlooked a lot in 22 years. How could I expect her to come around and understand this psychological mess in her short life? Gina was a fine young woman. I had faith in her. I had faith in us.

It was time for me to work on healing myself after all the years of pain Captain X had inflicted on me. It was time to go, to get far away from Captain X and the reminders of the 22-year fraudulent marriage. I needed to find a place to heal, write, and find peace.

Chapter 20: A Run for the Border

WHEN MY FINANCIAL settlement arrived, suddenly everyone wanted to help me manage my finances. I wound up at a local branch of a national brokerage firm, looked directly at a financial advisor and said, "Think of me as your mother. You wouldn't screw your mother out of her life savings, would you?" He handled my brisk question quite well. He got my business.

I negotiated down my part of the credit card debt I was assigned in the divorce and paid it all off. I was taking care of business. It felt good.

Earlier I'd flown to Costa Rica on airline miles I'd accumulated from charging my costly divorce on my business credit card. While there, I checked out an ex-pat area I researched on the Internet, staying at a bed and breakfast. I was welcomed by American and Canadian ex-pats who gladly answered questions about relocating as an ex-pat. It was a whole new world with a fantastic climate just waiting for me. It took me only one day to conclude I would make it my new home.

With a major airport nearby, Gina and I could easily fly to visit each other with our airline passes. That is, *if* she would visit me. I hoped she would. Surely she had to understand that I could no longer live in Phoenix, which only held bad memories for me. I also needed a consistently warm climate for my painful arthritis, and a place where medical care was afford-able. I would not be eligible for full Social Security benefits for a few years, so I had to stretch my money.

One morning I was sitting on my tiny balcony with my morning cup of coffee watching the sun come up. I wondered what was still keeping me in Phoenix. It was my apartment lease. I was only three-quarters into it. Breaking it would cost me $2,400.

As the sky lightened I realized I needed to leave Phoenix. I couldn't wait any longer to take control of my own destiny. I was active on many Costa Rican Ex-Pat Internet bulletin boards looking for someone who was moving down, driving through Phoenix, looking for a ride share. There I found Chuck, a Canadian, a recent widower who was retiring in Costa Rica. He had room in his huge van for my belongings I had already started to box up.

After numerous phone calls I was sure I would be comfortable traveling with him. I made it quite clear that although we would be sharing motel rooms, I had just come out of a "horrible divorce" in no emotional shape for *anything* other than a ride-share relationship.

Chuck was a big burly man with a shaved head, a former correctional facility guard, and he looked every bit the part. "Look, I'm glad to have your company. People think I look like a narcotics dealer. Having a woman next to me makes me look less suspicious during the drive," he said, smiling. "All I'm asking is for you to pay half the expenses of the trip and make sure your stuff is boxed and ready to go so I can load it in my van and hit the road. I figure it will take us five days or so."

I called Joan, telling her my plans to leave Phoenix. I gave her a check to pay off my remaining apartment lease obligation. Unlike Captain X, I *do* abide by rules and I didn't want debt following me. I called the electric and cell phone companies, cancelling my service. I am not like Captain X. I have a conscience. I pay my bills.

I called my friends, telling of my move. They thought I was crazy. They didn't know the first thing about crazy! I gave them carte blanche to take anything I left behind. Many of my boxes hadn't been unpacked from my move out of the Captain's House. I wasn't sure if I was moving to escape my past life, or if I was moving to start a new chapter. Most likely it was both. My psychologist friend Martha's words "*get as far away from him as you can*" played an important part in my decision to move. The more I read about psychopaths, the more I realized how Captain X still terrorized me. I would be moving to a place he didn't fly to. I could feel safe.

I sat on my tiny balcony with a stiff drink as I pondered the last night I would spend in Phoenix. *I'm really moving to Costa Rica*, I told myself. Moving to another country can be scary. "Aren't you afraid of the crime driving through Mexico?" people asked. They didn't know I had been living my own battle. Nothing to me was as scary as having been married to a psychopath.

At the crack of dawn the next morning Chuck showed up at my apartment. He was physically strong, lifting my heavy boxes with ease, loading them into his two-seater gray van. My emotions were high as we moved remnants of my past life. It took 2 hours to move everything out of the building I had just moved into nine months earlier.

I packed two rollaboard suitcases, the same suitcases I used to fly around the world, filling them with as many clothes and personal essentials to live in Costa Rica until I found a place to live. Chuck would drive me to a storage locker where my belongings would stay until I found an apartment.

Chuck slammed closed the two back doors of his van, which was filled to the brim. "Ready?" Chuck asked as he checked his watch and started the ignition. "Yes, let's go!" I said, firmly planted in the passenger seat next to him.

Our conversations were enjoyable as we headed south, to Tucson and the interstate to Nogales, Arizona. There we entered the US/Mexico border crossing where officials scrutinized the van's contents, our paperwork and passports. Then we proceeded to cross the border into Nogales, Mexico. Chuck was amazing. He had our route perfectly planned with a GPS system. My job was to keep track of the receipts and expenses in a notebook. It would be a long drive but I was lucky finding someone nice who also making a major change in his life.

By late afternoon we were exhausted. We checked into a small Mexican motel with twin beds and a pool. Chuck suggested we go for a swim to enjoy the remaining sunshine and take my mind off this monumental move. Afterwards we had fast food and cervezas while we watched TV from our respective beds. "Time to hit the hay," he said after he got out of the bathroom wearing checkered pajamas. That was comforting. I slept very little that night; I kept glancing at Chuck. *He's normal, a person with empathy and a conscience.* Being in such close proximity to a normal man was foreign to me.

The next morning we were up at the crack of dawn. Dressing quickly, we ate breakfast nearby and were back on the road again. I was in awe of the desert scenery. I was actually beginning to enjoy this adventure.

For safety reasons we didn't drive at night. Chuck and I spent the night in Mexican no-tell motels, often used by locals for private sexual liaisons. Ex-pats find no-tell motels perfect because they can park loaded vehicles safely out of sight in an enclosed garage. Most were clean, cheap, with plenty of hot water and oddly enough, twin beds.

I glanced over the room service menu listing prophylactics and Viagra! We laughed. Since the TV provided only pornographic movies, we turned it off and went to sleep. I was positive Captain X had frequented similar establishments while flying to Mexico.

Again, we hit the road early, driving on efficient Mexican toll roads. Our gas and food stops were quick. Chuck skillfully avoided the Mexico City traffic. The most annoying part of the journey was the border crossings. Officials examined our papers and the van contents with suspicious eyes. Chuck was right. He needed a woman by his side so I took on the role of his love interest at each crossing. He loved it!

I really don't remember much of Guatemala, Honduras or Nicaragua. Chuck was hell-bent on us not wasting time. I was too.

Finally we made it to Costa Rica, where we found a storage locker in the ex-pat community of Alajulea, where I planned to live. I paid for a month's storage locker rental and we unloaded my belongings into it. Then we went to the final hotel we would be sharing the night together. Over dinner, we did the math, dividing the trip expenses. "Been fun, babe," he said playfully that night in his now-familiar pajamas. Chuck was continuing on the next day to a different area. The next morning I hugged him hard, thanking him as we said our goodbyes.

Within a few days I found a beautiful rental casita for $500 a month plus utilities. The cost of living in Costa Rica was definitely cheaper than the U.S. My casita was near a bus stop and was fully furnished all the way

down to silverware and linens. It even came with high speed internet and
cable TV, with CNN!

My *Tico* landlord spoke English and helped me get my possessions out
of the storage locker and into my casita. Most of the boxes were not
marked. Somewhere was my laptop computer. I needed to locate it. I had to
open each and every box containing the remnants of my past life. While
searching I opened a box with Gina's Hong Kong dolly and her doggy scarf
from Frankfurt. Tears filled my eyes. I quickly shut it. Next I came across a
box containing evidence of Captain X's deception. I needed it to write my
story. More than anything, I needed it to *believe* my own life story. The very
last box contained linens. Nestled in the middle was my trusty laptop.
Success! I was now ready to start my new life. *Poco a poco*, little by little, as
they say in Spanish.

It took months to adjust to my new ex-pat life, with much to do. I had
to apply for legal residency and learn the money, so when my financial in-
stitution deposited a monthly sum in my bank account I could use ATMs
for cash withdrawals in colons. I opened a mail service account allowing me
to maintain a U.S. address. Since Captain X had ruined my credit, I had only
one credit card to my name, but most financial transactions were in cash. I
was thrilled to discover how much cheaper living in Costa Rica was.

The area was beautiful. The climate and exotic flowers reminded me
daily I was no longer in Phoenix. I spent many days sitting at an outdoor
cafe, watching ex-pat seniors holding hands. One day it hit me like I was
punched in the gut. They were living the life I thought I would be having
with Captain X when he retired. I was still hurting, even in the tropical paradise. I ordered a Tico Sour, pretending I was on vacation, instead of a
woman who had gone through hell.

Once I met a Vietnam vet named Ron at a café. I was lonely and
poured out my story to him while we nursed Imperial beers. He handed me
a cocktail napkin to dry my tears. Ron was from the South, as his thick accent made obvious. Of those with whom I shared my sordid story, Ron's
response was the best. "Laydee, you've been blindsided." He hugged me,
wished me well and left. *You're so right Ron, I was blindsided!*

I decided not to buy a car. I bought a mountain bike instead, since
there had been no room to bring mine. I walked, biked and took the bus

everywhere. I wanted to live as economically as possible. My main goals were to take care of myself, become financially secure, get counseling, and write.

I located an ex-pat psychologist, sharing my story with her. I had great hopes that I could make some headway in healing from the aftermath of life with a psychopath. After four visits, she made it clear I should get on with my life. No one victimized by a psychopath for so long can easily get on with their life. I never returned.

The only way I felt I could heal was by writing. I maintained a self-imposed exile. Call it cathartic, but writing helped me understand what had happened to me. Writing is a lonely process. The pain of reliving both a psychopathic relationship and child alienation was difficult, but I had to write, even when I didn't feel up to it. I continued to read everything I could on psychopaths on my Kindle.

I put all my evidence of Captain X's secret life into a cabinet. While organizing it, I came across an old external hard drive I barely remembered, so I connected it to my computer. On it was an old "Works" document from Captain X's computer I had never opened. It was dated 5/1/89:

Like a GUY in UNIFORM? 34 yr. old Airline Pilot with successful and secure career looking for success motivated, emotionally secure, fun loving lady for fun, friendship and impossible long future. I am over 6' tall and about 180 lbs, black hair and green eyes. Attracted to cute as well as sophisticated, preferably slender, non-smoker, social drinker. I am a sensitive and emotional man with an unpredictable sense of humor and a predictable habit for being spontaneous. I enjoy fine dining, exquisite wines, light jazz, computers, winter sports and the surroundings that come with them. I am only looking for one woman. If that woman is you, then please let me know by responding with a letter and the means with which to contact you. Looking forward to talking with you so that we can arrange to meet.

We had been married only 226 days when Captain X wrote this advertisement. It was one more reminder of why I moved to Costa Rica.

Chapter 21: Crashed with Gina
but Trying to Heal

I TRIED TO phone Gina about my move to Costa Rica. She never answered calls or emails. I was hurting terribly. I had no direction or professional help on how to get closer to her. I was flying by the seat of my pants. Months after the move she resumed brief contact with short emails or short phone calls, speaking only a minute or two. She'd say, "Hey Mom, I'm on my way to my job and have to go." She always sounded guilty when she talked to me. I believe Captain X, the psychopathic alienator, made her confused to have contact with me. He controlled where she lived, what she drove, her phone (she was on his cell phone plan so he could monitor her calls to me), her school plans, and her choice of a college.

I had a Magic Jack phone system with a Phoenix number so that we could talk anytime. "Hi Gina, how are you? I just want to hear what you're doing. I love you so much," I would say each and every time I called. Most every call went directly to her voice mail.

One day she called me and berated me for moving to Costa Rica. I tried to explain my arthritis was bad and I needed a consistently warm climate. I also tried to explain that Phoenix held too many bad memories for me. I couldn't tell her I had to get away from her father; instead I continued to provide her with other reasonable explanations for my move. I couldn't find work at my age, lacking marketable skills and a degree. I mentioned the cost of living was much better in Costa Rica and that I no longer had medical insurance. Medical care was cheaper in Costa Rica. I lived close to the airport where we both could fly to see each other in just a few hours. I made it clear that if she wanted me to live in Phoenix with her or near her, I would be there in a heartbeat. She was crying on the phone. My heart was breaking. I sent her a lengthy, well-thought-out email repeating the same set of reasons. Later, on one short phone call she said, "I understand why you moved to Costa Rica." I hoped she did.

Captain X had new plans for Gina. Gina told me he had moved her into an apartment a few miles from him so she could live on her own while attending the local community college. Gina told me she had been accepted to a business school in California, but that never materialized. I had no information about her college courses, grades and future plans.

Months passed with no word from Gina, but I never stopped emailing or trying to call her, always telling her I loved her. I had a terrible time glancing at the happy Costa Rican families with brown-eyed, dark-haired girls. Gina's face appeared on every teenage girl in jeans who passed me.

Christmas time was approaching. Once a holiday junkie, family holidays were empty for me. Then, out of the blue Gina phoned me and said she would fly down to spend Christmas with me. I was shocked and thrilled at the same time.

When Gina arrived she was suffering from a sinus infection and was moody and sullen. I was suffering from a terrible lingering bronchial infection, on antibiotics, and coughing constantly. The timing of her visit couldn't have been worse. Since I didn't own a car, I asked a male friend to drive us around the area and dine with us.

The entire visit was unsettling. I tried to stay in the moment, showing her the highlights of my Costa Rica. I tried to ask her about her school and future plans but she wouldn't divulge anything. I worked hard to think of an appropriate Christmas gift. Her father continually bought her the latest cell phone or gadget as soon as it was on the market.

I was searching my brain for a clever Christmas surprise. I purchased a huge piñata that looked like a teenager and filled it with $200 USD in twenty dollar bills. Again I hated giving her cash but I was left with little choice since she had everything given to her by her father or grandparents. I hung her childhood Christmas stocking on the front doorknob, filled with socks, panties (a family tradition that somehow emerged through the years), headbands, local jewelry and candy, all in the hopes of providing some holiday spirit, but it was not to be. Gina was too ill during the visit, spending most of her time either watching TV or sleeping. The visit had little warmth. My heart ached. A few days later, she flew back to Phoenix.

I broke off my relationship with the friend who had taken Gina and me around during Christmas, but not before he told me, "Your daughter said you're bipolar."

"WHAT?" I said.

"She said it when you were in the restroom," he said. "No!" I yelled. Captain X must have told her I was bipolar! He was still spreading lies about me to my daughter, yet I couldn't say a word to her about him. My life was still filled with confusion and stress, even in Costa Rica.

Emails and phone calls with Gina continued throughout the year, but only in brief spurts. She shared so little of her life with me. I tried to make my life sound interesting, but it was far from that. I was distraught over losing her. I tried another therapist but she, too, lacked knowledge of how to help a victim of a psychopath and child alienation. Again I terminated future sessions.

When Gina was 19, out of the blue she phoned me. "Mom, do you want to come here for Christmas? It will be a 'Gina Christmas.' We won't talk about the past."

"I'd love to!" I said, thrilled by her invitation. At the time Captain X had refused to give me the court-mandated airline passes so I paid a hefty price for a last-minute flight. I didn't care. My daughter wanted to see me! I was elated! Gina had broken up with her boyfriend Chad and she was lonely. She was still oblivious to the fact that I had a hole in my heart from missing her.

Again I thought hard to figure out a Christmas gift for Gina. At the local junk store I found a dark-haired Ken-like doll and attached two hundred dollar bills to his hands with rubber bands. I also brought a tiny plastic tree for us to decorate and her Christmas stocking filled with little treats. I crammed it all into my rollaboard and flew off to Phoenix.

When Gina picked me up at the airport, I hugged her tightly. We drove off to her apartment Gina said was being paid for with her college fund, the one Allegra and George had established years back.

Why in the world does she need this big place, I thought. I bit my tongue and never asked. Gina's apartment was a mess. I didn't say a word, just cleaned everything in sight. I taught her how to get her new dog Petey's pee stains out of the carpet. I understood her need to have a pet, someone to love, all while my heart ached seeing the result of her lack of parental supervision from her father. Cleaning her apartment kept me busy and my anger at Captain X at bay. Soon the apartment was presentable for our holiday together.

In good spirits we drove to the market. I bought a turkey, stuffing mix and everything needed to keep us happily housebound during the holiday. While putting food in her refrigerator I noticed a magnet holding a wedding invitation. Captain X was getting married. It was no surprise he would be remarrying. Psychopaths usually have a new victim waiting in the wings. I didn't care. I just felt sorry for the bride.

Gina expertly made spaghetti dinner for Christmas Eve. "This is the best spaghetti I've ever had," I told her proudly, and it was. I remembered back to when I taught her to make 'sketti.'

The weather was dreary. Gina had been working long shifts waitressing after school and was tired. All she'd planned for us was to lie low and watch movies. I was happy just to be with her watching anything with Petey on my lap.

We decorated the tiny tree with miniature ornaments and candy canes from the Dollar Store. The tree took 10 minutes to decorate, but it added holiday spirit. Gina slept on her couch downstairs with the TV on. I slept in her bed upstairs. On Christmas Eve I tackled cleaning her master bath.

She was still asleep Christmas morning with Petey snuggled next to her when I put the gift-wrapped doll and other goodies next to the tree.

"Merry Christmas baby," I said to my drowsy 19-year-old daughter. "Santa came!" I said, pointing to the wrapped packages by the tree. A smile appeared on her face as she pulled off the wrapping paper revealing the cash-holding doll she named Mario.

She gave me Christmas socks and candy. Would she ever know that just being with her was the best gift ever? I told her it was the best Christmas I ever had as we kissed and hugged goodbye at the airport.

Again I hoped that this Christmas visit would mean she was back in my life, but it didn't. She went back to not answering for weeks and sometimes months at a time. When I did get her on the phone asking about school, friends or her plans, she hedged, saying she had to go. She was still under Captain X's spell.

The mixed messages I got from Gina continually confused me. Again, I read everything I could that addressed my situation. I tried to be the best mother I could under the circumstances. On her birthday, I sent Mario a pair of blue jeans with cash in the pocket. I was doing the money thing but at least I did it with humor. She surprised me with a phone call. "Thanks Mom, for Mario's new outfit and the cash." We chatted a bit about her fun childhood birthdays. Then she told me she was going out to dinner with Dad and his new wife for her birthday. At least we talked.

I buried myself in my writing. I made a handful of friends but had no one to confide in. Again I sought out another psychologist and again, they hadn't a clue how to help me.

One day out of nowhere Gina phoned and asked what I was doing the following weekend. "Let me check my calendar," I joked. "Nothing honey, why?"

"I want to come down and visit you for Mother's Day," she said. I was elated!

As soon as she arrived, we walked around Alajuela. Her visit made it the happiest Mother's Day ever. I was drinking cocktails with my grown-up daughter at a sidewalk café. I was thrilled! At one café, she grabbed my camera and asked a waiter to take our photograph together. My heart burst with happiness.

We hugged and kissed goodbye as she entered the waiting taxi to take her back to Phoenix. *I have my daughter back!* I said to myself. I was floating on air again.

May passed quickly into June and our communication by phone and email slightly increased. I urged her to get a credit report on herself. I also told her she should know more about her college fund, since it was hers.

Months later Gina called, sobbing. "Mom, I'm so lonely. I asked Dad if I could move back in with him but he said no. He won't let me move back unless I get rid of Petey and I just won't," she sobbed. Her call was heartbreaking. "Can I come down there with Petey and stay a few months?" she asked.

"Of course baby, of course," I said. We talked about the logistics of bringing Petey to Costa Rica. I also slipped into the conversation that she should do a credit check on herself. Captain X had ruined my credit; I feared he was using hers. I also asked her to bring her college fund information. She agreed.

My neighbor drove me to the airport to pick up Gina and Petey, who was dying to get out of his flying crate. I was excited but also very confused. Gina was constantly dropping in and out of my life. Now, with just a few days' notice, she was dropping in again. My stress level was high.

Gina plopped her rollaboard down while Petey sniffed out my casita. "Gina, did you bring the credit report and college fund information with you?" I asked. "Here," she said, handing me a large envelope. I put it on a bookshelf to review later.

We spent the afternoon walking around the Alajuela, with Petey happily sniffing everything. Waiters even provided bowls of water for dogs. I was in a shocked state of happiness.

After having lunch we walked around before returning back to my casita. There Gina showed me she that she had indeed done an online credit rating of herself. It appeared OK, thank God. We ordered in a pizza and watched TV sitcoms. Gina curled up with Petey on a lounge chair and was soon fast asleep.

As I gazed at her I thought of her college fund. Then I recalled a horrible memory. Gina was about 10 years old. Captain X was doing his usual "money is tight" talk and said, "Maybe we should borrow some money from Gina's college fund." I was so naive at the time I remember saying, "Is that a good idea?" I didn't know how college funds worked. I didn't realize penalties were involved. It was entirely plausible that he had taken money from it. Out of fear I opened the envelope. It contained only her birth certificate and a photograph of Gina when she was born, no college fund information.

I became enraged. Three years of anger, hurt and frustration caused by her psychopathic father alienating her from me was bottled up inside and was coming up. I'd asked Gina to bring the college fund information to protect her, but she didn't understand that.

I woke her up. "Gina, where's the college fund information?"

"Dad showed it to me last night and he said it's all OK," she said in a tone that communicated her belief in every single word he said. I once believed every word he said too.

"How much money is left in it? Do you know?" Then I lost it. Before I knew it the words just flew out. "I don't trust your father. He spent all our money on prostitutes. That's why he divorced me, I found out. He ruined my credit. I know you don't believe me but it's the truth," I spewed out. I couldn't stop. "Look," I said as I went into the cabinet with the evidence and I pulled out a photo of Tiffany Sparks. "This was your father's favorite prostitute. She was 20. You were 17 at the time." I tried to show her the photo but she wouldn't look at it. I tried to show her my attorney's long list of prostitutes he visited, but she wouldn't look up. Everything went downhill from there. I had just ruined everything.

Doors slammed. She screamed, "I'm leaving tomorrow."

"Noooooo. I'm sorry, I'm sorry. Please forgive me! *PLEASE, GINA!*" I cried. "I'm sorry. Please, I'm begging you, stay. I won't say another word to upset you." She had just locked herself in the guest bedroom.

Why can't I find anyone to help me? I screamed to myself. Frozen in grief over wrecking my relationship with my daughter, I didn't sleep at all that night.

Early in the morning Gina grabbed a business card for a taxi from my bulletin board and phoned a cab to take her and Petey back to the airport. In tears I begged for forgiveness. She opened the house door and left. I leaned into the backseat of the taxi and cried, "I love you." I *think* I heard her say it back.

I had just ruined everything. Gina was gone. Never had my heart been heavier as I grieved that day. I tried phoning her but she had blocked me from her phone. I sent her carefully worded emails apologizing profusely. I cried endlessly. I didn't leave my casita for days, constantly trying to figure out what to do next.

In another carefully worded email, I attached the scan of a 2008 quarterly statement from her college fund I had just found buried in my computer. I also sent her a link listing colleges that accepted pets so she could have Petey with her if she decided to change colleges. I desperately wanted her to get out from Captain X's clutches. If Captain X hadn't gone into her college fund and she kept her grades up, she should be able to get into a good school away from him. I'd been helpless for years, not knowing what she was doing.

I knew I had just made a horrific mistake during Gina's visit. I was determined to fix it and get her back into my life. I may have just crashed and burned, but I was determined that we would both survive.

Chapter 22: Working to Undo the Alienation

PARENTAL ALIENATION HAS been called the ultimate hate crime. I couldn't agree more. I'm not alone in the misery of its effects. With more than 50 percent of marriages ending in divorce, many children become victims of parental alienation. When a psychopath is involved, it can be extremely damaging.

I often wondered what I could have done differently in the divorce. Even if my attorney upheld the court-mandated therapy sessions and joint custody, it probably would have been useless. I had to face the fact that early on, Captain X started alienating Gina from me. My inability to parent while recuperating from surgeries provided him the perfect opportunity to polish off his alienating skills.

I was on a mission to find someone who could provide parental alienation counseling over the phone, someone to whom I could tell my story as concisely as possible, and receive guidance to undo the damage I had just done with Gina. I hoped to find someone who could grasp the fact that I was positive my ex-husband was a psychopath. Life had dealt me a double whammy but I was bound and determined to persevere.

I listened to a YouTube lecture by a parental alienation expert. She explained that an "alienating parent" uses strategies to turn the child against the other parent. During my surgeries Captain X filled Gina with lies about my emotional stability, an alienating strategy. A normal husband would have shown love and empathy during my medical procedures, displaying this to Gina. But he didn't. He was never there for me. Captain X was never a

normal husband or parent. I was the "targeted parent." I was unduly tar-
nished when he fed Gina lies about me. This is a heart wrenching position
to be in, especially when the alienating parent is a psychopath.

I booked a phone session with the parental alienation expert from
YouTube. I had jotted down notes and questions to ask. My voice was filled
with emotion while we talked. I tried to explain that my emotional state was
the result of *finally* finding someone who might help me. I liked the professional voice on the other end of the phone. I briefly went through my story.
Although she could not address the question of psychopathy, since it was
outside her field, she appeared to be familiar with psychopathy in alienation
cases.

I learned a lot from our sessions, including that I'd expected far too
much from Gina. She was still confused about what happened to our family, and caught up in the alienation. She was 20 but may be emotionally the
same young girl Captain X had taken from me three years before. I had no
way of knowing this; had I known, I wouldn't have made any demands of
her. I would never have acted the way I did. I would have shown her empathy, love, and support. The parental alienation expert said I must keep my
emotions intact, adding that I "should never give up loving her." *That's easy*,
I thought. *I could never stop loving her.* Despite all I'd been through, and the
recent mistakes I had made, I was still her healthiest parent.

When Gina left Costa Rica I continued to have no way of contacting
her except through email. After discussing my situation with the alienation
expert, we decided I would send Gina a weekly email filled with positive
news in my life, always reassuring her that I loved her. After my first session
with the counselor, I carefully worded an email to Gina telling her that I
was sorry I had been so emotional that I gave her too much information,
and that it would never happen again. I stressed how much I loved her and
wanted to hear from her any time. I kept the rest of the email lighthearted,
asking about Petey and telling her I would pay for her to visit, or would visit
her anytime she wanted. As I expected, the email went unanswered.

During our phone session the expert said, "You made a tactical error
in telling her about the prostitutes, but all in all I think there's much to be
hopeful about. It's a process." This was the first time in three years I had
heard the word "hopeful." I *am* hopeful. Psychopath Captain X cannot

keep up his mask of sanity all the time, pretending he cares about Gina. When his mask slips, and I'm sure it will, he will be revealed as a controlling, malevolent bully with no capacity for love or empathy. I continue to try to get Gina back in my life. I love her. That's just what mothers do.

I continue to send her loving birthday and holiday gifts. I continue to invite her to visit me and ask her to allow me to visit her. I will continue to suggest we spend vacations together. I will never stop trying to get her back in my life.

If Gina were to have an emergency, a terrible accident, or become deathly ill, I have no idea if I would be contacted. If Gina continues not to share news of her life with me, I am fully prepared to hire a private investigator to find her. I will do whatever it takes to maintain a connection with her.

Gina still goes in and out of my life with short emails. My heart goes out to her. I have no idea if she will ever comprehend who her father is, that he turned her against me, and that what he said about me was not the truth.

Some might ask if it really matters that she learns the truth about him someday. In a sense it does. His psychopathic behavior defined our family dynamics. He made me the targeted parent, filling Gina with lies about me. I had 22 years of lies with Captain X, and Gina's entire life with him was filled with lies. He put her on a pedestal as a golden child in order to appear a normal loving father. I know Gina still believes he loves her, just as I did for so many years. When Captain X quickly remarried a woman with grown children and one child a year younger than Gina, he moved Gina out of the Captain's House and into an apartment of her own nearby, all under the guise of making her independent and on her own. I cannot imagine how confused Gina must have felt to learn that she was being replaced in the Captain's House by a whole new family with a new teenage girl sleeping in her childhood bedroom. Her disappointment and confusion over his sudden marriage, replacing our family with a new duplicate family she hardly knew, must have been difficult to absorb.

Some say Gina probably has some idea, deep down inside, of Captain X's true nature. I really don't know. I do know she filled her time with school, an assortment of part-time jobs and boyfriends whose parents soon became surrogate parents. I can't imagine how sad she must have felt when she told her dad she was lonely and wanted to move back with him and he said no, supposedly because of her dog. I am thankful she had the unconditional love Petey provided.

I will work the rest of my life to undo the alienation. According to experts, unlike psychopathy, child alienation can be undone. When Gina comes back to me, I will be prepared and filled with a love I've never lost for her.

Chapter 23: Grounded with Answers at Last

IN 1998 I read *The Pilot's Wife*, a bestseller by Anita Shreve. I remember thinking how flawed the plot was. In Shreve's book, Kathryn Lyon's pilot husband dies in an airplane crash. She uncovers his secret life in the IRA with another wife and children in Ireland. A promotional piece about the book said "it explores the question of how well we can ever really know another person."

I scoffed at the book, smugly telling myself, *come on now, she would have known.* After being in a marriage to a pilot with a secret life, I no longer scoff. The premise of *The Pilot's Wife* is not flawed. Secret lives occur all the time. Of course the book *The Pilot's Wife* is based on politics, not psychopaths.

How did I not know about Captain X's secret life? The answer is simple: psychopaths are masters at deception and can easily escape scrutiny.

In her book *Love Fraud: How Marriage to a Sociopath Fulfilled My Spiritual Plan,* Donna Andersen tells of her ex-husband James Montgomery, who, during her two and a half year marriage, cheated on her with six different women and fathered a child with one of them. Ten days after she left him, he married the mother of the child, committing bigamy for a second time. He entertained the other women with a quarter of a million dollars of Ms. Andersen's money. Ms. Andersen and I are just two of millions of people who have been victims of psychopaths.

Why didn't I know Captain X was a psychopath? I thought a psychopath was a serial killer, or that the term was slang for someone who is crazy.

I had no idea that some people have absolutely no conscience. I had always maintained the belief that there is good in everyone. Unfortunately this is not true; there are people among us who are socialized psychopaths, people without a conscience who blend well into mainstream life. These charming people are talented at projecting a normal outward appearance and behavior.

Captain X is a perfect example of a socialized psychopath, someone who fits in, someone you would never suspect to have what the American Psychiatric Association refers to as ASPD, antisocial personality disorder. Ironically, the Internet prostitution organization Captain X belonged to had those same initials!

Some researchers believe that both nature and nurture could be responsible for a psychopathic personality. In his book *Without Conscience: The Disturbing World of Psychopaths Among Us,* expert Dr. Robert Hare says, "Although psychopathy is not primarily the result of poor parenting or adverse childhood experiences, I think they play an important role in shaping what nature has provided. Social factors and parenting practices influence the way the disorder develops and is expressed in behavior."[1]

I tried to remember everything I knew about Captain X's childhood. He revealed virtually nothing of his past. Every time I questioned him or his parents about his childhood, they glossed over his youth, providing me with just a handful of sentences before quickly changing the subject.

When we first met, Captain X stressed how wonderful and close his family was. I now realize he only told me what he knew I wanted to hear. He mirrored and parroted what I projected, what I wanted. His family never displayed the strong emotional ties associated with a close family. They themselves showed signs of being antisocial when they saw no reason to spend holidays or family celebrations together, or to be together in family times of need. Love—especially from Allegra—was shown with money, not emotions.

---

[1] *Without Conscience: The Disturbing World of the Psychopaths Among Us,* Robert D. Hare. 1993. Copyright Guilford Press. Reprinted with permission of the Guilford Press.

Working backwards from my certainty that he is a psychopath, the combination of his childhood with what must have been a psychological predisposition produced his psychopathic personality. Most researchers agree that a psychopath's bond progresses through three predictable stages: **idealize, devalue** and **discard**. These three stages are believed to be natural to a psychopath's personality.

When I first met Captain X, I was vulnerable, needy, lonely and looking for love. I was a psychopath's perfect victim and easy prey. I projected what I wanted in life—love and a family—and he mirrored back these expectations as his own. This was the start of his **idealize** stage, sometimes called the honeymoon stage. It was then that Captain X love bombed me.

Love bombing is a deliberate show of affection in order to influence someone. He charmed me with his witty and entertaining conversations, making me feel secure, loved and appreciated in ways I had never felt before. Like all victims of psychopaths, I was swept off my feet, fast and furiously. Soon after we met we became engaged to be married. Psychopaths work with a vengeance to gain control of their victims very early in the relationship.

During my whirlwind courtship I was so mesmerized by his constant phone calls, gifts, attention and flattery that the love cocktail of adrenaline, dopamine and serotonin swirled around in my brain. Soon I felt addicted to him. I was in love. Psychopaths expertly love bomb their victims very early in the relationship, sometimes even before they meet in person, as he did with me on the telephone in the pre-Internet days. I fell in love with Captain X but Captain X never loved me. I thought I had found my soul mate. He could never be a soul mate; he doesn't have a soul.

Empathy is a prerequisite to love. Psychopaths cannot feel empathy, so they cannot love. They can only *appear* to love and they do so with the skill of an Academy Award-winning actor.

Captain X married me to look respectable, to create a positive image he wanted to present to his family and the community. I was pretty, smart, loving, trusting and hardworking. I provided him with a perfect cover for his psychopathic lifestyle. He exploited me so he would appear as a loving husband and family man. He was *so* charismatic that everyone who met him told me how lucky I was to be married to him, and how much he loved me.

This only added to my confusion in the marriage. Psychopaths want someone committed to them, but they will not return the commitment. As soon as we were married he cleverly began to use distractions to keep me off balance.

His profession as an airline pilot provided him with the perfect opportunity to maintain a mask of sanity, a mask of normalcy, covering his true pursuit of a secret promiscuous life with prostitutes. He used my trust and credit to cover his financially draining prostitution habit. Psychopaths are easily bored. His secret life with illegal sexual partners fed his need for excitement. He frequented prostitutes before we were married and through elaborate ruses and manipulation, he continued his prostitution habit during our entire marriage, filling his sick need for excitement.

Psychopaths are rarely monogamous. The marital vow of "forsaking all others" means nothing to psychopaths, who are known to continue their sexual promiscuity soon after marriage. Captain X must have gotten quite a rush when he told me he had "a tough three-day trip," when in reality he had spent his layover with one or two prostitutes, feeding his sexual addiction and using family money to pay for his habit. Experts believe psychopaths get an emotional high from deceiving their victims.

Captain X repeatedly mentioned his birth date and profession on Internet prostitution sites, web postings and in emails, all which helped uncover his secret life. Because of his psychopathic super-inflated ego, he believed he was capable of getting away with anything.

Captain X's profession also answers the question of why our marriage lasted so long. Because he traveled away from home on flights lasting three or four days at a time, for fifteen days a month, I was constantly in and out of his psychopathic control and crazy-making. When he perpetually changed his flying schedule, he added even more confusion to my state of mind, all while convincing me the relationship was normal.

Although I came into the marriage with little money, I maintained an excellent credit rating. I was extremely frugal and very trusting. Captain X knew I would never question him. He was free to abuse my trust and credit. With me on his arm, he could constantly ask his family for more money under the guise of my medical expenses or our family needs.

My first sudden memory took me back to the day we looked for a new house in the upscale Elmdale neighborhood. Captain X duped me into believing he'd bought the huge mansion in front of us. I remember the weird smirk on his face as he enjoyed the fact that I had fallen for his lie. Dr. Robert Hare refers to this as a psychopath's "duping delight." When Captain X took pleasure in duping me, he was working on me, making me feel inferior for not being able to take a joke. He constantly duped me during the entire marriage from something as outlandish as tricking me into thinking he bought the mansion, to the enormous deception of his double life. Psychopaths love the thrill of the game, pulling one over on people.

Captain X used gaslighting tactics to manipulate me, to destroy my perception of reality. The term gaslighting comes from the 1938 stage play and subsequent 1944 movie *Gaslight*, starring Ingrid Bergman. In the plot, the husband turned the gas lamps lower than normal to convince his wife that she was crazy. Captain X used gaslighting to convince me I was responsible for him not getting the check airman job with Major Airways, when in fact he didn't get the position because of his own inadequacies. Captain X used gaslighting to get me into therapy and to convince me, as well as my therapist, that I had mental issues.

He used gaslighting when he told me Dr. Bob's office had called to report that my pre-op blood work was problematic. I should have known a physician's office will only speak to the patient, not to their spouse, but at that point my life was filled with his crazy-making so I never even considered this. He used gaslighting to convince me that our financial problems were due to our infertility treatments, the adoption costs and his Major Airways pay cut, when in fact he had been spending enormous amounts of money for his prostitution habit. He constantly gaslighted me, twisting situations to make me feel inferior or off guard. The more he used this technique, the more vulnerable I became to it.

Psychopaths only do things for personal gain, not out of love. When he finally agreed to adopt a baby I'm sure it was only to look good in the eyes of his family and co-workers. Being a father added to his persona of a family man, aiding him in obtaining more money from his family. Psychopaths are selfish. He showed this as he skillfully continues to alienate Gina from me.

When I went through the painful and emotional infertility treatments, a miscarriage, and endured three major surgeries in 14 months, Captain X showed absolutely no empathy whatsoever. The marital vow "in sickness and in health" is empty gibberish to a psychopath since they cannot feel empathy. Little is worse than the pain of being with someone who shows no empathy when empathy is greatly needed.

Stockholm syndrome also played a huge role in my staying with Captain X. Stockholm syndrome was named after an August 1973 incident in Stockholm when an armed Swedish robber held bank workers captive for six days. The hostages began to identify and form sympathetic bonds with their captor. I was held hostage by Captain X in the Captain's House.

I had no support system. I was very much alone when we married, having come from the transient theatrical world, and living in a new city. Most all of my friends were in different cities or countries. Locally I had friends in infertility and adoption groups but after achieving our goal and leading vastly different lives, we parted. Early on when we moved into the Captain's House I had a good friend, but she moved away after her divorce.

Susan was my closest friend for 10 years until I showed her proof of my husband's secret life. Then, for some reason, she no longer cared to be a part of mine, refusing to be a character witness in my divorce. I lost contact with my antique friends. I just couldn't express what happened to me. Most victims of psychopaths have few friends who understand what they have been through.

As much as I desperately tried for us to have a social life together, Captain X used his flying schedule as a constant excuse to avoid building a network of shared friends. As a psychopath, he has no need for anyone in his life unless he can use them for his personal gain. As a result I was isolated in the Captain's House. My only reward was when I flew on vacations or trips to see my out-of-town friends. It was only then, and when I was alone with Gina, that I truly felt alive.

I was grateful to Captain X for allowing me the opportunity to fly, to travel and see the world. This feeling goes back to our first year of marriage when I remember thinking how lucky I was to be able to sip champagne in a Major Airways first class cabin. I didn't realize psychopath Captain X dangled the opportunity to travel on Major Airways in front of me as a reward for being a good captive, also allowing him time for prostitutes.

Thomas Sheridan's book *Puzzling People: The Labyrinth of the Psychopath* helped me understand why Captain X took over the cooking in our household. Sheridan says,

> "One skill that some psychopaths have learned to capitalize on is their ability to cook. This is not out of any joy derived from culinary pursuits. They are only too well aware that people nearly always trust someone who feeds them. It is a primal response in all of us to nurture and nourish. The psychopath can often produce elaborate meals and dinner parties and keep their guests up all night with feeding them. However the 'windbag' nature of the psychopath constantly praising themselves can make the most impressive culinary presentation distasteful after a while."

Sheridan was right. Our visitors never reciprocated with dinner invitations.

Sheridan's book also shed light on Captain X's habit of being able to instantaneously fall to sleep, something I erroneously assumed was a pilot's trick. Sheridan says, "Psychopaths do not have that moment of internal reflection with their inner thoughts at the end of the day. They sleep and wake instantly, similar to a machine turning on and off."

I even found answers for his "airline voice." Psychopaths often have emotionless or monotone voices and facial expressions, called a flat affect, unless they become enraged. They are insensitive to the emotional connotations of language. Captain X's flat affect left me confused, while it helped him control and manipulate his personal interactions with me.

When I questioned him about why he had no friends, or more importantly, why money was tight, Captain X, a true psychopath, began the **devalue** part of the psychopathic bond. He started telling friends and family behind my back that I was bipolar (a mental illness difficult to prove or disprove to casual acquaintances and a tactic often used by psychopaths) sending me to a therapist to reinforce his story. With all his crazy-making he almost convinced me I was mentally ill.

After my 60th birthday, when I finally found the necessary strength and demanded to see the family finances, psychopath Captain X started the **discard** phase of the psychopath emotional bond. As is true in the majority of romantic relationships with a psychopath, he had already found a new victim, a new target, and wanted me out of his life. I was no longer useful to him. He knew I was on to him, that I no longer trusted him.

I was extremely fortunate to have uncovered Captain X's secret life with prostitutes throughout our marriage. If I had gone through the **discard** period without uncovering the scale of his deception, I might never have understood who he really is, a psychopath. Had I not uncovered his secret life, I would have gone through the rest of my life as a bewildered, confused and destroyed woman trying to understand why I was discarded after 22 years of being told "divorce is not an option." I was a good and loving wife. His enormous deception made me search for answers and thankfully, I found them.

I endured emotional and physical abuse and Stockholm syndrome while being married to psychopath Captain X. After discovering the scope of his financial and sexual deception, the stress of a horrific divorce, and being alienated from Gina, I was finally diagnosed with post-traumatic stress disorder, the result of long-term exposure to emotional trauma.

I now realize how very lucky I am to be alive. I came close to taking my life twice. Only the thought of leaving my daughter Gina in grief prevented me from doing so. I can truly say Gina saved my life.

Does Captain X love our daughter? Most psychologists say psychopaths think of people as acquisitions, discarding them when they are done using them, when they no longer suit their purpose. Captain X grabbed Gina as a marital acquisition during the divorce when he alienated her from me. Someday he will have no need for her, unless she has money or power, something as a psychopath he covets with a vengeance.

Everyone will come across a psychopath at some point in their lifetimes. It was just my turn, just my misfortune. I went into the marriage without knowing that socialized psychopaths are among us. Everyone who has ever lived has had personal struggles. Being married to psychopath Captain X was mine. I cannot forgive Captain X. You cannot forgive someone who lives life without a conscience. He does not deserve pity because he cannot understand pity.

It took three long years of hard work to fully understand what happened to me. Now I have the answers. I am a woman who, through no fault of her own, married a profoundly flawed man. Sarah Strudwick, author of *Dark Souls: Healing and Recovering from Toxic Relationships*, said it best: "The superficial façade that they portray to suck you into their game falls away and you are left with the image of a cardboard cut-out, without any substance whatsoever." I am now grounded with answers. I survived a marriage and divorce with Captain X, a psychopath, a man without substance.

Chapter 24: Understanding and Avoiding Psychopaths

PSYCHOPATHY IS BELIEVED to be one of the most highly publicized yet most misunderstood of all mental illnesses. Because of the mass media and Hollywood's misrepresentation of psychopaths, they are far too often depicted as criminals, distorting the public's perception of these unstoppable, untreatable social predators present in our everyday lives. Most psychopaths are not criminals, but are rather socialized and living among us.

Psychopaths are found in all walks of life and in every country in the world. Researchers believe that as many as four percent of the world's population could be psychopathic. Within this population of psychopaths there are three times as many male psychopaths as female psychopaths. These social predators are masters of deception, charming us while they wreak havoc in our lives, leaving us in a state of emotional and financial ruin. If you think back to people in your life, to someone who caused you trouble, you might have known a psychopath.

The brain of a psychopath does not function in a normal manner. Dr. James H. Fallon of the University of California, Irvine uses Post Emission Tomography Imaging (PET scans) while Dr. Kent Kiehl of the University of New Mexico uses Magnetic Resonance Imaging (MRI) technology to detect differences in the brains of psychopaths compared to non-psychopathic individuals. Their studies indicate that psychopaths have structural abnormalities not found in normal people. Some researchers believe psychopaths have a malfunctioning or underdeveloped amygdala, a structure in the brain that processes emotions.

Because psychopaths don't process emotions normally, they do not understand the feelings of others and feel no empathy and no remorse. Psychopaths *do* understand the difference between right and wrong, but they just don't care. They have no concerns about the consequences of their actions. They have no moral compass, no conscience. Psychopaths are pathological liars with no stress reaction, so they are often able to pass lie detector tests.

The *Diagnostic and Statistical Manual of Mental Disorders* (DSM) is published by the American Psychiatric Association and is used in the United States and, to varying degrees, around the world to classify mental disorders. The current version of the manual, the *DSM-5*, doesn't even mention psychopaths in its index, but rather clumps psychopathy, sociopathy, and dissocial personality disorder under an umbrella term, Antisocial Personality Disorder (ASPD). This is confusing because the wording of the term antisocial in itself suggests that people with these disorders do not interact well with others.

Psychopaths do interact with people. The *DSM* states that an individual with antisocial personality disorder may exhibit the superficial charm of a psychopath. Again this is confusing and it's partly because of this confusion that there is much disagreement about the way the American Psychiatric Association handles the issue of psychopathy.

Psychopaths are found in all professions, and in positions where they can wield power. Your doctor, lawyer, psychiatrist, professor, police officer, politician, your charitable organization leader or your co-worker may be a psychopath. Psychopaths can be found in the workplace as well as in the religious community. Extreme cases of "spiritual psychopaths" include Jim Jones, the leader of the Peoples Temple known for the 1978 mass suicide of 914 of its members in Jonestown, Guyana, and David Koresh, the leader of the Branch Davidians religious sect who, in 1993, led many to death under his spiritual guidance. Sadly, charismatic *socialized* psychopaths exist in the religious community where they destroy their victim's core beliefs, fleece them of their money, and have been known to sexually abuse young children.

Psychopaths use their social skills and circumstances to construct a facade of normalcy, placing themselves in positions of influence—not for their service, but rather for the power. People find them exciting and dynamic, not realizing that they are climbing up in leadership in an effort to control and destroy people below.

Children exhibit psychopathic traits, but until they reach the age of 18, when their brains are fully developed, they can only be considered to have a conduct disorder. These children are often thought of as fledging psychopaths. *The Bad Seed,* a 1954 novel by William March, subsequently adapted to the stage and film, was an early commercialization of childhood psychopathic behavior. A more recent example is Lionel Shriver's 2011 novel *We Need to Talk about Kevin,* which was made into a feature film the same year. These days we only have to watch the news to see how fledging psychopaths have done the unthinkable.

We cannot fix these evil people. There is no cure or effective treatment for psychopaths. Psychopaths who undergo traditional talk therapy are said to become even more adept at manipulation. Some researchers believe that therapy actually appears to teach psychopaths better skills at manipulating people.

While Dr. Robert Hare's work helped in diagnosing psychopaths, Thomas Sheridan, researcher and author of *Puzzling People: The Labyrinth of the Psychopath,* developed a simple but effective approach to help victims of psychopaths recover: NCEA, No Contact Ever Again. Sadly the NCEA approach is impossible for the parents of children who display psychopathic traits, as well as for those who share child custody with a psychopathic partner.

Because psychopaths are social predators, they are quite prevalent on social media and Internet dating sites. Listen to your instincts and set boundaries when using social media and dating sites.

Psychopaths often prey on the vulnerable elderly with no family, under the guise of friendship and caring, all while manipulating them and bilking them out of their life savings. This elder abuse often goes unreported because seniors are too embarrassed to admit being duped at a time in their life when they should be enjoying their golden years.

There are indeed bad people in the world. Psychopaths are a menace to society. We owe it to ourselves to learn all we can about these social predators and share this knowledge with those we love and trust. A selection of books on the topic can be found in the back of this book under *Suggested Reading and Viewing*.

We must remain vigilant in our daily lives. Psychopaths are overtly charming. A quick promise, unusual flattery and a sudden gift might be an attempt to manipulate you. Be wary of any personal relationship that progresses too quickly. Slow down. Ask questions and get answers. There's nothing wrong with a reasonable investigation of a person's background before entering into a close relationship or business deal. If a person seems far too perfect and everything they say sounds too good to be true, you just might have met a psychopath.

Know yourself and your vulnerabilities. Psychopaths know how to spot your vulnerabilities quickly, allowing them to mirror your needs in an effort to manipulate you. Set boundaries when embarking on a personal relationship. Most of us are trusting souls, forgetting that our trust should be earned and not assumed. We must pay more attention to our gut feelings, since our unconscious can be a good guide in making decisions. If you think you may have come in contact with a psychopath, avoid him or her at all costs.

If you are a survivor of the heinous experience of being with a psychopath, keep in mind that there is no real closure with a psychopath. Although they may have progressed on to their next victims, they still might contact you in a week, month or even decades later, all in an attempt to control or add chaos to your life.

If you know a victim of a psychopath, keep in mind that they are suffering terribly from the loss and confusion of their horrific experience. As Noelle R. Andrews states so eloquently in her book *The Aftermath of Rock 'n' Roll*, "Unless you have been the victim of a psychopath you cannot accurately understand the hopelessness, the helplessness of the person who has been wronged. Persons of conscience may sympathize, but the act of lending an uncritical ear is even more important. If you know someone who has suffered the inevitable harm from a relationship with a psychopath, I offer this advice to you. Listen. Be there. Don't judge."

After the experience of being in a psychopathic relationship I follow the advice of Thomas Sheridan, author of *Puzzling People: The Labyrinth of the Psychopath*: "Stop thinking of yourself as a victim. You were a target that is now no longer being hit."

Chapter 25: Epilogue

AS SOON AS our divorce was finalized, Captain X married Sonia from Argentina, one of only four of the hundreds of women he contacted through the Internet who was not a prostitute. They met on the singles website eHarmony while he was still married to me. Sonia was a woman looking for love, just as I had been, more than two decades earlier.

According to Sonia's Facebook page, he proposed to her while vacationing in the Grand Canyon. Six years earlier, we had vacationed there as a family. I was emotionally struck by the beauty of the site. I remember asking Captain X, "If you knew it was so romantic, why didn't you propose to me here?" I had given him the idea to propose there. Later Captain X took Sonia on a trip to China, the exact same Yangtze River cruise I had given him for his 50th birthday. Psychopaths are emotional recyclers.

Sonia has three grown children and one teenage daughter who still lives with them in the Captain's House. Gina is still in the rented apartment near Captain X. When he remarried, he replaced Gina and me with an entirely new family the exact same size in the Captain's House. Psychopaths repeat the same relationship cycle over and over.

I'm positive he has filled Sonia's head with lies about me, that I'm emotionally ill and spent all of his money. Psychopaths lie and badmouth all their past relationships. I desperately wanted to warn Sonia about him, but that would have been impossible since I'm not allowed to talk to anyone about our divorce, according to our final decree of divorce. Even if I could, she wouldn't believe me. She's in the idealize stage of their relationship and undoubtedly believes everything charming and convincing Captain X says.

Soon Sonia will be confused about why he never kisses or embraces her, why there's no intimacy in their marriage. She'll wonder why he's not empathetic to her illnesses and why he has no friends. She will be exposed to his crazy-making with his constantly changing schedule, and his insistence that "money is tight." By now he's added his name to her credit cards or opened new ones in her name. Eventually her credit will be ruined. Captain X, like all psychopaths, will continue to feed his need for excitement by continuing his secret sexual life with prostitutes. This time he has most likely taken better precautions to conceal his "hobby." I am sure he's still a financial parasite, constantly asking Allegra for money, despite making a substantial income as a pilot.

When Captain X and Sonia argue, I have no doubt he puts his hands on her shoulders, looks hypnotically in her in the eyes and says, "Divorce is not an option." It worked for me, and psychopaths repeat successful deceptive strategies. Sonia doesn't know she married a man without a conscience.

According to Sonia's Facebook page she was a psychology major. She must have studied psychopaths. When she is a devalued and discarded victim of Captain X, it still might take her a long time to put the pieces of her puzzle together. Captain X fooled everyone. He even fooled my psychologist. He's that smooth, charming and dangerous.

Psychopaths are extremely litigious and crave drama. Captain X sued me twice since our divorce. The first case was over $1,700 in damages he said I had done to my luxury car. I have no doubt he found someone to inflate any miniscule damage that was done to the vehicle. I had no strength to fight and simply paid him and his attorney.

The second time he sued me was over auction proceeds from my small antiques collection. He said I hadn't fully disclosed them in the discovery process of the divorce. These antiques were from my original collection prior to my marriage and netted more than $17,000 at a European auction. Captain X only purchased a few as gifts for me over the years. My attorney assured me that I was fine in using my photo book of these antiques in the discovery process. This second lawsuit came shortly after I moved out of the country. I had no strength left to put up a fight and fly back to the States to do so. I sent off a check for $17,000 to his attorney. I was so emotionally distraught by this lawsuit that I became physically ill. My friends in the antique world cannot understand how and why he would take what was mine. They don't know that Captain X is a psychopath. He feels entitled to everything and anything he wants.

As per our final decree of divorce I was allowed four airline passes on Major Airways each year until Captain X retired. I flew on the first pass to London to see my antique friends. Upon my return and after paying Captain X the fees incurred, he notified me that the money I sent him came late (a lie) and therefore he was terminating the pass privileges. I hired a new attorney to help file contempt of court charges and get my awarded airline travel passes back. When the court date arrived, Captain X brought to court a Major Airways gate agent I had never seen before who claimed I was rude to her, and that I had mentioned I was flying on passes for business purposes (which is against company policy), both lies. The judge was ill that day and so the case was postponed. I had no strength to fly back to Phoenix and face Captain X in court again. As a result I lost all my airline flight pass privileges. You cannot win with a psychopath.

I recently attended a retreat for victims of psychopaths, trauma survivors. Eleven of us gathered together with two professional counselors to better understand psychopathy, what happened to us, and how to get past the pain and manage the emotional distress we all suffer from. I finally felt I was not alone. I was, however, the only attendee who had been alienated from her child by a psychopath.

It was there that I was officially diagnosed with post-traumatic stress disorder (PTSD) as a result of the prolonged trauma and abuse I received while married to and divorcing Captain X. It was comforting to know there is a name for what I had been and still go through. The memories still occur, but less often because I have consciously worked hard to understand what triggers them.

As suggested by my parental alienation counselor, I stay in contact with Gina by sending weekly emails and birthday and holiday gifts, always telling her I love her. Since the mistake I made during her last visit with me, causing her to leave abruptly the very next day, I feared I would never hear from her again. I continued to send her weekly emails and I occasionally receive replies. I remain blocked from her cell phone so I can't call her, but I continue to show my love in the best ways I can through emails and birthday and holiday gifts.

Subsequent emails from Gina have been sporadic. I carefully word each and every email I send her. This past birthday I received a gift from her, the first since she was taken from me by Captain X. It was a 5x7 framed photo grouping in four parts, one photo of us together, one of her dog Petey and two of her, one as a child and a current photo of herself. At the top of wood picture frame is metal attachment with the word "Family." It is my most prized possession.

Everything I went through pales in comparison to what Gina is still going through. All I can do is write her my weekly emails (hoping Captain X has not intercepted them) filling her in on the news of my life and telling her I love her forever and always will, and if she needs me, to contact me. I make it clear that I will return to the States if she wants me to. Like the parental alienation expert said, I think there's much to be hopeful about regarding our future together.

I have been asked, "How do you think Gina will react when she reads this book?" I really don't know. My heart goes out to Gina when that time comes. My decision to write this book and tell my story weighed heavily on my heart. I had to think of readers who may be victims of psychopaths or those who know someone in a psychopathic relationship. Education is the answer. I wrote my story to shed some much-needed light on the topic of psychopaths. I might still be foundering, wondering what had happened to me, had I not read Barbara Bentley's book *A Dance with the Devil: A True Story of Marriage to a Psychopath*.

I am a member of a writers group that meets bimonthly. I shared the nature of my writing project with only a handful of very close people. Months later I was shocked to be asked how my revenge book was coming along. This is not a revenge book. There is no revenge with a psychopath. If I think of revenge, I think of the old adage "living well is the best revenge." I am doing that the best I can.

While settling in Costa Rica I once again came in contact with a male psychopath suitor. At the time I was still suffering from the long-lasting effects of the discard phase of Captain X's psychopathic bond with me. Again, I was vulnerable with the stress of adapting to my new home and new culture in Costa Rica, as well as Captain X's constant court litigations. As soon as I realized I had been targeted yet again by a psychopath, I immediately broke all contact with him. I was proud of myself that I caught on so quickly. This is a sign I'm well on my way to my recovery.

When meeting single mature adults, past histories immediately come up in conversation. When it's my turn to share my past I quickly say, "I went through a very difficult divorce." When I get to know someone better, I reveal more of the truth, that I was married to a dangerous manipulative man who alienated me from my daughter, and I am working to get her back into my life.

I have run across people who poured out stories of their own about psychopathic relationships, without ever divulging mine. On two different occasions I met people so traumatized by their association with a psychopath that all they could say in conversation was that they were "victims of a psychopath," leaving it at that. One chatty ex-pat told me she had been befriended by a suave local man. "He was just so charming. I can't believe he stole my car and now he's gone. Now I can't find him," she confided with embarrassment.

I didn't move to Costa Rica to escape psychopaths. They are everywhere, easily blending into a crowd. We shouldn't live in fear, but we must be aware that up to four percent of our population is made up of these social predators, and we should avoid them at all costs.

My life has changed drastically for the better. I enjoy walking, hiking and biking. I am very involved in my finances, and thankfully my credit rating has vastly improved. I plan to travel, visiting countries I've never been to before. I will continue to write and get back my creativity, painting or decorating again. I take each day as it comes, fully recognizing that each day is better than the last when there's no psychopath in my life to control me.

I often meet a group of emotionally healthy happy ex-pat retirees at a nearby outdoor café for lunch. I welcomed the social life after working many long hours daily on this book. Last month we gathered at a long patio table shaded from the warm tropical sun by an overhanging roof. There we enjoyed the delicious local cuisine of *casados* with meat, fried plantains and corn tortillas, all washed down by *cervezas*.

A group of young street musicians suddenly appeared with a guitar, violin and melodica to serenade us. As soon as the talented trio began playing "Por Una Cabeza," the tango music I love so much, I wanted to dance. I grabbed John, a senior in his 70s, insisting he be my partner without waiting for his reply. I had only one tango lesson and John was not at all a dancer. The patio wasn't even designed for dancing but I was living in the moment, and would make the area work. I pushed and pulled John back and forth, our eyes locked and our heads held up high in a playful romantic way to the rhythm of the music, all while I gave him verbal instructions to move forward and back in the basic dance steps I barely remembered. This time I danced the tango to celebrate living well, reclaiming my life and moving on.

Chapter 26: Suggested Reading and Viewing

If you believe you may be a victim of emotional and/or physical abuse due to a psychopath or non-psychopathic partner, contact **The National Domestic Violence Hotline** (24-hour support) http://www.thehotline.org 1-800-799-SAFE

BOOKS

By academic clinicians and researchers

Without Conscience: The Disturbing World of the World of Psychopaths Among Us
Robert D. Hare, PhD (Jan 8, 1999)

Snakes in Suits: When Psychopaths Go to Work
Paul Babiak, PhD, and Robert D. Hare, PhD (May 9, 2006)

The Sociopath Next Door
Martha Stout, PhD (Feb.8, 2005)

Women Who Love Psychopaths: Inside the Relationships of Inevitable Harm with Psychopaths, Sociopaths & Narcissists
Sandra L. Brown, M.A (2010)

Thinking about Psychopaths and Psychopathy: Answers to Frequently Asked Questions with Case Examples
Ellsworth Lapham Fersch, Editor (October 23, 2006)

The Mask of Sanity, An Attempt to Clarify Some Issues About the So-Called Psychopathic Personality
Hervey Cleckley, M.D (1941)

Puzzling People: The Labyrinth of the Psychopath
Thomas Sheridan (March 1, 2011)

The Psychopath: Emotion and the Brain
James Blair, Derek Mitchell, and Karina Blair (Sept.23, 2005)

The Science of Evil: On Empathy and the Origins of Cruelty
Simon Baron-Cohen (May31, 2011)

The Psychopath Test: A Journey Through the Madness Industry
Jon Ronson (May 1, 2012)

Dark Souls: Healing and Recovering from Toxic Relationships
Sarah Strudwick (August 25, 2010)

Memoir

A Dance with the Devil: A True Story of Marriage to a Psychopath
Barbara Bentley (Nov. 4, 2008)

Love Fraud: How Marriage to a Sociopath Fulfilled My Spiritual Plan
Donna Andersen (August 25, 2010)

The Aftermath of Rock 'n' Roll
Noelle R. Andrews (May 29, 2012)

FILM

"I am <fishead("
www.fisheadmovie.com, documentary about how psychopaths and anti-depressants influence society, Misha Votruba, Vaclav Dejcmar, Directors/Producers

RECOVERY WEBSITES

Aftermath: Surviving Psychopathy Foundation
http://www.aftermath-surviving-psychopathy.org

The Institute for Relational Harm Reduction & Public Pathology Education
http://saferelationships.com

Donna Anderson's Lovefraud Blog
http://www.lovefraud.com

Psychopath Free Recovery Forum
http://psychopathfree.com

Made in the USA
San Bernardino, CA
30 June 2018